FIRE ACROSS THE SEA

FIRE ACROSS THE SEA

THE VIETNAM WAR
AND JAPAN

1965–1975

THOMAS R. H. HAVENS

PRINCETON UNIVERSITY PRESS

ALL RIGHTS RESERVED
Library of Congress Cataloging in Publication Data will be
found on the last printed page of this book

ISBN 0-691-05491-6 (cloth)
0-691-00811-6 (pbk.)

This book has been composed in Linotron Bembo

Clothbound editions of Princeton University Press books are
printed on acid-free paper, and binding materials
are chosen for strength and durability. Paperbacks,
although satisfactory for personal collections,
are not usually suitable for library rebinding

Printed in the United States of America by
Princeton University Press
Princeton, New Jersey

CONTENTS

CONTENTS

PREFACE

"Fire across the river" or "fire on the opposite shore" (*taigan no kasai*) is how Japanese often describe a major event that does not affect them directly. Watching a blaze from a safe distance may imply indifference to the suffering of the victims; at the very least it connotes remaining a spectator who does not intervene in someone else's problems. Even though Japan grew more and more entangled in the endless conflict that raged in Southeast Asia between 1965 and 1975, the nation tried its best to stay aloof from the fire across the sea.

A narrative of Japan's involvement in the Vietnam War, this book studies the impact that war had on Japanese politics, foreign relations, trade, society, and culture. My aim is to discover what the Indochina conflict meant to America's chief Pacific ally. This task is an important one because historians are increasingly coming to recognize that the United States intervened in Vietnam after 1950 mainly to protect Japan. A National Security Council memo on January 27, 1950, said that "Japan's economic recovery depends upon keeping Communism out of Southeast Asia, promoting economic recovery there in further developing these countries, together with Indonesia, the Philippines, Southern Korea and India as the principal trading areas for Japan."[1] After the Chinese communists came to power in October 1949, America's strategy of regionalism centering on Japan required that Indochina and Southeast Asia be kept free of communism so that the Japanese could have the resources and markets necessary for prosperity through trade. Much of the tension in the Japan–United States relationship during the Vietnam War stemmed from this strategy. The Japanese were sometimes regarded by Americans as ungrateful for the sacrifices the United States was making to safeguard Japan's interests. Many ordinary Japanese, by con-

vii

trast, believed that the United States was acting in its own interests, not Japan's or South Vietnam's, by joining in the Indochinese conflict.

Japanese scholarship on Vietnam, Southeast Asia, and their country's relations with the region is no further advanced than in the United States or most other nations. More than 300 new titles on Vietnam, including translations from foreign languages, appeared in Japan during 1965–1975, including at least fifty on the war itself, and more have come out since. Yet only nine universities and research institutes do significant work on any part of Southeast Asia.[2] What is more, attitudes toward the conflict are almost as polarized in Japan today as they were during the war itself. Each side remains firmly dug in, certain of its moral correctness and reluctant to leave its comfortable vantage point in order to walk back through the recent past for a fresh look at what happened.

In mapping some of the most controversial terrain in contemporary Japanese history, I have benefited from the kind help and generous hospitality of many friends in Japan, especially Isamu Amemiya, Kazuko Amemiya, Delmer M. Brown, Mary L. Brown, Kawahara Hiroshi, and M. William Steele. For advice about my work I am also indebted to many colleagues in the United States, particularly Sheldon Garon, Gary G. Giachino, Marius B. Jansen, Daniel I. Okimoto, T. J. Pempel, Donald M. Peppard, Jr., and Valdo H. Viglielmo.

Some of the information in this book is based on interviews conducted in Japan during late 1984 and early 1985 with persons who are well informed about the effects of the Vietnam War on Japanese life. Without exception the individuals listed among the sources at the back of the book answered my questions with candor and courtesy. The directors and staffs of the following libraries provided unstinting help with research materials: National Diet Library, Waseda University Library, International Christian University Library, and Connecticut College Library, especially Helen K. Aitner. Yoshikawa Yū-ichi kindly lent photographs from his personal collection.

Funds from the Japan–United States Friendship Commis-

sion awarded through the Joint Committee on Japanese Studies of the American Council of Learned Societies and the Social Science Research Council, from the American Philosophical Society, and from an anonymous alumna of Connecticut College have speeded my studies, and I am grateful to each of these sources for indispensable assistance.

Except for citations of Western-language publications, the personal names of Asian nationals are given in the customary Asian order, with surname first. Abbreviations used in the text, as well as Japanese-language titles of organizations, are listed in the index.

I am grateful to Margaret Case, Marilyn Campbell, and the staff of Princeton University Press for their customary expert editorial and production care.

March 1986

FIRE ACROSS THE SEA

INTRODUCTION

Japan, the United States, and Vietnam

SPRINTING and jumping with amazing ease, blue-shirted athletes from the U.S.A. dominated theater screens for two hours of physical superiority and competitive heroics in one of the top Japanese movies of 1965, *Tokyo Olympiad* by Ichikawa Kon. A montage of highlights from the flawlessly staged games of October 1964, the film and its musical soundtrack evoked with shrewdly selective memory the images the Japanese wanted to recall. In those Olympics such clean-cut exemplars as the selfless basketball player Bill Bradley, the versatile swimmer Don Schollander, and the persevering vaulter Fred Hansen suggested some of the best qualities of America, the country that to nearly all Japanese had gone faster, farther, and higher than any other nation.

Even though they also scored superbly at Tokyo, only a handful of Soviet athletes made it into the movie—often as losers. Theatergoers felt particularly proud as they watched Ichikawa's excerpts from the gold medal victory by Japan over Russia in the women's volleyball final. The film was a deft mix of visual and aural patriotic symbols—although few in the audience realized that Japan's governing party, the Liberal Democrats, had persuaded Ichikawa to recut it before it was released in order to inject more nationalism.[1] The message of *Tokyo Olympiad* was clear: U.S.A. was number one, but Japan was catching up fast.

AMERICA in early 1965 was at the pinnacle of its popularity in Japan. In monthly polls taken the year before, an average of 49 percent of the public listed the United States as their favorite

3

foreign country, and only 4 percent said they disliked America. Both figures were new records since World War II. But suddenly in 1965 the relationship between the two nations began to change. Until then, Japan had run a big deficit in its trade with the United States; from 1965 on the Japanese had the upper hand. Economic relations soon grew cloudy, and then they turned downright stormy as the decade ended. A brewing movement to regain the Ryūkyū Islands from American control quickly boiled up after Satō Eisaku, the Japanese prime minister, visited Naha on August 19, 1965, and told Okinawans that World War II "will not be over for Japan until Okinawa is restored to the fatherland."[2] Joined closely with these frictions over trade and autonomy, yet for many people more disturbing than either, was the shuddering jolt to the psychological relationship between America and Japan that occurred when the United States abruptly escalated the Vietnam War early in 1965.

In the next eight years the popularity of the United States among the Japanese public dropped to its lowest point since 1945. By 1973 only 18 percent of those polled listed America as their favorite foreign country, in third place behind Switzerland and France, and 13 percent now said they disliked the United States. Surveys of this sort tell little about the United States, but they reveal a good deal about how ingenuous and idealistic most Japanese perceptions of America were before the mid-1960s. Public images of other countries are uncertain in what they reflect; in this case many reasons explain the tarnish after 1965, including race riots and political assassinations in the United States, trade disputes between the two nations, growing Japanese self-confidence, and the diplomatic surprises unveiled by President Richard M. Nixon in the summer of 1971. But the most powerful shock to the idealistic, almost serendipitous view most Japanese held of America came from the rolling thunder of bombers over North Vietnam, starting on February 7, 1965.

Japanese and Americans had agreed on most international issues after World War II, with the partial exception of Wash-

ington's Cold War policies in Asia.[3] The Vietnam War soon prompted the Japanese to see themselves, the United States, and the rest of the globe in more realistic terms. One of the chief aims of this book is to explain how the war in distant Indochina forced people in Japan to come to grips with the United States as a pragmatic participant in world politics rather than the genial model of democracy and fairness they remembered from the American occupation of their country during 1945–1952.

Japan's entanglement with the Vietnam War quickly formed a maze of puzzles. Article ix of the postwar Japanese constitution ruled out sending troops abroad, but the Japan–United States Security Treaty of 1960 allowed America to use bases in Japan as prime staging areas for ground and air operations in Indochina. Very few Japanese had much taste for communism or wanted the communists to win in Vietnam, but progressives and conservatives alike were haunted by memories of how the Japanese armies had bogged down in China during World War II as they watched the Americans fight Vietnamese guerrillas on TV. The Japanese government often spoke of looking for a peaceful settlement, but its diplomacy did little to foster one. Its export policies did not permit arms to be sold abroad, yet Japanese industries took in at least $1 billion a year from providing goods and services to the United States and South Vietnamese forces. Many Japanese took neither side in the conflict, simply hoping for peace as soon as possible, but their foreign minister, Shiina Etsusaburō, frankly told the national parliament in May 1966 that "Japan is not neutral" in the Vietnam War.[4]

Another conundrum was more subtle: for many Japanese with long memories, the specter of American violence against Vietnam probably "helped lighten Japan's guilty conscience about its own behavior in a guerrilla war in China" two decades earlier.[5] But for others who worried about how their government was quietly abetting the United States in Vietnam, the war increased their sense of guilt. The art critic Haryū Ichirō believes that "the main influence of Vietnam on Japa-

5

nese intellectuals was to discover ourselves as cooperators in the war. Ever since World War II we had seen ourselves as victims of war, but with Vietnam we began to see that we were now perpetrators of war"—by failing to stop American procurement and the use of bases in Japan.[6] Many such intellectuals and many more citizens from other backgrounds rallied, marched, and agitated against America's actions in Indochina in the late 1960s, forming the biggest antiwar movement in Japanese history. So Washington's chief Pacific ally faced the paradox of heavy public protests but also tidy industrial profits during the Vietnam War. As a wry journalist for *Mainichi* put it, "this country, just like a magician, satisfied both its conscience and its purse."[7]

Unpacking these puzzles is the task of this book. The focus in the pages that follow is on what the war reveals about Japan: its elitist leadership, ambivalent views of the United States, clubby social cohesion, and basic cultural insularity. What were the war's direct and indirect effects on Japanese foreign policy, industry, society, and culture? Why did elite perceptions of the outside world differ so greatly from the views held by the general public? What difference did the frustrating war in Vietnam make to Japanese political behavior? The well-known Marxist historian Inoue Kiyoshi wrote in 1965 that "this is the first time in the history of our country that the overwhelming majority of people have opposed a war the government supports."[8] Yet no member of parliament was ever turned out because of his or her stand on Vietnam. Dilemmas like this are reminders of the big gaps in what is known about how the war affected America's major allies throughout Asia and the rest of the world.

Vietnam was just one of several key issues facing Japan during the decade 1965–1975. Other powerful factors included economic prosperity, security relations, trade ruffles, the reacquisition of Okinawa, and recognition of the People's Republic of China. In light of these multiple elements, it is worth remembering that "to the average Japanese person," as the political scientist Sodei Rinjirō wrote in 1975, "the Vietnam

6

experience was not as traumatic as it was to the American public. It did not cut deep into the mind of the Japanese, and never 'came home' as it did in America."[9] Even though many anti-war intellectuals in Japan believed that United States imperialism was oppressing Vietnamese national aspirations, very few of them turned to outright anti-Americanism. Maruyama Shizuo, chief editorial writer for *Asahi shinbun* and a relentless critic of United States policy in Vietnam, wrote that "certainly America is an important country for Japan. Needless to say, it is essential to have trade and cultural exchange with the United States. The existence of America is also indispensable for Asia."[10] To readers today, the Vietnam War is both a looking glass for reflection on how Japanese viewed the conflict and a prism for refracting the historical experience of the Japanese people during ten critical years of self-examination and redefinition of their place in the world.

The Security Treaty and the Peace Movement, 1952–1964

Except during World War II and the occupation, Japan has been linked to the United States by treaties of various sorts ever since the Kanagawa pact of 1854. From the moment Japan regained autonomy on April 28, 1952, the controlling influence on its foreign policy has been a bilateral security treaty with the United States. The agreement, known to Japanese as Anpo, was signed at the San Francisco Peace Conference on September 8, 1951. It allowed the United States to station its military forces at bases in Japan to prevent domestic rebellion fomented from without, to protect Japan from outside attack, and to assure peace in the Far East. A revised version of the treaty, approved in 1960, removed the right to intervene in internal affairs. Because Japan's defenses were insufficient to guarantee its protection, the nation even after regaining independence remained subordinate to the United States. The treaty implicitly defined the scope of Japanese diplomacy as well as making explicit security arrangements; separately the

two countries reached agreements that acknowledged an unequal economic relationship characterized by American domination. It is small wonder that the Japanese, whose economy
did not regain its prewar level of output until 1955, felt psy-
chologically dependent on the United States.

The security treaty, which they were powerless to refuse,
made obvious financial sense to most Japanese, and it also
shielded them against possible threats from powerful neighbors on the Asian continent. But, as tribute for these benefits,
the United States forced Japan to recognize the Kuomintang
government in Taipei, not the communist state in Beijing, as
the legitimate government of China. Yoshida Shigeru, the
prime minister, reluctantly reconciled himself to this stubborn
outcropping of America's Cold War policies.

Soon President Dwight D. Eisenhower and his secretary of
state, John Foster Dulles, urged Japan to forgo trade with
mainland China and to cultivate Southeast Asia instead as a
market, helping to fend off revolution there. According to the
Pentagon Papers (1971), the joint chiefs of staff feared in 1954
that if communists overran Southeast Asia, "the communiza-
tion of Japan would be the probable ultimate result."[11] Based
on this premise, according to minutes from an Eisenhower
cabinet meeting on April 6, 1954, Dulles believed "that there
was little future for Japanese products in the United States and
that the solution lay in developing markets for Japan in pres-
ently underdeveloped areas such as Southeast Asia." A top secret—eyes only memo from the National Security Council
dated September 12, 1954, reveals: "Dulles told Yoshida
frankly that Japan should not expect to find a big U.S. market
because the Japanese don't make the things we want."[12]

Under the security treaty Japan (excluding Okinawa)
hosted 40,000 American military personnel and became part of
the mightiest peacetime military empire ever built. At its peak
in the late 1960s, the United States had 3.5 million troops under arms, of whom 1.1 million were stationed abroad—twice
the combined figure of all other countries. The United States
had defense pacts with forty-two nations and maintained

2,200 military bases in thirty-three countries. Through 1970, the direct costs of the Vietnam War were little more than a tenth of the total United States defense bill after 1945.[13] Although the purpose of these outlays was not to impose imperial domination over other states, the opposition parties and labor unions in Japan were dismayed at the security treaty and its anticommunist assumptions. The main parties not in power, the Japan Socialist Party and the Japan Communist Party, resented how the Americans had seemingly backtracked on democratic reforms halfway through the occupation. The JSP and JCP were afraid that if their country cooperated with American Cold War policies in Asia, autocracy and militarism might once again flourish in Japan. They also favored friendlier relations with the Soviet Union, and especially with China, than were possible in the 1950s because of the American bear hug.

The Left mounted a strong campaign against nuclear weapons in the mid-fifties and an enormous cacophany against the security treaty at the end of the decade. Both movements tapped a deep current of postwar pacifism among the public, symbolized by the no-war clause in the constitution. The ban-the-bomb campaign began in earnest after high radioactivity from an American hydrogen bomb test on Bikini atoll in the South Pacific showered a Japanese tuna boat, the *Lucky Dragon No. 5*, on March 1, 1954.[14] A group of housewives in Suginami, a comfortable surburban district of Tokyo, started collecting signatures on an antinuclear petition. Within a year 32.3 million people had signed their names. The first world conference to abolish nuclear weapons was held in Hiroshima during the summer of 1955, sponsored by ninety-six civic, farm, labor, religious, and women's groups. Politicians from the ruling conservative party, the Liberal Democrats, as well as from the JSP and JCP took part, lending a nonpartisan tone to the occasion.

But the antinuclear movement soon became politicized. In September 1955 the Japan Council against Atomic and Hydrogen Bombs (Gensuibaku Kinshi Nihon Kyōgikai, usually

called Gensuikyō) was formed, and it immediately began agitating against United States bases in Japan as well as planning the annual antibomb rallies. Arguing that the revision of the security treaty proposed for 1960 might lead Japan to adopt nuclear weapons or use its troops overseas, Gensuikyō joined the outcry against the pact in 1958. The ruling Liberal Democrats, denouncing Gensuikyō as a "camouflaged peace movement," immediately cut off their financial support and withdrew from the council. From this point on, the "peace movement" usually referred to partisan sloganeering against weapons, bases, and the treaty by the Old Left—ban-the-bomb groups, leftist parties, and labor unions—whose main objective was to embarrass the party in power. As a result, opponents of the Vietnam War in the 1960s spoke of themselves instead as the "antiwar movement."

The clamorous struggle led by the Old Left and student groups against the ratification of the revised security treaty in 1960 was the largest mass protest to that point in Japan's history. It reached its climax in a general strike by 6.2 million workers (according to labor leaders) on June 22.[15] The crisis was energized by various fears and frustrations: resentment at the continuing presence of American troops in Japan, worry that the country might become an innocent victim of a future war because of its defense ties with the United States, disapproval of America's foreign policy, and outrage at the high-handed way the prime minister, Kishi Nobusuke, rammed the treaty through the parliament on May 19. But the tumult was not fundamentally prompted by disagreement about foreign affairs or external threats. Instead the real concern was internal: the apprehension that the Liberal Democrats might revise the peace constitution, beef up the police, and restore despotism and fascism at home.[16] This preoccupation with domestic agenda helps to show why labor, the opposition parties, and even the antinuclear organizations were often ineffective vehicles of protest against the Vietnam War.

Both the labor unions and the campaign to ban atomic weapons suffered from inner bickering and underwent splits

in the early sixties. The main labor group was the General Council of Trade Unions of Japan (Nihon Rōdō Kumiai Sōhyōgikai, or Sōhyō, founded in 1950), which was closely affiliated with the Japan Socialist Party. Early in 1962 the Democratic Socialist Party, barely two years after splitting off from the JSP, helped to form a rival labor alliance, based on non-Marxist principles, that soon became known as the Japan Confederation of Labor (Zen Nihon Rōdō Sōdōmei, or Dōmei, formally constituted in 1964). Unlike Sōhyō, whose members were mostly public employees, Dōmei drew its strength from workers in private industry, and it upheld labor harmony and the anticommunist outlook of the Democratic Socialists.[17] This division in the union movement made little difference to national policies, which the Liberal Democrats controlled, but it further weakened labor's voice when the debate about Vietnam began.

Denouncing the antibomb movement led by Gensuikyō as too partial to communist countries, various members of the DSP, the LDP, and private labor unions set up a second antinuclear group in November 1961, the National Council for Peace and against Nuclear Weapons (Kakuheiki Kinshi Heiwa Kensetsu Kokumin Kaigi, or Kakkin Kaigi). Gensuikyō itself was ripped by disputes between socialists and communists, especially after the Soviet Union resumed bomb tests in September 1961 and then the Americans, British, and Russians signed a limited test ban treaty in July 1963. Gensuikyō had always favored a complete prohibition on nuclear weapons, whereas the JSP and Sōhyō supported the test ban treaty as a good first step. The socialists split off from Gensuikyō after its ninth world conference in 1963, and two years later they founded a third antibomb group, the Japan Congress against Atomic and Hydrogen Bombs (Gensuibaku Kinshi Nihon Kokumin Kaigi, or Gensuikin). As a result, the JCP took charge of Gensuikyō mainly by default in 1965, and the organization began to draw a reasonably large following the next year after the party stopped defending China's nuclear tests and declared its independence of both Moscow and Peking.[18]

11

Such factionalism and ideological quarreling sapped the resistance the Old Left could offer against the security treaty, American bases, nuclear weapons, and United States policies in Indochina. So did rising standards of living under Prime Minister Ikeda Hayato (1960–1964), by making theories of class conflict seem old-fashioned. Disputes between the Soviet Union and China showed that pacifism would not work even among communists. What is more, the new United States ambassador to Japan, Edwin O. Reischauer, went on the offensive in 1961 against opponents of the treaty by promoting American liberalism among Japanese intellectuals. Reischauer, who told Congress in 1963 that classical Marxism was America's real enemy in Japan, was widely credited with improving his country's image among the general public—until an unpopular war in Indochina, whose wisdom he questioned but whose intentions he defended, burst forth in 1965 to nullify many of his efforts.[19]

Still, the antinuclear movement and the leftist parties were important voices on public issues in the early 1960s. Article IV of the security treaty called for consultations between Japan and the United States about implementing the pact; a separate status of forces agreement (U.S.–Japan Administrative Agreement, signed January 19, 1960) and accompanying exchange of notes specified the conditions under which prior consultation was needed. Article VI of the treaty defined its purpose as "contributing to the security of Japan and the maintenance of international peace and security in the Far East."[20] When the United States became actively involved in Laos in 1961, a socialist member of parliament named Morishima questioned whether under the security treaty American bases could be used for operations outside the Far East, which Japan had previously defined as the area north of the Philippines. A foreign ministry legal expert replied that in exceptional cases the United States could take military actions short of actual combat in areas surrounding the Far East from its bases in Japan, if the security of the Far East itself was threatened. The govern-

ment implied that such moves did not require prior consultation.[21]

Again when the United States moved troops from Japan to Thailand in 1962, the government brushed aside the objections from the JSP member of parliament Hozumi, on the ground that no prior consultation was needed because the troop deployment did not directly originate in Japan. The authorities also dismissed objections when the United States, in mid-1962, moved part of its air force stationed in Japan to Thailand because of the situation in Laos. The cabinet's position was that prior consultation was never needed before withdrawing American forces from Japan unless they were to be used directly in combat roles.[22] These examples show that by 1962—almost three years before America intervened in Vietnam with major military force—the persistent pressure from the Left had already forced Japan's leaders to reveal nearly all their ways of interpreting the security treaty so as to let the United States have maximum use of bases in Japan for operations in Indochina.

VIETNAM AND JAPAN BEFORE 1965

Japan had little contact with Indochina before occupying the French possessions there during World War II. This lack of interaction stemmed mainly from distance and trade restrictions. The ancient imperial city of Hue, in Annam (central Vietnam), was 4,000 kilometers to the southwest of Tokyo. Even the Japanese ports nearest to Vietnam lay 2,500 kilometers distant in Okinawa. Most relations before the twentieth century were indirect because Annam was a tributary of China. Small enclaves of merchants from Japan sprang up at Da Nang and Hoi An in the later sixteenth century, but they withered after Japan cut back on trade with Vietnam and most other overseas regions in 1640. France seized full control of the Indochinese peninsula in the 1880s, adding the rich resources of the area to its empire but allowing only meager trade with Japan until a tariff barrier was removed in 1932.

Japan at the turn of the twentieth century was a magnet for youthful reformers from all over Asia. They studied engineering, finance, and the other modernizing skills that Japan had put to use in building a powerful state after 1868. Japan's unexpected victory over tsarist Russia in 1904–1905 churned up nationalist feelings throughout Asia, particularly among the future Chinese revolutionaries then living in Tokyo and Yokohama. About 200 Vietnamese were also in Japan during 1905–1908, including the monarchic reformer Phan Boi Chau, who hoped that independence and prosperity could happen in Vietnam without a revolution. Fearing subversion, the French colonial administrators crushed a series of free schools set up in 1907 by Vietnamese who had returned from studies in Japan to teach science, languages, political economy, and Vietnamese culture. France tightened its rule after weathering large Vietnamese demonstrations in March 1908, and it also persuaded the Japanese to cancel the residence permits of the Vietnamese still in Japan that spring. Tokyo's new impulses toward empire, fed by success in the Russo-Japanese War, had just been confirmed in the Franco-Japanese agreement of 1907 to respect each other's spheres in East Asia. In this fashion the young Vietnamese nationalists, so recently inspired by Japanese modernization, became victims of its growing imperialist dreams.[23]

This same imperialism, when fully formed, victimized both France and Indochina when Japanese forces stepped in to take control of northern Vietnam in 1940. On June 19, three days before the French surrendered to Hitler at Compiègne, Japan demanded that their governor-general in Southeast Asia, Gen. Georges Catroux, sever all supply routes to the Nationalist armies of Chiang Kai-shek in China and allow a Japanese military mission to be posted to Hanoi. Catroux reluctantly accepted the demand, hoping to minimize the problem. He was quickly dismissed from office by the new French state at Vichy, which still aspired to protecting French interests from Germany and its treaty partners. Vichy soon enough backed down, instructing the new governor-general, Vice Adm. Jean

Decoux of the French Far Eastern fleet, to honor a Franco-Japanese treaty signed on August 30, 1940. The agreement permitted Japan "certain military facilities in Tongking for the liquidation of the China incident."[24] It might have added "the liquidation of the French empire in Asia" as well.

Quickly General Nishihara stationed 6,000 troops in the Hanoi area, sealed off the Chinese border, and cowed the French into ordering an end to all resistance against the Japanese occupation of northern Vietnam. Japan set about exploiting the concentrations of minerals that had drawn the French extractive interests sixty years earlier, and it also insisted on a virtual right of first refusal for acquiring four-fifths of Vietnam's exports in most commodity lines. Governor-General Decoux continued to run the French administration in Indochina but by 1941 was in no position to disregard Japanese instructions. Nor could he protest when Vichy signed a treaty with Tokyo on July 29, 1941, awarding Japan the use of all ports, bases, and airfields throughout Indochina. Japan was now set to strike through Thailand to the Malay peninsula, Singapore, and the oil fields of the Dutch East Indies. French troops in Indochina stood by without firing a shot as the Japanese forces moved south from their Vietnamese and Cambodian springboards on Pearl Harbor Day.

Japan's five-year dominion over Indochina ruined the local economy, undermined French rule, stimulated Vietnamese nationalism, and earned much resentment from residents of the region. Standards of living fell, as they did in other parts of the Greater East Asia Co-Prosperity Sphere, and at least a million people died from starvation in northern Vietnam after dreadful harvests in 1944–1945.[25] Japanese Pan-Asianist propaganda against white-man's imperialism helped to discredit the French, as did Decoux's dispirited capitulation to General Nishihara in 1940. The following year Ho Chi Minh and other communists formed the Viet Minh, a popular front of antiforeign groups who wanted independence from both France and Japan, national unification, and a democratic republic.[26] Partly because Ho Chi Minh was imprisoned by the Chinese Nation-

15

alists throughout 1942, the Viet Minh armies became a major force only toward the end of the war, particularly after the Japanese suddenly abolished French rule in March 1945 and tried to govern the region themselves. Japan considered backing the noncommunist patriot Ngo Dinh Diem as the leader of a "free" Vietnamese state but found him to be too independent—as the United States learned a decade later.[27] Many local residents felt bitter toward the Japanese for substituting a new imperialism and for draining the area's riches while returning so little. But their misgivings were relatively milder than in other occupied countries because rather few Japanese were present in Vietnam during World War II and because Japan's new policies helped to get rid of the French.

The first postwar contact between Japan and Vietnam took place in the austere setting of the San Francisco Peace Conference of September 1951. The French-backed State of Vietnam, led by Bao Dai in Saigon, was one of forty-nine governments that signed the Treaty of Peace with Japan. Cambodia and Laos were also parties to the agreement. In this manner the United States, which arranged the conference, made sure that Japan officially recognized the Saigon regime, not its rival founded at Hanoi in 1945 by the Viet Minh. Formal relations between Tokyo and Saigon began in 1953, and full embassies followed two years later. The first item of business was to complete a pact about restitution for wartime damage done to Vietnam.

It was France, not the State of Vietnam, which insisted at San Francisco that the Japanese start negotiations for reparations payments. The initial demand was for $2 billion. The compromise settlement, reached with great difficulty because of political instability in Saigon, called for $39 million in reparations ($37 million for a hydroelectric power plant at the Da Nhim dam, $2 million for factories), $7.5 million in Japanese government loans, and $9.1 million in private economic cooperation loans. The total payment of $55.6 million was duly completed by Japan on January 11, 1965, just two days before the first Satō-Johnson communiqué on the Vietnam War.[28]

16

Tokyo also agreed in 1959 to make grants of "gratuitous economic aid" to Cambodia ($4.2 million) and Laos ($2.7 million) but carefully avoided calling them reparations, on the grounds that Japan had caused no war damage in either country and that each had waived its claims to reparations.[29]

The payments to South Vietnam struck a note of controversy appropriate to the whole postwar record of Japanese relations with the region. Both leftists and rightists in Japan thought it remarkable that Vietnam got as much as it did, considering how little physical destruction the country suffered in World War II. For the same reason, few Japanese felt much guilt at their country's wartime actions in Indochina, especially compared with how their imperial forces treated the Chinese. The opposition parties denounced the Kishi government for excluding the Democratic Republic of Vietnam (Hanoi regime) from the reparations. The agreement, they reasoned, clearly showed that Japan was cooperating with America's anticommunist policies in Vietnam as well as in China. But nearly everybody in Japan applauded one motive for the reparations program: to clean the slate from World War II and regain full sovereignty by hastening the return of Okinawa. The Vietnamese themselves understood that the payments amounted to a form of investment sought by Japanese exporters who were looking for markets in Indochina.[30] The accumulation of United States and Japanese government aid funds in Saigon after 1954 created a purchasing power for imports that Japanese businesses hoped to supply.

After the occupation ended in 1952, Japan was concerned primarily with its immediate neighbors, particularly Korea and Taiwan, and paid little heed to the Geneva agreements of 1954 or the new Government of Vietnam in Saigon under Ngo Dinh Diem. Diem's failure to hold national elections in 1956, as provided for at Geneva, and the subsequent rise of the National Liberation Front at the end of the decade were noted even more fleetingly in Japan than in France or the United States. But even though the Japanese were content to follow

American political guidance about the region, they increasingly developed their trading ties with both Saigon and Hanoi.

The reparations system provided the main frame for commerce with South Vietnam. Between the end of World War II and the early 1970s, Japan was relatively uninterested in acquiring resources from the south but very eager to open new markets there. In 1961, the peak year before the Vietnam War escalated, Japan sold goods worth $65.7 million to South Vietnam (and bought products valued at just $2.8 million).[31] The Japanese also joined the Mekong River project, founded in 1957 by the Economic Commission for Asia and the Far East under the direction of the United Nations, to build dams, generate electricity, and control irrigation. By 1967 Japan was the third largest contributor. In 1964 Japan began building sugar mills in South Vietnam capable of giving the glutted world market an additional 150 tons per day, but all such Japanese projects and investments soon ran head-on into the chaos of warfare. By 1963 Japan's exports to South Vietnam were barely half their level two years earlier; some of the dams and many of the factories started by the Japanese are still unbuilt.[32]

Japan officially recognized only the Saigon government, but it dealt privately with Hanoi after 1955 through the Japan-Vietnam Trade Association (Nichietsu Bōekikai, at first called the Friday Club out of political delicacy). Tokyo had traded unofficially with the People's Republic of China since 1952 (known after 1962 as Liao-Takasaki memorandum trade), and it also regularized its ties with the Soviet Union in 1956. By the late 1950s Japan had an active commercial relationship with a number of communist states, even though it conducted diplomacy with only some of them and adhered closely to the anticommunist political and military policies of the United States. This scheme was known under Prime Minister Ikeda in the early sixties as the separation of politics and economics (*seikei bunri*), but its foundations were already in place under his predecessors. The United States was unwilling to antagonize the leftists in Japan any further and did not object to these dealings with the communists.[33]

North Vietnam earned a steady surplus in its trade with Japan until 1969, the height of wartime destruction. The most valuable export was Hongay coal, which the Japanese had purchased since the French era for coking. The volume of two-way trade in the late fifties and early sixties was only one-quarter to one-third the value of the trade between Japan and South Vietnam. In May 1964, "because international conditions are unfavorable," Japan refused to admit any more trade representatives from Hanoi (the ban was not lifted until 1970). Once the United States entered the war with full force in March 1965, goods had to be shipped between North Vietnam and Japan by roundabout routes in third-country vessels. Under pressure from the Americans, Japan curbed the export of war-related products like copper and electrical wire, and the level of trade was sliced in half for most of the war.[34] Once again, as was often true in the past, political restrictions held contacts to a minimum.

THE IKEDA YEARS: STRENGTH AND PRIDE

Superficially, the four years after the security treaty demonstrations of 1960 were calm, stable, and prosperous for Japan. Prime Minister Ikeda Hayato, who succeeded Kishi Nobusuke on July 19, 1960, deflected attention from the defense question by announcing a hugely popular plan to double incomes within a decade. Ikeda cultivated a soothing image because the public had tired of the arrogance of his predecessor. He undertook a studied humility, in foreign as well as domestic affairs, which he called "low-posture politics." Abroad he extended the principle of separating politics and economics beyond Asia, eventually including Japan's most important partner, the United States. The Tokyo Olympics of October 1964, preceded by a cyclone of improvements in subways, highways, hotels, and conversational English skills, symbolized the new economic strength and public pride that Ikeda's affable approach nurtured. Good will and good relations between Japan and the United States reached a zenith almost unimagi-

nable four years earlier—although strong feelings of competition were also irrepressibly evident in Japan, as Ichikawa's movie on the Olympiad showed.

Actually Ikeda did much more than boost workers' paychecks and pursue "no foreign policy except to follow America's lead," as one respected Japanese scholar put it.[35] The program of doubling incomes would not work without free access to consumers in the United States, so Japan tried hard to cement economic relations across the Pacific. The Joint Japan–U.S. Committee on Trade and Economic Affairs, with six cabinet officers from each country, was founded in June 1961 and met nine times in the next twelve years. This committee was proof that the Americans respected Japan's premise that politics could be separated from economics: its agenda never included Vietnam War policy at any point. The Japanese did not mean by separating politics from economics that trade was apolitical or value-free. Instead the policy allowed Japan to rely on American military protection, send more and more exports to the United States, and also develop markets in communist countries. Far from claiming that *sei* (politics) could really be divorced from *kei* (economics), the Japanese by adopting this principle were making an explicitly political statement. As Shibusawa Masahide, a commissioner of the Trilateral Commission, has noted, "the concept of *seikei bunri* represented a widespread skepticism in Japan about the efficacy of cold-war premises."[36]

For public consumption Prime Minister Ikeda maintained that the security treaty was a medium-range expedient until the United Nations worked well enough to assure Japan's safety. He tried to pull away from diplomacy defined exclusively by the security framework, especially in his policy toward the People's Republic of China. Although the moment was not yet right for normalization of relations, Japan broadened its commercial activities with China in the Liao-Takasaki memorandum of November 1962. This agreement provided for two-way trade valued at more than $80 million a year for the next five years.[37] It signaled the hopes of a minority within

20

the Liberal Democratic Party for restoring full ties with the PRC despite bleak and unrelenting disapproval from Washington.

A major Japanese goal since 1952 was to retrieve the Ryū-kyū Islands (Okinawa prefecture) from American control. In the early 1960s Tokyo increased its economic aid to Okinawa, reminding the United States that Japan was ready to accept responsibility for economic development and social welfare in the Ryūkyūs. The Ikeda cabinet also tried to cut its reliance on the American military shield and improve its case for reclaiming Okinawa by revising the self-defense law in 1961 and adopting the second defense plan. This program expanded the Self-Defense Forces by 15,000 troops and called for acquiring Nike and Hawk missiles from the United States. Ikeda had promised President John F. Kennedy in June 1961 that Japan would be a fortress against communism. He underlined this commitment the next October by resuming discussions with Seoul about restoring normal relations between Japan and South Korea, a task finally accomplished in 1965. The prime minister asserted his country's strength and pride even more optimistically in October 1963 when he stated that Japan had the intention of "assuming the role of leader in the Western Pacific, just as Britain had been the paramount power in Europe in the 19th century."[38] People in nearby Asian countries who recalled World War II thought this a rather highhanded pronouncement from a supposedly low-posture politician.

When North Vietnamese PT boats exchanged gunfire on August 2, 1964, with the United States destroyer *Maddox* in the Gulf of Tonkin, Japan was puzzled but remained publicly loyal to its ally. The government accepted Washington's explanation of the incident: "we trust the American statement. America's actions were unavoidable."[39] Shiina Etsusaburō, who had become the foreign minister three weeks earlier, told the foreign affairs committee of the House of Representatives on August 10 that the American reprisal attacks on North Vietnam after the *Maddox* episode and a second apparent raid two days later "fall within the sphere of self-defense rights."[40]

21

Yet Shiina conceded that "there is no way to ascertain for sure, based on reports currently available to us, the true facts about whether an attack from North Vietnam was carried out on the high seas. We can only rely on the announcements of our ally, the United States."[41] Prime Minister Ikeda reportedly conveyed his concern in private to Ambassador Reischauer.[42]

The Japan Communist Party, the Japan Socialist Party, the Sōhyō labor federation, and 134 other organizations sponsored a rally on August 10 to protest the American reprisals. As he had in 1962, the socialist representative Hozumi asked in parliament if the government interpreted the Far East in the security treaty to include the Gulf of Tonkin and North Vietnam. The answer in 1964 was the same: events just outside the Far East might threaten its peace and security, allowing the American forces to use their bases in Japan for noncombat purposes without consulting with Japan in advance.[43] From this point on, one Japanese cabinet after another used legalistic reasoning to justify its cooperation with the United States, well aware that the general public would accept arguments about treaty obligations much more readily than ideological or moral assertions as a rationale for supporting the Americans.

Apart from the issue of the bases, Japan's backing for United States activities in Vietnam during most of 1964 was the minimum necessary to keep defense relations from souring. The cabinet agreed readily enough to send medical aid to Saigon when the United States asked twenty-five of its allies to help solve the Vietnam problem in April 1964. Japan sent medical teams to South Vietnam in August and October of that year and also provided the Government of Vietnam with $1.5 million in goods such as medicines, prefabricated buildings, twenty-five ambulances, and 20,000 transistor radios. Ikeda justified the aid on the ground that North Vietnam had broken the Geneva agreements of 1954.[44]

After the Gulf of Tonkin clash, the cabinet gave in to requests from Washington dating back to January 1963 for permission to use the American naval bases at Yokosuka and Sasebo for port calls by nuclear-powered submarines. The United

States waited until November 12, 1964, well after the Tokyo games, to send the *Sea Dragon* to Sasebo, where it met with vast protests. William F. Bundy, the American assistant secretary of state, visited Japan at the end of September to spur on the discussions of normalization between Tokyo and Seoul, and stated that "it would be more of a blow in the long run to Japan than to the U.S. if her smaller Asian neighbors should fall under the dark shadow of militant communism."[45] The Japanese gave more attention to another message from Washington: a warning from Secretary of State Dean Rusk on September 29 that China would explode an atomic bomb "in the immediate future."[46] Many Japanese were piqued when the Chinese upstaged the Olympics in midcourse with their nuclear test at Lop Nor on October 16, only days after the downfall of Premier Nikita S. Khrushchev in the Kremlin.[47] The Japanese government felt less pique than fear at being suddenly enclosed in a nuclear triangle among China, the Soviet Union, and the United States. Two weeks after the Olympics ended Prime Minister Ikeda resigned in poor health. Satō Eisaku took office on November 9, 1964, determined to draw closer to the United States. The war in Vietnam soon gave him the opportunity—and the risks that went along with it.

CHAPTER 1

The War Comes to Japan

SATŌ EISAKU served so long as prime minister that the pundits called his leadership "the politics of waiting." As a party sultan he outlasted his top rivals Ikeda, Kōno Ichirō, and Ōno Banboku, whose deaths one after another in 1964–1965 left Satō in full command of the Liberal Democrats precisely when the socialists in parliament were split into two parties and the Left as a whole was stunned by political upheaval in revolutionary China. Satō, who was the younger brother of former Prime Minister Kishi, graduated from the elite law faculty of Tokyo University and became a career bureaucrat in the transportation ministry. After the war he became the protégé of Prime Minister Yoshida Shigeru and a party loyalist to the core. His peers knew him as a master schemer who united the party through his skill at human relations, under the motto "tolerance and harmony." Satō's patience helped him survive a corruption scandal, student demonstrations, and another potential treaty crisis. Although he was often chided for inaction and his economic program was ridiculed as a "nonpolicy,"[1] Satō's perseverance allowed him to ride out the storm over his Vietnam policy, and it also produced the chief accomplishment of his career: the reversion of Okinawa on May 15, 1972.

OKINAWA, CHINA, AND VIETNAM

During his term of seven and one-half years, Prime Minister Satō continued Ikeda's policy of separating politics from economics. He managed to draw closer to the United States on military issues without jeopardizing Japan's trade with communist countries. *Seikei bunri* was popular in Japan because it

24

helped the economy prosper. The Vietnam War was highly unpopular, but the Satō cabinet continued to support America's policies there in order to achieve two goals: 1) heading off future trade conflicts with the United States, and 2) regaining control over Okinawa. Soon after he took office on November 9, 1964, Satō tipped his hand about Vietnam. He warned that the foreign ministry was wrong in showing "a lack of determination to establish peace and freedom in Asia," adding that Southeast Asia should not "be considered only a market."[2] Satō put the Okinawa issue to President Lyndon B. Johnson at the White House on January 12–13, 1965. Reversion had first been raised when Kishi met Eisenhower in 1957, and later between Ikeda and Kennedy. The Satō-Johnson communiqué of January 13 at least recognized Japan's desire to regain Okinawa and the Ogasawara (Bonin and Volcano) Islands, and the scope of the standing bi-national committee on the Ryūkyūs was broadened. The Satō-Johnson agreement also reaffirmed that the American military facilities on Okinawa were vital for preserving peace in the Far East. Many Japanese inferred that when tensions in Asia relaxed, Okinawa would be restored to them.[3] The communiqué also emphasized that the Taiwan regime was the recognized government of China but Japan traded privately with the People's Republic.[4] Finally, both countries "agreed that continued perseverance would be necessary for freedom and independence in South Vietnam."[5] In exchange for American flexibility on Okinawa and China, Satō now seemed to be marching jowl to jowl with Johnson on the war.

Actually the prime minister's endorsement of American policies was still almost as guarded as the response of most of the other major allies. He said in January that although Japan could not constitutionally send military assistance, "I shall be happy if we can provide something more than moral support."[6] The cabinet on January 28 gave 11,645 radio receivers to the psychological warfare ministry of the Saigon government so that citizens could listen to broadcasts from Japan—or announcements their rulers wanted them to hear. It also con-

tinued to send medical supplies and other humanitarian aid.[7] Even though Satō defended America's intentions in January 1965 when he addressed the Diet (parliament), on other occasions he was cautious about the use of outside forces. He declared that Asian problems needed Asian solutions and that he would give Johnson some ideas.[8] Foreign Minister Shiina traveled on to London after the Satō-Johnson talks and pointed out that "in China there is the expression 'three parts military, seven parts politics.' . . . isn't the United States doing just about the opposite in Vietnam, just like the old Kwantung Army? The United States understands this, but the problem is how to put it into practice."[9]

Both Satō and Shiina were anxious to defuse the situation. They sent Noda Uichi, a Liberal Democratic member of parliament, to Saigon in late January to see what could be done. The next month they dispatched a member of the parliamentary House of Councillors, the prominent Buddhist Ōtani Yoshio, to talk with South Vietnamese politicians and clerics. These emissaries found that the real problem was the political fragility of the GVN. Gen. Nguyen Khanh carried out a coup on January 27, 1965 to regain his eroding power but yielded three weeks later to Premier Phan Huy Quat, whose government lasted until June. At that point he was replaced as premier by the young air force general Nguyen Cao Ky.[10] The opposition parties in Japan did not take these missions seriously, calling them a sop to domestic opinion. Japan was only one of many countries that tried to mediate the conflict, and its occasional peace efforts were inevitably tarred by the government's close economic and military ties to the United States.

Even though Satō had moved a few steps closer to Washington during his first months in office, he backed the war without enthusiasm and for very specific, instrumental goals: trade and autonomy. His ill-starred attempts to arrange a settlement, which were partly intended to silence a small coterie of dissidents in his own party, showed that he was determined not to be a meek hostage of American foreign policy in early 1965. Still, in spite of the prime minister's hesitation, Japan

was drawn by degrees into more active support as the war widened. Speaking two decades later in the alumni club of Satō's university, the antiwar leader Oda Makoto conceded that Vietnam for Japan was a piece of tragic theater: "our country was a kind of 'forced aggressor' in the war. Because of the security treaty, Japan had to cooperate with the American policy of aggression. In this sense Japan was a victim of its alliance with that policy, but it was also an aggressor toward the small countries in Indochina."[11]

THE FIRST JOHNSON SHOCK

"It is difficult to understand the minds of Buddhists fully if you have a Christian outlook,"[12] Prime Minister Satō told the press with considerable asperity the week after the United States began bombing North Vietnam on February 7, 1965. The aerial campaign came as a total surprise to the Japanese government, which reflexively defended its ally against a squall of censure but also said it hoped for a quick resolution of the conflict. Years later the *Pentagon Papers* divulged what many Japanese leaders had suspected: the Americans briefed Australia, Britain, Canada, and New Zealand before bombing Vietnam, and they also told the Philippines, South Korea, and Taiwan about the initial phase of the strategy only.[13] It is no wonder the besieged prime minister felt exasperated with the snub from Washington, which three weeks earlier had courted his cooperation on Vietnam.

Part of the reason the American bombardments shocked ordinary citizens in Japan so greatly was that before February 1965 they had taken very little interest in the war. A month or so earlier the press had begun carrying vivid accounts of the fighting, such as Ōmori Minoru's thirty-eight-part "Mud and Flames of Indochina" for *Mainichi* and Kaikō Takeshi's "Vietnam War Diary" in *Shūkan asahi*. The photographer Okamura Akihiko published his best-selling *War Report from South Vietnam* in January (*Minami Betonamu kara jūgunki*), and starting February 1 TBS television began showing a documentary on

the Viet Cong by the Australian communist Wilfred Bur-
chett.[14] But it was the bombing campaign that created the first
real public interest in the war. As the critic Owada Jirō noted,
"the newspapers died with the security treaty crisis but came
to life again with Vietnam."[15]

No major paper approved of the bombing strategy. The national dailies called for peace, as did the opposition parties in
the Diet. The foreign ministry at first tried to reassure the public that the air raids would not "escalate the war," but when it
became obvious that they had, Shiina on February 10 called the
bombardments "justified" and argued that they constituted
proper self-defense. Two days later Satō said he hoped the war
would not enlarge further.[16] The government was also dis-
comfited by the disclosure, on February 10, of a plan for joint
Japanese-American military operations in South Korea if another war should break out there. The Japan Socialist Party assailed the scheme, prepared in 1963 and known as the Three
Arrows Study, but Satō brushed it off as "merely a game of
war on paper."[17]

The Three Arrows Study had no real connection with Vietnam, but the furor helped to sharpen the debate in parliament
over how liberally the United States could use its bases in Japan for operations in Indochina. Shiina told the budget committee of the lower house on February 14 that Vietnam was
not within the Far East but that the security treaty could not be
limited to the Far East alone if nearby events menaced its peace
and security. Reaffirming the government's position since
1961–1962, he said that direct combat operations undertaken
from bases in Japan required prior consultation but that routine supply functions did not.[18]

The following month Shiina told the Diet that the government essentially accepted Washington's definition of the Far
East and that it would not ask for prior consultation when
bases in Okinawa, which was not covered by the treaty, were
used for direct combat.[19] When the Democratic Socialist representative Nagasue asked on April 7 how the Vietnam War
threatened peace and security in the Far East, Shiina replied

vaguely that Japan was affected by the war.[20] Later that day at Johns Hopkins University President Johnson set forth the terms acceptable to the United States for peace and postwar development in Vietnam, a speech "welcomed" by the Japanese state.[21]

Through this series of pronouncements, the Satō cabinet yielded to Washington's interpretations of the treaty, reneging on Kishi's promises to the Diet just five years earlier. Kishi had limited the treaty to the Far East, which he placed north of the Philippines, and he had insisted that Japan could veto American requests during advance consultations.[22] Now the government of Japan not only took a more expansive view of the geography involved but also practically wrote off the need for prior consultation. The result was that the United States never once asked for prior consultation throughout the whole war, and none was ever held. With such a broad and ill-defined security system that might embroil Japan in an unwanted conflict, many critics said they felt less secure under the treaty than without one.

THE EARLIEST PUBLIC PROTESTS

The struggle in 1960 over the security treaty, which was rooted mostly in domestic political rivalries, attracted unimagined throngs but in many ways resembled the strikes and hostile urban confrontations that erupted in Japan before World War II. The public commotion over the Vietnam War after early 1965 was different: it was much smaller at first, it was mainly a challenge to the foreign policies of another country, and it often used tactics not previously seen in Japan.

Both in and out of parliament, the Old Left had condemned the American advisers in South Vietnam long before Johnson ordered the Rolling Thunder bombings in the spring of 1965. Right after the escalation began, Sōhyō organized a rally against the war on February 26 in Tokyo, and together with another labor federation, Chūritsu Rōren, it sponsored a meeting there on March 27 to demand that the United States

withdraw. Two days later Gensuikyō sent a delegation to the American embassy to deliver a note of protest to Johnson.[23]

Apart from labor, the antibomb groups, and the opposition parties, the first widely reported public dissent came on February 13, 1965, when the Nobel Prize-winning physicist Yukawa Hideki and six other scholars appealed to Johnson to end the war. Another Nobel physicist, Tomonaga Shin'ichirō, formed a committee of scientists who called on world leaders to limit the conflict. This was the beginning of a fusillade against the United States from liberals, socialists, neo-nationalists, and uncommitted intellectuals. Some of the critics had strong ties to Japan's authoritarian regime that had seized Southeast Asia during 1941–1945, such as the leading journalist Ryū Shintarō, who ignited a letter-writing campaign with an attack in *Asahi* on American war policy. Soon the Harvard-educated scholar Tsuru Shigeto and five other leading intellectuals wrote to the editor asking that Japan steer clear of the war.[24] Even the usually pro-American Cultural Freedom group, including tough-minded scholars like Hayashi Kentarō and Inoki Masamichi (later head of the Defense Academy), asked the United States to withdraw from Vietnam at once.[25]

By far the biggest blasts of the spring came in late April, from groups of scholars, writers, and artists led by a seventy-seven-year-old economist, Ōuchi Hyōe, and a thirty-three-year-old novelist, Oda Makoto. Ōuchi, who was a professor emeritus at Tokyo University and a leading Marxist ideologue in the left wing of the Japan Socialist Party, presented a petition on behalf of ninety-two academic, literary, and cultural figures addressed to Prime Minister Satō on April 20. It asked him to explain to the United States that its policies in Vietnam were misguided and to take action so that Japan would not become involved. The appeal contained three main points: 1) "we demand that the Japanese government immediately make it clear" to all that "it will not sanction the use of American military bases in Japan for combat operations"; 2) "we demand that the Japanese government request the United States to immediately cease its bombing of North Vietnam"; and 3)

"we demand that the Japanese government" ask the combatants "to effect a suspension of hostilities and open diplomatic negotiations which include the South Vietnam National Liberation Front."[26]

This statement specifically addressed Japan's self-interest, rather than rejecting war in principle, and it also attacked concrete American actions in Indochina without lapsing into generalized condemnations of aggression or imperialism. Many of the ninety-three signers, and most of the 521 Tokyo University professors and lecturers who supported them in a petition the following month, were liberals who were normally well-disposed toward the United States. Although they disagreed with its current actions in Vietnam, a number of them supported the Johns Hopkins proposals of April 7, and most wanted to keep their campaign "from being transformed into an anti-American movement."[27]

Unlike the earlier protesters in letters to editors and street rallies, the ninety-three petitioners were too eminent to ignore. Satō replied at once that the Japanese government welcomed the Baltimore speech, that it hoped for peace, and that it felt hamstrung in trying to bring it about: "it is difficult for Japan to intervene directly on behalf of a peaceful solution, but for some time we have been taking every opportunity to make our opinions known to the American government."[28]

A far less diplomatic reply to the Ōuchi group arrived from the playwright Fukuda Tsuneari, who berated them for their naiveté and for the "uselessness" of their proposals. Vietnam was unready for independence, Fukuda contended, and granting its freedom would be "more criminal and cruel than what the United States is doing in Vietnam—including the bombing of the North."[29] If Tokyo did not stand by its ally, "Japan might end up as the orphan of Asia."[30] Although the writer Kaikō Takeshi quickly rebutted Fukuda in print, many other influential Japanese agreed that Satō was right to back the Americans. Two of the most prominent were Asakai Kōichirō, a former ambassador to Washington, and Matsushita Masatoshi, the head of Rikkyō University who founded the

Kakkin Kaigi antibomb group in 1961, ran for governor of Tokyo, and later joined the Unification Church. An important commentator on military affairs, Saeki Kiichi, tartly reminded the antiwar protesters of the domino theory and argued that bombing North Vietnam would have a restraining effect on communist rebels in Laos. Such rigorous scholars as Etō Shinkichi and Kamiya Fuji, writing in the spring of 1965, said the Vietnam situation showed that Japan should be far more active diplomatically and stop relying on the security treaty alone to defend its interests. Like their counterparts in other countries, Japanese intellectuals wrangled endlessly over the war. Some agreed with the Americans completely, some gave concrete aid to Hanoi and the NLF, and others could not abide either side and called for peace at once.[31]

The group of writers, artists, and scholars assembled by Oda Makoto on April 24, 1965 did not command the immediate access to Satō that Ōuchi enjoyed, but the movement they started on that date in Shimizudani Park, near the New Otani Hotel in Tokyo, turned into the most powerful antiwar campaign in the country. It was characteristic of this decentralized, largely unstructured movement that it did not settle on an official name for nearly a year: Citizens' Federation for Peace in Vietnam (Betonamu ni Heiwa o! Shimin Rengō). But formality was beside the point in this near-clone of the early peace movement in the United States. From the start everyone called it Beheiren for short, and anyone who wanted peace in Vietnam was free to join in. "Raise your cry as an individual Japanese concerned about Vietnam, as an individual human being," read the invitation to Beheiren's first rally.[32] A pamphlet distributed at the event urged everyone to learn more about how to stabilize South Vietnam "and advise our friends the Americans" on what to do.[33]

Most of the organizers were young writers and artists who had close contacts with the antiwar movements in Cambridge, Ann Arbor, and Berkeley. They often scheduled their demonstrations to coincide with protests held in Europe and the United States. Their compass was nationwide and their style

was deliberately casual compared with the carefully choreo-
graphed, whistle-driven processions of zigzagging street
marchers who resisted the security treaty in 1960. As they
walked to Shinbashi after the first Beheiren gathering on April
24, carrying flowers and white balloons, the 1,500 demonstrators called out to passers-by, "please take part as ordinary
citizens."[34]

There were many reasons why people in Japan might oppose the Vietnam War in 1965. Pictures of the death and destruction from American B-52s reminded Japanese of how
helpless they had been twenty years earlier during daily raids
by B-29s and reinforced the strong pacifism most of them had
embraced since 1945. As the scholar Michio Umegaki has
pointed out, the Japanese often feel "almost uncritically sympathetic" toward the people who live in divided countries with
competing regimes.[35] Some citizens no doubt sensed a racial
bond with the Vietnamese as fellow Asians, although most
people in Japan regard themselves as distinctly separate from
other nations.[36] Even if questions of race were absent, it was
easy for almost anyone to identify with the Vietnamese as underdogs.

Men and women born in the 1930s who experienced wartime as they were growing up often compared the Vietnam
War with Japan's fiasco in China during 1937–1945. Marius B.
Jansen has written that despite different goals, both Japan and
the United States became unexpectedly trapped in guerrilla
warfare, underestimated local nationalisms, fell victim to self-
doubt, and resorted to tactics of vast destructiveness.[37] It is
easy to understand why so many Japanese in 1965 tried to
warn the United States not to repeat such bitter mistakes—and
why so many antiwar intellectuals thought American imperialism was thwarting self-determination by the Vietnamese.

The general public in Japan was often accused of taking too
sentimental a view of the Vietnam War at the beginning, over-
reacting to stark newsphotos and brutal television footage.[38]
Actually much of the outcry was more pragmatic than indig-
nant or even principled, because it was based squarely on the

33

fear that the security treaty would drag Japan into the fighting. The American bombings were especially frightening because it seemed in early 1965 that China might be drawn in on Hanoi's side. If so, many Japanese were afraid that the Chinese would attack the American bases in Japan. Absolutely nobody in Japan relished being caught in the middle of a Sino-American war.[39] The eminent China specialist Matsumoto Shigeharu warned sternly that "a war between America and Communist China would split the nation in two," with the likelihood of "disturbances approaching a civil war in scale" throughout Japan.[40] There could scarcely be a greater disaster for Japan—or a more blundering misadventure for the United States.

Such worries receded by the end of 1965 when it became clear that China was not likely to join the war. In retrospect the public anxieties seem exaggerated, but to people living in Japan they were unquestionably real. Writing in an unrelated context, the sociologist Ronald P. Dore has pointed out how shared fears in a consensual society "can rapidly develop into a sense of crisis by the reverberating process of cumulative feedback."[41] Such a syndrome may have magnified the anxiety over Vietnam in 1965, especially with a newly nuclear China across the Yellow Sea. Long after the Vietnam War ended, the former dean of the Japan Defense Research Institute, Momoi Makoto, made light of the public's fears of war with the PRC. "Japan's leaders," he said, "knew that China lacked the capability to attack American bases in Japan" because its missiles were set on fixed targets in the Soviet Union.[42] Even had they known this information, many citizens might have wondered why the Chinese could not reset their weapons to fire in another direction.

Perhaps the most practical reason for dissenting from American policies in Indochina was the widely held belief that the United States had backed a loser.[43] Most people in Japan never dreamed that the United States could snarl its goals so badly by supporting a regime as unpopular as the Saigon government. At the same time it was almost incomprehensible

that the debate between hawks and doves was getting out of hand in the United States, especially since very few Japanese under similar circumstances would have wanted it known to outsiders that they thought their own country's policies were wrong.[44]

THE MEDIA TAKE AIM

The Vietnam War was a big story in Japan from start to finish. Star reporters like Tokuoka Takao of *Mainichi* and Honda Katsuichi of *Asahi* became daily companions for many readers through their dispatches from the war zone. "TV sensationalized the war right in the average family's living room," the veteran journalist Roy M. Honda recalls.[45] Whether or not they favored American actions in Vietnam, most people would probably agree with the scholar Irie Michimasa that "the worsening of feeling toward the United States on the part of the majority of Japanese was a direct result of the Vietnam reporting by the Japanese mass media."[46]

The three largest national dailies, *Asahi, Mainichi*, and *Yomiuri*, had a combined circulation of 24 million, and the other 168 dailies had about 25 million.[47] Both television and newspapers reached nearly every home in Japan. Because they were better established and less dependent on advertising than broadcasting, Japanese newspapers were the main source of public attitudes on foreign affairs in the 1960s, although the press had even less influence over the government's foreign policy than in the United States. On international affairs, the American diplomat Richard L. Sneider observed, the newspapers saw themselves "as the surrogate of public opinion and more important than the Diet opposition parties in resisting any government tendencies to expand significantly the defense forces and budget."[48] Sometimes, too, even news correspondents became participants in the story instead of simply reporting it. For these reasons the press became snarled in controversy as the Vietnam War developed, and just as in the United

States its most acrid critics often denounced the medium because they could not abide its message.

Daily newspapers have been watchdogs over the Japanese authorities ever since the late nineteenth century, but not until after World War II did they begin to shed their reputations for sensationalism and concentrate on building their circulations through accurate, balanced reporting. The treaty crisis in 1960 relieved the papers of some of their postwar blandness, but the real shift away from the safe, reliable grayness of the fifties came in response to the growth of TV news and the weekly magazines in the mid-sixties. For all these media the events in Vietnam were a boon. Since reporting had been censored during both World War II and the Korean War, Vietnam was the first conflict covered on location by a free Japanese press and the first portrayed with graphic pictures of dead bodies and burning houses.[49]

Several hundred Japanese reporters and photographers were stationed in Vietnam at various times during the war. A number of Japanese journalists were killed or missing in action. Correspondents vied with one another to cover the National Liberation Front (Viet Cong), and all the news organizations regularly carried dispatches from Hanoi as well as from the daily press briefings held by the United States military command in Saigon. Most writers filed their stories by telex, in Romanized Japanese.[50]

Were the Japanese reporters biased? Seeing the grim destruction at first hand undoubtedly honed their perspectives and sometimes evoked their sympathies for the suffering of the Vietnamese. Japanese newspapers invariably gave their correspondents wide latitude in the choice of topic, angle of approach, and critical interpretation. Editors back in the newsroom rarely had enough personal experience in Vietnam to question a dispatch; instead, most of them concentrated on scrupulously presenting the views of both Saigon and Hanoi each day. The scholar Jung Bock Lee surveyed the political attitudes of 177 journalists from five major Japanese dailies in 1973, finding that three-quarters of them placed "themselves

in either the center or the moderate left" on politics.[51] Most were critical of the Liberal Democrats but also skeptical of all the parties. Without a doubt there was some one-sided reporting from Vietnam and some slanted judgment about the news value of certain stories in the makeup rooms back in Tokyo. But it is worth remembering the warning against self-delusion offered by the distinguished journalist and friend of the United States, Matsumoto Shigeharu of International House, in late 1965: unlike the American press coverage of the NLF and Hanoi, he said, Japanese writing from North Vietnam "has been highly objective and humanistic in its approach . . . in no sense the work of reporters who are Communists or fellow-travelers."[52]

Far more outspoken than the news stories were the editorial columns of *Asahi, Mainichi*, and *Yomiuri*. Japanese publishers usually allow their editorial boards great freedom in expressing opinions about public issues. In the case of Vietnam, they used it for perhaps the first time ever to criticize an issue of foreign policy itself, rather than making the war a stalking horse for their inveterate opposition to the government at home. Nearly every paper in the country weighed in editorially against the American involvement in Vietnam, none more so than the flagship of the industry, *Asahi*. Maruyama Shizuo, who wrote 270 of the newspaper's 280 editorials on Indochina during 1962–1974, consistently called the conflict a civil war and relentlessly castigated the Saigon regime. Maruyama also wrote off the PRC and the Soviet Union as "no good" on the Vietnam question, but he shot nearly all his arrows at the United States for its sustained bombing campaigns.[53] (Along with many Japanese war critics, he spoke constantly of "the bombing of the north," even though far more explosives fell on South Vietnam, Laos, and Cambodia—over 14 million tons on all of Indochina, several times the total dropped on Germany and Japan in 1939–1945.) Like most newspaper editorialists in Japan, Maruyama called for an end to the bombings, a cease-fire on the ground, the removal of United States forces but not those of the DRV, and a political settlement agreeable

37

to the Vietnamese. He railed against the United States for demanding picky concessions inappropriate for a superpower. Most of all, he wrote in a postmortem on the war, America's "falsehoods" were hateful. He believed that the United States perpetrated aggression while claiming to defend freedom and saying it was using war to build peace.[54] Clearly *Asahi* and other papers of its stripe differed from American policy not just on the details of a peace program but in fundamental world view. Almost no Japanese leaders shared *Asahi*'s basic assumptions about international politics, nor did a majority of the people at large. This chasm between outlooks was unbridgeable; time settled the Vietnam issue but did not do much to reshape the viewpoints.

What effect editorials, news reports, and other sources had on the staggering flood of letters to editors cannot be calculated precisely, but a number of the major dailies received more correspondence than ever before. More than 60,000 letters on all subjects reached *Mainichi* in 1965, triple the usual volume, and 74,411 arrived at *Asahi*. As always, most of those who wrote were students and housewives, but there was a tall stack from persons who almost never wrote: prominent scholars, politicians, and religious leaders. The voice of the people (Koe) column of *Asahi* became a choice forum for individuals from Beheiren and other antiwar organizations. Weekly and monthly magazines quickly sensed the same wave of public concern. *Shūkan asahi* received 178 letters in 1960 when it asked readers to write President Eisenhower about the security treaty; five years later it collected 1,233 addressed to President Johnson about Vietnam.[55] The monthly journal of opinion *Sekai* quickly sold out its April 1965 number on the war, the first such special issue in its twenty-year history, and magazines like *Asahi gurafu, Bungei,* and *Chūō kōron* ordered extra printings to meet the demand for their specials on Vietnam.[56]

Still, the Japanese journalistic parish was not quite unanimous about the war. Both *Tōkyō shinbun* and *Kumamoto nichinichi shinbun* remained editorially anchored to the American policy in Vietnam, and new tabloids such as *Sekai shūhō* and

Genronjin carried reports that were usually favorable to the United States. Eventually critics of the big three dailies charged that the press was variously too sentimental, too gullible about communism, too wedded to ritualistic peace formulas, and too idealistic in its understanding of democracy, freedom, peace, and human nature. But noisiest by far were the hecklers who gathered daily outside the sooty *Asahi* headquarters at Yūrakuchō, chanting "*Asahi* is red" (*aka da, aka da*).[57]

Japanese television also opened many people's eyes to the savage fighting in Vietnam, yet most media people agree that TV had a relatively slighter impact on public opinion than was true in the United States.[58] Film clips appeared almost daily on the 7 P.M. and especially the 9 P.M. news. Their effect was as undisputed as it was hard to measure. Roy Honda believes that "the impact of the print media is more lasting; the effect of TV is more immediate but more transient."[59] A public opinion poll taken right after a brutal documentary on television usually turned up strong antiwar feelings, but the daily papers seem to have been the single most persuasive influence on people's outlooks. Like the newspapers, television also thoroughly covered the protests in Japan against the war, to the point of giving officials at the American embassy "the impression that the whole country was up in arms" over Vietnam—although Prime Minister Satō quickly assured them that things would simmer down.[60]

The television world itself was thrown into turmoil on May 11, 1965 when Nihon Terebi (NTV) canceled a rebroadcast of part one of Ushiyama Jin'ichi's graphic documentary, *Diary of a South Vietnamese Marine Battalion (Minami Betonamu kaihei daitai kiroku)*. Chief Cabinet Secretary Hashimoto Tomisaburō, who learned of the original May 9 showing from a reporter at an Akasaka teahouse, called the president of NTV on May 10 to remonstrate because the film was said to be rife with violence, including the execution of a VC suspect by a South Vietnamese marine. Tokyo Gas Company asked that its name be removed as a sponsor after the first broadcast. Part one was

shown only once, in Tokyo alone, and parts two and three were never seen. Such pressures from the government and big business were fairly rare during the 1960s and 1970s, but the threat of them unquestionably caused the stations to exercise self-censorship as they reported the war.[61]

There is very little to suggest that the state interfered with how the newspapers covered or interpreted the events in Indochina. Even though Japanese journalists have used press clubs for many years to ingratiate themselves with bureaucrats and other government officials, no one in the Satō cabinet expected the unwritten policy of press cooperation with the state to reach as far as the editorial pages. Apparently overt threats from the government were rarely felt at *Asahi* during the war, even when the authorities were completely dismayed at instances of sloppy reporting.[62]

The cabinet was unhappy, but not surprised, when *Asahi* carried an exclusive interview on April 16, 1965 with the diplomat Matsumoto Shun'ichi, who had just returned to Japan on April 1 from a two-week fact-finding mission to Saigon as the prime minister's personal emissary. Matsumoto had once served in Vietnam and later became Japanese ambassador to Great Britain. Suspicious of the advice coming from Japan's foreign service officers in Saigon, Satō dispatched Matsumoto to scout the prospects for peace and meet with leaders of the Government of Vietnam. He also conferred with the American ambassador, Gen. Maxwell D. Taylor, and the top United States commander, Gen. William C. Westmoreland. His report to Satō and the nation was brusque and pessimistic.

Matsumoto told *Asahi* that "the Japanese government understood nothing at all about Vietnam" and that it naively expected the Americans to win.[63] On April 23 he told the foreign affairs committee of the lower house that no amount of bombing would weaken the communists' will because "the core of Vietcong is the nationalist movement that is growing in South Vietnam."[64] Soon after the *Pentagon Papers* vindicated his report almost point for point in 1971, Matsumoto disclosed that Satō had asked him almost no questions after hearing his

findings in April 1965; instead the prime minister ended the meeting with: "America is not making a mistake in what it is doing in Vietnam."[65] Obviously the cabinet ignored his advice, Matsumoto wrote in 1971, concluding rhetorically, "doesn't the public place too much trust in the government and foreign ministry?"[66]

The Matsumoto report caught the United States by surprise. Its glum forecast was one reason why a stream of top officials visited Tokyo in late April and early May. Another was to persuade the Liberal Democratic Party to stop showing "virtually no interest" in defending the Pacific, as Assistant Secretary of State William P. Bundy put it.[67] Henry Cabot Lodge arrived on April 24, 1965 to explain on Johnson's behalf why the United States had just intensified the Rolling Thunder campaign. Walt W. Rostow, chair of the policy planning committee of the state department, spent several days in Japan at the end of the month conferring with leaders of the LDP and the opposition, as well as with diplomats, about the Vietnam situation. Tokyo, Waseda, and Kyoto universities all canceled lectures he was scheduled to deliver, with the terse excuse that certain students might harass him. Patrick Gordon Walker, a special British envoy, also came to Japan in May to explain his country's support for the United States in Vietnam. The foreign visitor who seemingly had the greatest cachet with the public was Edgar Faure, the former French prime minister, who presented President Charles de Gaulle's plan for ending the bombings and starting peace talks.[68]

Another task for the delegation from Washington was to help smooth over the rumpus in the newspapers when they learned on April 28, 1965 that two high American officials had recently accused *Asahi* and *Mainichi* of harboring communists in their newsrooms. On April 7 George Ball, the undersecretary of state, and Douglas MacArthur II, a former ambassador to Japan, testified to the Senate foreign relations committee that the two papers were hostile to American policies in Southeast Asia because of communists on their staffs. MacArthur said that *Asahi* alone had more than 200 of them. Sen.

J. William Fulbright, the committee chair, was not fooled by these fanciful and unfounded charges.

Ambassador Edwin O. Reischauer, who had often sparred with the Japanese press over Vietnam, quickly defended the two papers in a statement cleared with the state department: "even when it [the press] disagrees with or criticizes U.S. policy, we admire its professionalism and enterprise, welcome its independence and forthrightness and respect its political integrity."[69] *Asahi* reaffirmed its "impartiality and nonpartisanship" in an editorial on May 1, pledging "to print strictly fair and unbiased reports and comments" but also calling once again for an end to the war.[70] Ball and MacArthur eventually withdrew the charges, which apparently reflected an old grudge from 1960. The Japan Communist Party, which had been a legal political group for nearly twenty years, turned out to have only a few members among the staff of either paper. Throughout the procession of visitors and swirls of controversy, Prime Minister Satō remained vague and noncommittal, shifting a step or two to the right and practicing the art of waiting while his party refined its position on the war and prepared to face the first national election since he took office.

Vietnam and the Parties

The war in Indochina finally took center court in the Japanese political arena when the governing Liberal Democratic Party came up with a united strategy in May 1965 for supporting the United States without entangling Japan directly in the conflict. Almost immediately after Lodge and Rostow departed, the LDP took a right turn on the war issue when party secretary Miki Takeo told the *Asahi jānaru* that the NLF was violating the Geneva provisions with military help from North Vietnam and China—a common refrain in Washington at the time.[71] Foreign Minister Shiina told the Diet on May 7 that "the reasons for the American bombings of the north are proper" and that Japan was cooperating through the treaty framework "because America is taking these military actions

on behalf of the peace and security of the Far East."[72] On the same day Satō gave an unusually forthright talk to young Liberal Democrats, defending the bombings and insisting that "the thing we should fear most is red imperialism."[73] By now the government had slowly inched away from its nonchalant position at the time of the Satō-Johnson meeting the previous January.

Facing protests in the streets, drum-beating by the press, and an election for members of the House of Councillors on July 4, the LDP chiseled out a unified viewpoint on Vietnam that could mollify the Americans and ease the bickering among factions within the party about Japan's Asian policy. One group thought that the nation should take a hard-line, pro-American stand on the war. It consisted of about 160 LDP members of the lower house belonging to the Asian Problems Study Group (Ajia Mondai Kenkyūkai), led by senior right-wing figures such as former Prime Minister Kishi Nobusuke and Kaya Okinori, who headed the finance ministry during 1941–1944, was convicted of class A war crimes, and yet somehow became the minister of justice in 1963. The world view of the Asian Problems Study Group was rooted in anti-communism stemming from the 1930s, when Japan increasingly used force to expand its economic influence over the Asian continent. Conservatives like Kishi wanted their country to rearm rapidly after the American occupation ended in 1952, and they were also convinced that in the long run Japan's closest trade ties should be with its noncommunist neighbors in Asia. Although the LDP right wing was usually more neo-nationalist than pro-American in the 1950s and 1960s, its study group in the House of Representatives backed the United States unflinchingly on the Vietnam question.

Its opponents, the Asian-African Problems Study Group (Ajia-Afurika Mondai Kenkyūkai), criticized the "passive and evasive attitudes" of Satō and insisted that Japan press both Washington and Hanoi to stop the fighting.[74] The Asian-African group, led by Utsunomiya Tokuma and Fujiyama Aiichirō, included roughly 120 Liberal Democrats in the House of

CHAPTER 1

Representatives whose real concern was not war in Vietnam but trade with China. The influence of this second organization was modest; it was Richard Nixon, not the Asian-African clique, who eventually made it possible for Japan to recognize the PRC in 1972.

So long as no mainstream factions within the LDP turned against Satō, he could pretty well ignore the views of the Asian-African members and concentrate on keeping the hawkish Asian Problems Study Group from pushing Japan into even deeper involvement in the war. As the scholar John Clark has pointed out, Satō's power would have been threatened if additional factions in the party had shifted away from supporting the United States after the Tet offensive in early 1968.[75] The shift did not happen until the spring of 1972, when irritations in the Japan–United States relationship finally eroded the party's confidence in the prime minister.

With the Asian and Asian-African groups far apart in outlook and unequal in power, a true party consensus on Vietnam in May 1965 was neither intellectually possible nor tactically necessary from the standpoint of inner party politics. The umbrella position announced by the LDP on May 18 was a public relations gesture to the press, the Americans, and the electorate. The party statement repeated the government's recent opinions that Hanoi had violated the Geneva arrangements, that the Americans could use their bases in Japan for noncombat purposes without prior consultation, and that South Vietnam should be secured against outside attack. The document took a swipe at the Japanese writers and scholars who had criticized American actions, calling their attitude "unjust" in light of communist "aggression from the north."[76] It concluded with "earnest hopes for the earliest possible international talks" to end the fighting, after which "Japan expects to contribute to the economic and social development" desired by the region.[77]

Careful as the Liberal Democrats may have been to temper their backing of the United States, this unified position placed them on very different ground from any of the opposition par-

44

ties concerning Vietnam. The largest was the JSP, which denounced the war continuously after 1964 but split over what priority it should occupy. A left-wing group led by Sasaki Kōzō emphasized struggle against American imperialism and the security treaty that was forcing Japan to endorse the conflict. The JSP Right, headed by Eda Saburō and Katsumata Seiichi, rapped the war but did not expect it to engulf China or Japan. The Eda-Katsumata wing stressed domestic economic and social reforms that might break the grip of the great corporations. Sasaki, the party chair, loudly attacked the Americans on May 6, 1965 for "playfully bombing North Vietnam" and expressed his fear that "we are getting involved in World War III."[78]

The party joined in a number of peace rallies that spring with its labor allies, and during the next months it stepped up the salvos as the United States poured in more troops. In a policy statement released in 1966, the JSP declared that "American imperialism is expanding its war of aggression in Vietnam" and that Japan should promote peace by insisting that the bombings end and the United States withdraw.[79] The deepening war helped to push the party to the left ideologically, satisfying its soul more than its electorate. In April 1966 Prime Minister Satō mocked the socialists in parliament for "making a laughing stock of themselves" by endlessly deriding American imperialism, but for the rest of the decade the party showed no inclination to change its tune.[80] Its firm doctrines, quarrelsome leaders, preoccupation with subverting the security treaty, and strict neutralism in international affairs cost the JSP much favor with the public. Many politically unaffiliated individuals in the antiwar movement rejected the socialists and all the other opposition parties because they had seemingly been co-opted into joining a repetitive chorus of parliamentary dissent.

The Sōhyō labor alliance, which provided many of the votes for the JSP, condemned the war with rhetoric and rallies to the very end, but Sōhyō too was rent with disputes over how much attention to devote to matters of war and peace. "We

45

strongly oppose the policy of the Sato government which sides with the aggressive actions of America in Vietnam," declared a resolution of March 4, 1965.[81] Although it turned out hundreds of thousands of demonstrators (usually paid) at protest meetings, Sōhyō's main purpose was to improve wages and conditions for its members, most of whom were based in large cities. Along with the JSP and the JCP, it was less concerned to oppose the Vietnam War than to defeat the security treaty when the pact came up for possible abrogation in 1970, since doing so might topple the ruling conservatives.

What is more, many opponents of the war thought that the union leaders suffered from middle-aged spread, losing interest in resisting a conflict that was helping them prosper through procurement contracts. Haryū Ichirō, the art critic and Beheiren activist, recalls that the chair of Sōhyō told him near the end of the war, "we too want to send our sons to university and play golf."[82] The organizational strength of the Old Left should not be minimized; the labor federations kept up their pressure on American bases and sponsored an annual antiwar day each October throughout the war. Yet eventually Sōhyō grew alienated from some of its younger unionists over tactics for resisting the war and became a relatively soft voice in the debate over Southeast Asia.

The Japan Communist Party, like the left-wing socialists, regarded Vietnam as a war of aggression by American imperialism. At its ninth party congress on November 25, 1964, the JCP said that events in Indochina already showed that the United States was in the process of "the deepest decay and decadency"—a theme it sounded more loudly as the war escalated.[83] The JCP completed its break with Beijing in 1966, by which time it had tried but failed to revive the united front of communists, socialists, and workers that had lapsed after the treaty demonstrations of 1960 were over. The party inveighed against American foreign policy through debate in parliament and editorials in its widely circulated newspaper, *Akahata*. It also worked against the war through the Democratic Youth League (Minsei) on university campuses and through its shard

of the fragmented antibomb movement, Gensuikyō. Both Minsei and Gensuikyō faithfully spoke out against the American actions in Vietnam. The JCP itself was hampered by its relatively small size, its abstract interpretations of American misbehavior, its preference to refight the treaty battle in 1970, and most of all its determination after 1966 to design an appealing economic and social platform that would make it a credible and fully indigenous party at last.

The other minor parties in the Diet took a more insular view of the Vietnam question. The Democratic Socialists, who supported the LDP on certain domestic matters, condemned both sides in the war but did not make it a campaign issue. Like the other opposition parties, the DSP grew more irritated with the United States by the late 1960s, but it did not believe Japan had much leverage in promoting a cease-fire. Kōmeitō was a newcomer to national politics and very cautious about international questions that did not involve Japan directly. Founded in 1964 by the lay Buddhist organization Sōka Gakkai, Kōmeitō normally lined up on important issues against its archrival, the JCP. But Kōmeitō was also a party of peace, and it agreed with all the opposition parties that an end to the fighting was called for.[84]

Single-issue movements entered the political process only very slowly in any of the major democracies in the 1960s, because parties by definition were clusters of interests that were susceptible to compromise. In the Japanese case, factions based on personal loyalties, especially in the largest parties, made it even harder for an isolated issue to win support. It was customary to interpret any fusillade of policy opposition, no matter how principled, as a smokescreen for wresting power from those who held it. The antiwar protesters had even greater difficulty gaining entree to the established parties because their cause involved a foreign policy emanating from another sovereign state and because those who opposed the war, like both sides that fought it, were unyielding in outlook and unwilling to subject their demands to consensual modification. To some degree all the parties regarded any antiwar sentiment ex-

pressed outside the familiar mechanisms of the Old Left as potentially antiestablishment, so it is natural that the smallest parties with the most to lose from embracing controversy shied away from the Vietnam question and tried to broaden their allure with less dyspeptic menus.

VIETNAM AND THE POLLS

Prime Minister Satō prepared for the upper house election of July 4, 1965, by trying to placate his doubters through assurances that the war would not spread further. His aging predecessor and patron, Yoshida Shigeru, told Satō privately that he was not satisfied with Satō's recent forthright approval of the American bombings because he thought Japan's foreign relations would be impaired by such echo-like support. On June 9 Yoshida said publicly that what the United States was "doing comes from a sincere wish to aid Vietnam," but he scolded the Americans for failing to understand the country: "they have preconceived ideas about what should be done in Vietnam and try to impose them."[85] That same day Sōhyō, the JSP, and the JCP as well as smaller civic groups held the first big nationwide rally against the war, drawing 108,000 people (according to the police). In the campaign itself, the Liberal Democrats tried to emphasize income doubling and soft-pedal their unified position. As a senior diplomat, Miyake Wasuke, later said of the war era overall, "we told the opposition parties that we supported what the United States was seeking to accomplish in Vietnam but not necessarily its methods, such as bombing the north. We supported the American effort to achieve self-determination for the people of South Vietnam."[86]

The voting results on July 4 showed little if any fallout from choosing this approach. The Liberal Democrats won 71 of the 127 seats contested, leaving them with four fewer than before the election but still comfortably in charge of the upper chamber. The JSP and Kōmeitō each gained seats. Compared with the previous election in July 1962, the LDP's share of the popular vote dipped slightly, from 46.8 percent to 45.7 percent,

part of a long-term pattern of gentle decline.[87] The political analysts who rehashed the outcome barely mentioned Vietnam. One reason why the war was hardly an issue is that it had not been festering long enough to affect voting behavior in any country very greatly. Another is that foreign policy is rarely decisive in electoral politics anywhere in times of peace. In the Japanese case, party identification is relatively weak and candidate recognition is quite strong, so that politicians with active local organizations based on personal ties tend to win, regardless of their party's—or even their own—positions on specific issues. According to the political scientist Rōyama Michio, in Japan there is a "low correlation between the preferences of individual voters vis-à-vis foreign and defense policies, and the declared policies of the respective political parties to which they give their support."[88] This axiom probably held true in other countries during the war as well.

Another piece in the voting puzzle is the lack of an appealing alternative on the ballot. The scholar Kamiya Fuji concedes that there was a "true dilemma" to be found in the gap between growing public worries about the war and the increasingly pro-American policies of the state. "But even though the public didn't support the government's Vietnam policy," he observes, "neither did it support the opposition parties."[89] Many people at various levels of society apparently remained dubious of the minority parties and kept on supporting the familiar LDP, no matter how much they questioned its position on Southeast Asia. It is also true that antiwar feelings were strongest in electoral districts where the LDP was historically weakest, so that the Vietnam issue would have to penetrate the conservative rural areas where the party had its deepest roots. Only then could the Liberal Democrats' power be threatened. As the literary critic Katō Shūichi puts it, "the LDP view is that the only public opinion that counts is the wishes of the voters in its election districts"[90]—perhaps an extreme interpretation for a normally consensual political system, but one that indicates why the party never worried too much at the polls about Vietnam.

Like the Nakasone cabinet two decades later, the Satō government faced a good deal of pressure from agricultural cooperatives, the business sector, and factions within the LDP over economic policy but very little from these sources on defense or foreign policy. So long as the party, bureaucracy, and corporate world closed ranks on the issue, it was smart politics for Satō to overlook the public protests and to downplay Vietnam in election campaigns. Such maneuvers are subject to very little risk in a culture of one-party rule. This strategy worked well enough throughout the war, but growing evidence from public opinion surveys taken during the summer of 1965 showed that, no matter how people voted in elections, the war was much on their minds.

Opinion polls are sometimes used by newspapers in Japan to stir interest or generate momentum for a partisan viewpoint. Both government and newspaper surveys in 1965 showed that Vietnam was the number one international cause of concern to the public. *Asahi* questioned 3,000 adults throughout the country in early August, finding that 94 percent were aware of the fighting. Of this group, 75 percent disapproved of the bombings of the north and 4 percent favored them. The stated reasons for opposing the air raids were mainly pacifist and humanitarian, but *Asahi* attributed the antagonism to fears that Japan might be drawn into the war.[91]

Sixty percent of those who knew of the conflict said they thought its escalation might engulf Japan and 19 percent thought it would not. By a 42 percent to 17 percent margin they disagreed with the view that a Viet Cong victory would cause other Asian countries to turn communist.[92] For the first time in a decade, the *Asahi* survey found that a majority of Japanese thought that there was a danger of world war within the next twelve months (57 percent agreed, 20 percent disagreed).[93] If bombing might spread the conflict to China and drag Japan in against its wishes, and if the Americans were responsible for the bombings, then it is predictable that 33 percent of the respondents who knew of the war chose the United States when asked which country was most at fault in the Viet-

nam situation. The Viet Cong, who were not a nation, placed second at 8 percent.[94]

It is easy to understand that a self-interested wish to stay out of wars should dominate people's reactions to a distant conflict, especially in the early stages when no one knew how fast or far the Pentagon might expand its attacks. But the connection between attitudes and behavior is unusually hazy in the case of Japan and the Vietnam War. Opinion anonymously volunteered to a poll-taker does not necessarily translate into electoral behavior via the secret ballot, let alone into positive actions that cost individuals time, money, or the potential embarrassment of stepping out of line—especially in a society that lionizes conformity. Even if you favor a bitter war, it is very hard to tell an interviewer this fact amid the cascade of negative publicity about the conflict without seeming callous.

The least charitable view of how to interpret public opinion in Japan comes from Ambassador Douglas MacArthur II, who told Douglas H. Mendel, Jr., in December 1957 to "forget about what the mass public tells you in your opinion polls, because the men in Japan who really count are all on our side."[95] More to the point is an ingrained reluctance to become politically committed, an outlook inherited from premodern ideas about the proper roles of officials and citizens. This attitude is reinforced in child-rearing and other forms of cultural conditioning. Just as workers in Japan prefer to let the payroll office withhold taxes so that they can leave everything to the government, without having to think about how their taxes are spent, so individuals may tell a pollster their opinions about issues but in practice stay uninvolved.[96] This propensity is universal in contemporary bureaucratized society, but it seems to be particularly strong in Japan, where the cult of the uncommitted was celebrated in the early 1980s in a book called *Nantonaku kurisutaru (Vaguely Crystal)*.

On the other hand, the combined weight of public opinion expressed in attitude surveys, rallies, letters to editors, and the media probably set limits on how far the government could go in materially supporting the United States forces in Vietnam.

The Kaya-Kishi group within the LDP, for example, wanted to send Japanese troops to Vietnam in a noncombat capacity, but the outcry over Article IX in the constitution would surely have been deafening. Public opinion probably made "even less difference" in determining Japan's Vietnam policies than those of the United States, Katō Shūichi has observed, but it seemingly confined the Japanese government's role to one of "passive complicity" in the American war rather than active military assistance.[97] The crisis in 1960 showed the constraints that public attitudes and the opposition parties could place on official arrogance and highhandedness under the postwar democratic order, even though in the narrowest sense parliamentary institutions themselves were unequal to the task. The Vietnam case, although less weighty an example, suggests the limits that public sentiment can impose on government actions abroad. Satō dealt much less imperiously and far more astutely with protesters in the later 1960s than Kishi had in the treaty crisis. Whereas Kishi had tried to manipulate the Diet to his own advantage, Satō shrewdly used diplomacy (the Okinawa question) and economic policy (further growth) to appease the public.

Still, the government had little need to respond directly to the opponents of the war or to assuage the anxieties turned up by opinion polls. It knew that most citizens were wary of change and suspicious of communism. The LDP's electoral strength was substantial and its close relationship with the United States was intact, even if public confidence in America had drooped in the year since the Olympics. As Rōyama Michio puts it, "Vietnam was a big fire, but it was a fire on the other side of the river. So Satō could ignore it, knowing that it was a secondary issue for most Japanese."[98] Writing fictionally in 1972, the novelist and former Vietnam correspondent Kaikō Takeshi lamented:

> Forget about a war in another country. No one really takes it as seriously as they say they do. If they did, they wouldn't be able to sleep. The reason that everyone talks

about it so loudly is because it's far away and involves other people. Everyone wants to talk about other people's political problems; the farther the country, the more simply and heroically they can talk. When it comes to their own country, they are frightened to talk about the tiniest tremor and they begin to stutter right away. It's true. In other words, they can suffer without dirtying their hands, which is an attraction. They can speak eloquently without being held responsible and they won't be killed by either side.[99]

It was to overcome this armchair attitude and to offset the politics of waiting that the antiwar movement Beheiren was founded. Beheiren made only modest headway toward either goal, but it marked out a new course for citizens to take up public issues for themselves instead of leaving everything to the authorities.

The Protests Thicken

THE American-Japanese relationship suffered a bad attack of the jitters during the second half of 1965. Like nations everywhere, Japan grew suspicious when President Johnson sent 3,500 United States marines from Okinawa to South Vietnam on March 8, unleashing them "for offensive action" the following month. The public turned apprehensive when he announced on July 28 that an additional 50,000 troops would be sent. By the end of the year the figure had leaped to more than 184,000. By then American B-52s were flying about 300 sorties a month over North and South Vietnam (first from Guam, later Thailand), with bomb loads as great as twenty-nine tons per plane.[1] This dizzying buildup placed a huge strain on the logistical facilities at American bases in Japan, and it also winched more tautness than at any time since 1960 into the ties between the two nations. The gale of protests whipped up by Beheiren and other groups stretched the tension even further.

BEHEIREN: A MOVEMENT, NOT AN ORGANIZATION

In a rare moment of whimsy, the philosopher Tsurumi Shunsuke once wrote "I really don't know what Beheiren is."[2] Tsurumi knew more about Beheiren than almost anyone, since he not only helped to establish it but was also a founding father of its two most direct antecedents. One was the Society for the Study of the Science of Thought (Shisō no Kagaku Kenkyūkai), formed in 1946 by seven young intellectuals whose influence on postwar Japanese thought in some ways resembled that of the pathbreaking Meiji Six Society (Meirokusha, 1874–1875) on its era. The Science of Thought group consisted of

liberals who hoped to supplant both Marxism and German idealism with a pragmatism that was at once popular and academic. Unlike the Cold War liberals who plunged America headlong into Vietnam, these scholars eluded the snare of knee-jerk anticommunism and worked instead for world peace, Japanese-American friendship without treaty commitments, and a value-free social science known to its many followers as neo-positivism.[3]

The Science of Thought members made their political debut in June 1960 by helping to found the Voiceless Voices Society (Koe Naki Koe no Kai), the other main ancestor of Beheiren. Anticipating Richard Nixon and Spiro Agnew by a decade, Prime Minister Kishi brushed aside the treaty demonstrators that spring by saying "I think we must incline our ears to the voiceless voices."[4] Kobayashi Tomi, a schoolteacher, joined Tsurumi Shunsuke and others who had been on the sidelines to try to show Kishi that in fact the voiceless majority was opposed to the treaty too. No one paid them much attention amid the hubbub, but their wide-open and unstructured style turned out to be a sketch for the antiwar campaign five years later.

Members of Christian peace groups, housewives' circles, associations of World War II survivors, and a large number of unaffiliated individuals stood side by side with people from the Science of Thought and the Voiceless Voices groups when Beheiren held its first rally on April 24, 1965. Anyone was allowed to take part, and civic associations were invited to use the name Beheiren if they accepted its three aims: peace in Vietnam, self-determination for the Vietnamese, and an end to Japan's complicity in the war. Beheiren had donations but no dues, policy goals but no political affiliations, officers but no paid staff, and a commitment to individual action but no collective ideology. Takabatake Michitoshi called Beheiren a "passionate search for self-expression" and a flowering of individual "emotional sensibilities."[5] Referring to its lack of hierarchy and factionalism, Tsurumi Yoshiyuki (Tsurumi Shunsuke's cousin) called Beheiren an "action-oriented

movement," not an organization. "Our inclination toward concrete action sprang not so much from direct contact with the NLF as from latent dissatisfaction with the bureaucratic and doctrinaire character of the domestic political parties and the organized left wing."[6] Such impatience with the Old Left, in spite of its undoubted skill at mobilization, meant that Beheiren had to develop new strategies to entice rather than command support from the public.

The choice of leader reemphasized the point, Takabatake recalled: "we asked Oda Makoto, the popular novelist, to head Beheiren because he had done nothing in the 1960 struggle against the security pact."[7] Others who were present at the creation included the novelists Kaikō Takeshi, Ōe Kenzaburō, Nozaka Akiyoshi, Noma Hiroshi, and Komatsu Sakyō, the poet Nakano Shigeharu, and the playwright Terayama Shūji. Some of the founders were critics, such as Tsurumi Yoshiyuki, Mutō Ichiyō, and the film reviewer Satō Tadao; other early supporters were academics, like Tsurumi Shunsuke, his sister Tsurumi Kazuko, Hidaka Rokurō, Maruyama Masao, Takabatake Michitoshi, Umehara Takeshi, Kuno Osamu, Kuwabara Takeo, and Naramoto Tatsuya. The movie director Shinoda Masahiro and the painter Okamoto Tarō were also active from the start.

Many of them took part out of disillusionment with other means of protest. Iida Momo and Kitakōji Satoshi joined because they could no longer abide the Japan Communist Party; others like the political sociologist Ishida Takeshi were veterans of World War II who held deep pacifist feelings as a result. People such as the philosopher Sakamoto Yoshikazu were absolute pacifists who had become "radical liberals"[8] after turning against both the Soviet Union and China. Others were simply fed up with the war and wanted to do something to show it, like the mathematician Mononobe Nagaoki, who led processions of lantern-bearing citizens through the suburbs of Tokyo twice each month for eight years. Although he rarely attended rallies, even Utsunomiya Tokuma, head of the dissi-

dent Asian-African faction of the LDP, "helped us a lot during the Vietnam War."[9]

At some sacrifice of organizational effectiveness, the many strands of Beheiren were purposely allowed to flutter loose, rather than coiling back around a highly structured body. Except for small contributions from Sōhyō at the beginning, the local components of the movement were self-supporting, through thousands of modest donations each year from their supporters. Tsurumi Yoshiyuki and others, for example, worked as summer replacements for reporters on vacation from the major newspapers and used the proceeds to help Beheiren sponsor international conferences. When an antiwar tour by Jane Fonda late in the war piled up a ¥700,000 ($2,300) deficit, it was wiped out by royalties and honoraria contributed by the movement's best-known figures.[10]

Beheiren had no national headquarters, only a Tokyo office that published a monthly newsletter. Each of the 400 loosely affiliated groups throughout the country that eventually joined Beheiren planned its own activities and took responsibility for them. Individuals were free to take part anywhere they wanted and to decide for themselves which antiwar actions to take. Because of the diversity and decentralization, Tsurumi Shunsuke claimed, newcomers never seen before were constantly showing up at local Beheiren events, and the leaders did not always know one another either. On the other hand, as the political scientist Douglas Lummis points out, the top "movement people" popped up at rally after rally so often that they became known as Kintarō Ame, a long stick of candy with a miniature doll's head on the end: you break off the head and there's another Kintarō inside, and so on until the candy is all gone.[11]

ODA MAKOTO: INDIVIDUAL ACTION, NOT COLLECTIVE IDEOLOGY

Beheiren was a spontaneous alliance of people who loathed the impersonality of huge organizations, public or private, labor

or corporate. They took the Vietnam War to be an emblem of the evils produced by contemporary bureaucracies: anonymous warfare, in direction and execution, by the Americans and constant complicity by a monolithic Japanese state. Even the preestablished forms of protest were too hierarchical, or "pyramidal," as Oda termed them, because faceless participation in mass rallies called by the tightly disciplined Sōhyō labor federation usually amounted to mere role-playing (often for hire). Like many antiwar demonstrators in other countries in the sixties, Beheiren members were warned against becoming "structure freaks" (meekly accepting hierarchy), and they were urged instead to join what Tsurumi Yoshiyuki rather grandly called "a cultural revolution to create a new type of man determined to act, individually and voluntarily, on behalf of the cause of the antiwar struggle."[12]

Oda Makoto was the most recognizable and magnetic of the many people who made up Beheiren. Nearly everybody in the movement had read his best-seller, *I Want to See It All* (*Nan de mo mite yarō*, 1961), which frankly recounted his life as a Fulbright fellow at Harvard in 1958–1959 and his penniless travels in Europe and Asia on the way home.[13] Oda had majored in classical Greek thought and letters at Tokyo University and planned to become a novelist; his travelogue in 1961 also established him as one of the first postwar critics willing to write candidly rather than worshipfully about the United States. The conservative literary circles in Japan, which prefer polished prose, nonideological topics, and family situations within walls, have always denounced him for his innovating style and approach. Oda has written lengthy fiction about wars, revolutions, and social problems like the status of Koreans in Japan. "Everyone knows Oda," says the scholar Katō Shūichi. "He is very productive and is recognized as an established professional writer. Even his literary foes take him seriously, unlike certain obscure writers affiliated with the JCP who are more active in politics than in literature."[14]

Oda was as well connected with the international peace movement as any person in Japan. His energy was cyclonic: in

SANGFROID   Oda Makoto speaking beneath a
Beheiren banner at Shimizudani Park, Tokyo, December 1968.
(Photo: Yoshikawa Yūichi)

the first year and a half after Beheiren began, he not only launched a welter of protest activities but also took three trips abroad totaling nine months. In mid-September 1965 Oda, Tsurumi Yoshiyuki, and Kubo Keinosuke attended an international conference on the Vietnam War at the University of Michigan. During the fall and winter Oda traversed the United States, collecting money on streetcorners on Christmas Day to buy medical supplies for the Viet Cong, and then he toured Europe, the Soviet Union, and India before returning to Japan in April 1966. In mid-June 1966 he represented Japan at a world peace conference in Geneva, after which he traveled in Europe, and he returned to the Soviet Union in September to attend a gathering of writers concerned about Vietnam. Further trips took him to conferences in the United States, Cuba, Czechoslovakia, North Vietnam, France, India, and Sweden, where he flayed the Americans for their intervention in Indochina and expressed feelings of brotherhood with the Vietnamese.[15]

The secret to resisting the war effectively, Oda believed, was to take individual action, not to mouth ideological slogans. "Let's junk radicalism based on words" handed down by veteran agitators from the Old Left, he said, and instead let's encourage amateur protesters to act according to their inner feelings, not because of some cold, abstract doctrine.[16] Writing in the magazine *Gendai no riron* in August 1965, Oda said he refused to use terms such as imperialism and aggression because they turned away more people than they won over.[17] Critical though he was of American policies in Southeast Asia, Oda was also very anti-Soviet and never missed a chance to remind fellow intellectuals about the repressions in Hungary and Czechoslovakia. He was equally unswayed by the volleys of ideology coming from Beijing: "I am not a Marxist or a fan of Mao Zedong or the cultural revolution. We began our own cultural revolution before the cultural revolution in China started."[18]

Oda's principles of effective protest were astonishingly similar to both postwar European existentialism and the

introspective teachings of the Confucian revisionist Wang Yangming (1472–1528). Oda wrote in 1967: "I have two philosophies. One is long-term, without sudden changes, what might be called basic principles; the other is short-term, or situational, which does change quickly."[19] His enduring principles were democracy and individualism, which he pursued with a broad palette of tactics depending on the circumstances. Oda's situationalism (jōkyōron), based on his experiences in the 1950s and 1960s, declined fixed dogmas in favor of freedom of personal choice, in a manner remarkably similar to the existentialist art of the playwright Kara Jūrō or the vanguard choreographer Tanegashima Yukiko. Like the postmoderns in theaters and studios, Oda asked his readers to define their standpoints and accept responsibility for their individual actions depending on the circumstances of the moment. Oda's views were very consonant with the concrete, nonabsolute character of so much social thought in both Western Europe and Japan since 1945, and it was fitting that two of Beheiren's earliest foreign guests were Jean-Paul Sartre and Simone de Beauvoir.[20]

When Oda encouraged people who opposed the war to address specific problems, to act out their beliefs, "to like what you're doing," and "to finish what you start,"[21] he unwittingly evoked the Wang Yangming tradition as amplified by the patriotic restorationist Yoshida Shōin (1830–1859). Yoshida called on young samurai to look inward for inspiration from their own pure-hearted sincerity and then to act boldly and selflessly on their beliefs. This style of protest based on sincerity and action, so prominent among the young army officers who rebelled in February 1936 against the senior military command, reverberated once again in the Beheiren movement of the 1960s. But the resemblance ceased when Oda crossed the boundary from style to substance, since his goal of peace in Vietnam had no connection with the causes promoted by prewar followers of Wang and Yoshida. Oda sought responsible actions that avoided violence, mindless anarchism, and factional fights (uchigeba) among students. Activism, he said,

should never become a substitute for the goals it sought to accomplish.[22]

Under the circumstances, resisting the war was the task of the moment, he said; the long-range objectives were to establish democracy and create self-awareness in each individual. "What does democracy mean?" he wrote in early 1969. "As far as I am concerned, it is not so much a political ideology as a set of principles for how I live."[23] One was that people everywhere were equal; a second was that they should act on their own after making up their minds on their own. Important as majority rule was, the keys to democracy were respect for others combined with personal decisiveness. In this sense direct nonviolent action, demonstrations, and sit-ins were tools of democracy that were as valid as the Diet, elections, and voting on bills.[24]

"I believe in 100 percent freedom for the individual," Oda insisted a decade after the war. While it was still going on, he argued in utilitarian fashion that only if individuals willingly realized their own places in the antiwar movement would "strong solidarity be established."[25] The aim was self-awareness as a step toward helping one another build a society of democratic individualism. The purpose of joining a demonstration was not to merge with the mass of protesters but to achieve self-consciousness as an individual participant. Surrounded by people you often did not know, uncertain of how big the crowd was or where it was going, you sensed the importance of democracy based on actual experience. You were not sure whether the people near you were rich or poor, lofty or humble, well-educated or not—you knew them simply as humans. In this sense the size of the rally was unimportant; the crucial thing was what happened to each individual who took part. Once you created this democratic selfhood as a part of the antiwar movement, you were ready to risk arrest, bad publicity, perhaps losing your job—in short, you were personally committed.[26]

Like political activists in other countries in the 1960s, most Beheiren leaders believed that once the people themselves

were changed, then a fundamental transformation of society would be possible. Some persons mistook the idea of freeing the self from bureaucratism and hierarchy as license to engage in "immediate, sensory liberation in antiwar" actions that were little more than self-indulgence.[27] In fact, far from counseling a mindless age of sensation, Beheiren leaders told student radicals that they should form their own opinions thoughtfully and act decisively on them. They insisted that people could be free only when they acted of their own volition, not when they joined mass demonstrations because their bosses or their peers told them to.[28]

Five years after the United States intervened with bombers and combat troops in Vietnam, Oda admitted that "when I began Beheiren, I did not expect the movement would last this long or that I myself would still be a part of it."[29] He was still the central figure and the movement's biggest draw when the Paris cease-fire agreement was reached in January 1973. Yet Oda and Tsurumi Shunsuke were probably correct that most people joined because they hated the war, not because of a charismatic national leader.[30]

INTERNATIONAL TACTICS

The approaches Beheiren chose in the second half of 1965 more often than not reflected what peace groups were doing in North America and Western Europe. Like its counterparts in the United States, Beheiren tried to schedule daily activities against the war such as letter-writing and small meetings at community centers and college campuses. Instead of massive rallies once or twice a year, Beheiren groups in various cities sponsored small demonstrations at regular intervals that helped participants keep abreast of developments in the antiwar movement. The Tokyo Beheiren faithfully held its protests on the first Saturday of each month from September 1965 until October 1973, an extraordinary record of perseverance and routine considering the vicissitudes of the war. The Tokyo office also cranked out 101 numbers of its monthly bulletin *Be-*

heiren nyūsu between October 1965 and March 1974, and in 1969–1970 it also published a weekly on the Okinawa and security treaty problems, *Shūkan anpo.*[31]

Both the public meetings and the newsletters vociferously attacked American policies in Indochina, and they also accused the Satō government of turning the country into a co-conspirator and perpetrator of war, whereas the JSP, JCP, and Sōhyō still thought Japan was a victim of American aggression because of the treaty. The early Beheiren style of protest, with peaceful meetings in parks and plazas, improved the image of demonstrating in public immensely when compared with the hostile street confrontations five years before. The treaty opponents had often antagonized reporters in 1960, but the Beheiren leaders learned from the American peace movement how to use the media for an impact far greater than what could be achieved by a rally in front of a commuter station. The televised impression was much more upbeat: instead of zigzag dancing by tightly packed hordes of youths, Beheiren supporters often walked along, widely spaced, holding hands accordian-style like paper doll cutouts—a smart style the press dubbed French demonstrations. The prestigious intellectuals and writers who spoke at Beheiren assemblies carried far more éclat with the public than the ideologues and labor chieftains who had led the struggle in 1960.[32]

Another novelty introduced by Beheiren was the teach-in. Since many Japanese universities were jammed into the centers of huge cities, they often provided a less cloistered venue for antiwar events involving the general public than was true of campuses in other countries. Probably the most famous of the Japanese teach-ins took place not at a university but amid the Edwardian elegance of the Akasaka Prince Hotel in Tokyo on August 14–15, 1965. Oda and the other organizers chose the date for Japan's first twenty-four-hour antiwar teach-in to mark the twentieth anniversary of the surrender in World War II, filling an auditorium with 600 people and arranging for TV Tokyo to broadcast the entire event live over channel 12. It was a political assembly like none ever seen before in Japan.

Carl Oglesby, the former chair of Students for a Democratic Society, came at Beheiren's invitation and made a speech. Oda was the star attraction and a big reason why Kawade Shobō Shinsha, one of his publishers, sponsored the broadcast. Altogether twenty-one persons covering the ideological waterfront made presentations, including four Liberal Democratic Party officials and Diet representatives, three from the JSP, and one each from the Democratic Socialists, the JCP, and Kōmeitō. Dignified by such notables as the LDP leader Miyazawa Kiichi and the future prime minister Nakasone Yasuhiro, this splashy event gave Beheiren its first major exposure and had a big effect in publicizing the antiwar movement throughout Japan.[33]

Sakamoto Yoshikazu, the absolute pacifist and Tōdai professor, was one of the teach-in's most trenchant speakers against the war, at a session chaired by the philosopher Kuwabara Takeo. Rebutting him was Ezaki Masumi, who had just finished his term as head of the Self-Defense Agency. When Sakamoto asked what he thought of the Matsumoto report of April 1965 questioning whether the NLF could be defeated, Ezaki said "I can't entirely agree with it" and reiterated the LDP view that the Viet Cong were aggressors directed from Hanoi.[34] The discussion turned from Vietnam to World War II at midnight, long after Ezaki, Miyazawa, and Nakasone had gone home. Suddenly the broadcast was cut off at 4:08 A.M. while the educator Muchaku Seikyō was moderating an exchange about war criminals. Apparently someone at the studio pulled the plug because "some of the contents of the debates lost their impartiality," in *Asahi*'s delicate account of the affair.[35] Oda condemned the termination as symbolic of the same denial of freedoms that the Government of Vietnam and the United States were imposing on South Vietnam.[36]

Beheiren also sometimes bought advertisements in American newspapers to express its outrage at the war. Kaikō Takeshi was the moving spirit behind a campaign to raise funds for a statement in the *New York Times*. Within three months he collected enough for a full page, costing $6,000, in the edition

65

of November 16, 1965. The ad stressed that "America's best friends in Asia are the hundred million people of Japan," whose good will was vanishing because of the war. Declaring that "weapons alone are of no avail in winning the minds and allegiances of any people," the text appealed to America's "tradition of democracy and magnanimity" and called for a stop to the bombings and the opening of peace talks. A return coupon brought Beheiren about 130 letters and $500 in donations from readers. A similar but more pointed full-page ad from Beheiren appeared in the *Washington Post* on April 3, 1967: "Stop the killing! Stop the Vietnam War."[37]

This familiar American technique of speaking out against the war and giving encouragement to fellow protesters through newspaper advertisements proved hard to transplant to Japan. Katō Shūichi and others tried to buy space in big city papers to denounce the bombings in 1965, but they were turned away and forced to express their views in letters to editors. To accompany a teach-in held in Nagano City on November 16, 1966, the Shinano regional edition of *Mainichi* carried a large antiwar advertisement signed by seventy-four local residents, apparently the first such ad to run in a Japanese newspaper. On the whole Beheiren avoided them, Ishida Takeshi notes, "because ads were too costly" and "seemed too partisan and commercialized"[38]—perhaps also too assertive in a media culture where subtle mood ads are preferred to direct content ads. Instead Oda and the other leaders scored publicity coups with big events like the Sartre-Beauvoir visit in October 1966, a spectacle that generated megawatts of free attention from the press.

The antiwar movement used the media to influence the public, but unlike most people the activist community did not have to rely on television and newspapers alone for information about the war or about peace groups at home and abroad. Newsletters, correspondence, regular gathering places, and quiet support from small publishers all acted as alternative channels of information, as was true in other countries. The authorities kept a careful watch over Beheiren and other pro-

test groups, but direct repression by the police was rare because there was no military draft to invite resistance and because the antiwar community almost never broke Japanese laws or directly defied the power of the state.

Instead the leaders of Beheiren were determined to legitimize themselves and their cause, both in Japan and overseas. They tried to show interpersonal solidarity with dissidents abroad far beyond merely agreeing about the ultimate goal of stopping the war. This identity began, Oda wrote, with each individual who joined a demonstration; participating meant that "solidarity is established, strong solidarity" with fellow protesters everywhere.[39] Messages were regularly exchanged with peace groups at the University of California and read aloud at rallies, and quite a few Beheiren leaders toured Europe and the United States to make contacts in person with the antiwar movement.

International solidarity was important not merely because joint action was likely to have more impact but also because other postwar social and political movements, including the socialists and communists, were so insular. As Douglas Lummis has pointed out, antiwar people in Japan feared the national isolation of the Edo period and the years from 1937 to 1952. They knew it was easier for the state to control dissent by sealing it off from overseas support. Well aware of their isolation and vulnerability, the protesters focused their actions on harbors, airports, treaties, and traveling officials—the gateways, they believed, to internationalism and effectiveness.[40] These proved to be quixotic targets, since they were among the easiest for the authorities to defend.

A SWARM OF CRITICS

Apart from the flamboyant novelist Mishima Yukio and the scandal-tarred politician Tanaka Kakuei, Oda Makoto was probably the most controversial person of his era in Japan. Communists denounced him as soft on America; the Liberal Democrats attacked his sympathies for the Vietnamese. So-

cialists disdained him as petit bourgeois, and other writers panned him as an elitist. One group of thugs despised him so much that they came all the way from Nagoya one night "to smash up the desks and chairs in the Tokyo Beheiren office and throw them in the Kanda River near Ochanomizu."[41]

Conservative academic critics like Saeki Shōichi, Nishi Yoshiyuki, and Tonooka Akio generally assailed Oda's rhetorical style, finding his arguments long on passion but short on logic or proof. Tonooka, a political scientist, rejected Oda's claim that individual and state interests were incompatible, branding it "utter nonsense."[42] Other scholars who usually supported American goals in Vietnam, such as Etō Shinkichi, Kamiya Fuji, and Yano Tōru, were quite critical of Beheiren in general but agreed with certain points it raised about Japan's defense policies.[43] Within the state itself, Miyake Wasuke recalls, Beheiren members won scant favor: "they had little influence on the government's policy toward Vietnam. Such groups criticized the government but didn't propose any constructive alternative."[44] Mishima Yukio, an unswerving patriot, was surprisingly quiet. During a sojourn in Bangkok in the fall of 1967, where he waited for a Nobel prize that never arrived, he called Japan "a fool's paradise" where people naively demonstrated for peace without knowing the reality of communism.[45] Oda recalls that many people proposed a debate between the two—which would have been the media event of the decade. "I was willing, but Mishima always refused. Once I happened to run into him at Roppongi, I think it was, and he said 'I'm not going to debate that guy, he's too big.' "[46] Further to the right of Mishima there was less reticence. Since the early fifties the extreme nationalist Akao Bin, head of the Patriotic Party (Aikokutō), had sparred ceaselessly with the Old Left through counterdemonstrations, lamppost bills, and shrill military music. Soon after Beheiren started up, Akao began sending his khaki-clad followers in powerful sound trucks to disrupt its rallies.[47]

Oda and the Beheiren movement apparently were perceived as far greater threats by the JSP and JCP than by the Liberal

Democrats. They were suspect partly as newcomers on the Left and partly because the public seemed to be growing disillusioned with all the existing parties. The proportion of Japanese supporting no party at all had jumped from 19.8 percent in late 1964 to 32.5 percent two years later, a particular worry to small parties with little margin for shrinkage.[48] The Japan Socialist Party wasted little time before ripping into the newly formed Beheiren: "citizens' movements are based on a petit bourgeois ideology that destroys groups representing the viewpoint of the working class."[49] Both the socialists and the communists depended on tight party discipline and excoriated Oda's ideas of absolute individualism. The JCP, which bore a particular grudge against apostates like Iida Momo, blasted Beheiren as "Trotskyite" and called its leaders "anticommunist, antiparty bad elements." (Iida replied in 1970 that "the Communist Party has forgot about revolution.")[50] Even police groups were not sure how to classify Beheiren; one finally decided the movement was close to anarchism in its thinking.[51]

Oda and other antiwar leaders sometimes struck even their followers as elitist because many were graduates of Tokyo University, used its alumni club for press conferences, and maintained communications through their network of acquaintances. They were distinct, too, in that many spoke English, some had lived abroad, and most were highly accomplished professionals. "But what characterizes the group as a whole," Lummis observed, "is the fact that it maintains the movement tradition, not that it is 'elite.' "[52]

Insiders offered their own criticisms quite freely. Tsurumi Yoshiyuki admitted in retrospect that Beheiren failed to relate to workers and farmers, to whom the movement often seemed aloof because it did not acknowledge that they needed jobs and could not easily protest. Although this sort of *mea culpa* has been standard among exhausted reform groups in Japan since the 1920s, Tsurumi was doubtless right that to outsiders Beheiren, like its counterparts abroad, seemed to be top-heavy with intellectuals, white-collar workers, and students despite

its resolve to bring in persons of all backgrounds.[53] Ishida Takeshi reproved the Beheiren leaders less for elitism than for "not taking full responsibility for the movement." He thought "it was inadequate for them to say 'we don't know what will happen' at meetings." But Ishida credited Oda and the others for showing "good judgment at rallies by scheduling the moderate speakers first and the more radical people at the end."[54]

"Anti-American" was the label that stuck most persistently to Beheiren, but it was no more valid a criticism than calling protesters in the United States unpatriotic for questioning the policies of their government. In contrast with the Old Left in Japan, most Beheiren supporters thought that American values had gone awry in Indochina, suffocating Vietnamese national ambitions. Since the beginning of the twentieth century various Japanese reformers, including the early Japan Socialist Party, had been inspired by the American traditions of liberty and democracy. "Beheiren people believed in the ideals of American liberalism," Rōyama Michio points out. "Thanks to the new American-imposed constitution, they felt safe protesting U.S. policy. They believed in the ideals of America and felt close to American academic opponents of the war. Beheiren people were radical liberals, not communists."[55]

Both Oda Makoto and Tsurumi Yoshiyuki admitted that when the war began they and most other Beheiren supporters had no more awareness of Southeast Asia than the great majority of Americans. "I knew almost nothing about Vietnam when the war began," Tsurumi concedes. "I was at Harvard in 1965 and knew far more about the U.S. than about Southeast Asia."[56] Tsurumi Shunsuke agreed that their knowledge of the protest movement in the United States, not any familiarity with Indochina, was crucial for the Beheiren leaders: their views "are not necessarily anti-American at all, and they show support for the antiwar forces in the United States."[57] Yet by 1971 he himself was disgusted to the point of alienation: "nowhere can I recognize the America I knew in the America that has been pursuing this filthy war for more than ten years."[58]

Perhaps it is surprising that neither Tsurumi Yoshiyuki nor Oda was ever arrested for antiwar activities, even when Beheiren adopted the tactics of civil disobedience. But it was entirely predictable that Beheiren leaders started having difficulty getting visas to the United States when their antiwar efforts began to nettle the Americans. This happened the moment they started helping American military personnel in Japan to desert from the armed forces in October 1967. Even though he was born in the United States, Tsurumi Yoshiyuki (a Japanese citizen) as of 1985 could still count on receiving only a limited entry permit to attend academic conferences at set times. Yoshikawa Yūichi, the executive secretary of Beheiren during 1965–1973 while still an inactive member of the JCP, was forced to stay home when a Japanese peace boat left in September 1984 for China, Southeast Asia, Guam, and Saipan because the United States government held up his one-week visa to Guam until the day after the ship sailed.[59]

Japanese intellectuals and artists have been divided since at least the 1870s between political consciousness and an apolitical pursuit of pure art. Yet nearly all of them after 1945 regarded the United States as their liberator from militarism and authoritarian rule. At the same time they were less inclined than Western Europeans to think of America as their safeguard against communism, for several reasons: Japan was in diplomatic isolation during 1945–1952 and little buffeted by the Cold War; pacifism and neutralism had such strong appeal throughout the postwar era; the Soviet Union seemed only remotely threatening; many Japanese felt guilty about how their armies had pillaged China and minimized the dangers of revolutionary Maoism; and the security treaty with the United States often seemed more entangling than reassuring. To the extent that the predominant image was America as liberator, not America as protector, Katō Shūichi is probably right that for most "educated, politically aware Japanese, the Vietnam War was the first blow to American prestige in this country. By 1975 many of them were disillusioned with the United States."[60] To a number of Japanese intellectuals it seemed that

in the 1950s American democracy had enough self-correcting mechanisms to overcome aberrations like McCarthyism or brinkmanship, but then in the sixties the irony of Vietnam was that things went haywire and the American system no longer worked.

Yet, however crestfallen they may have been at losing their innocence about American democracy, the Beheiren leaders labored with mixed success to keep anger at the war from turning into generalized anti-Americanism. One reason for this circumspection was humanitarian, the assumption that a people should not necessarily be condemned for what its government did. Another was Beheiren's eagerness to distance itself from the JCP and JSP, both of which almost automatically opposed the United States on any major question. Moreover, anti-Americanism would lead to the trap of nationalism and isolation, robbing Beheiren of the solidarity it felt with individuals everywhere who resisted the war. In fact even at the height of the demonstrations in Japan, "the American style of life never lost its appeal to people in the movement, except for a few." After rallies, Douglas Lummis recalls, young people in jeans would sit about, laughing and chatting as they drank "Beitei Kōra"—classic American imperialist cola.[61]

ARTS AND THE WAR

The Vietnam War era was a cultural watershed of sorts around the world, part of a long skein of events that affected art no less than politics or society in most rich countries and yielded a revolution in pop culture in the Anglophone world. Few if any peoples outside that demesne were more transfixed by American and British mass culture than the Japanese, yet the world of the arts in Japan was curiously untouched by the roiling waves of protest during the Vietnam War. The Beatles, of course, stormed through Japan in 1966 and remained the best-known foreign musicians there for the next twenty years. But there was little Japanese antiwar art aimed specifically at the Vietnam situation; most of the cultural impact was second-

hand, via the United States, raising the suspicion that well-known protest songs or paintings were popular in Japan because of their provenance, not their message.

Much of the reason why artists were so reticent was historical. Until recent times the arts have usually been regarded as mere entertainments in Japan, pleasant diversions from the serious business of governing and making money. Only since World War II have the visual and performing arts emerged as valid careers worthy of aspiration by the youths of Japan's vast middle classes. Because writers, studio artists, and stage performers have striven for so long to win acceptance as respectable professionals, they have always been averse to risking their reputations by mixing politics and art. The idea of art for its own sake has also been nourished by the premodern Chinese amateur ideal, still widely admired in Japan, in which art is an avocation for relief from the routines of workaday occupations. And it is worth remembering that there was little precedent for antiwar art because Vietnam was the first war the Japanese were free to protest without censorship.

When artists took part in Beheiren, they usually did so as professionals rather than as plain citizens. Oda urged them to join instead as individuals, not as a status or role derived from an occupation. That line was hard to cross in any country but especially in the finely graded hierarchy of Japanese society, in which artists had struggled for many decades to find their crevice. Most of them stayed remote from Beheiren, Oda recalls wistfully: "many literary people criticized me for getting involved, saying I lost my literary independence."[62]

The Vietnam War had an effect on the authors of Oda's generation, a number of whom gave much time to the antiwar effort. But war writing in any national literature requires firsthand experience, and only Kaikō Takeshi among the first-rank novelists spent enough time in Indochina to write extensively about it in his fiction. Ōe Kenzaburō was active in Beheiren but remained absorbed in the theme of Hiroshima into the mid-eighties. The Japan P.E.N. Club, a pillar of the literary upper echelons, passed a resolution on May 1, 1965, calling

73

"on the countries concerned to take effective steps to restore peace in Vietnam,"[63] but few of its members chose themes from the war for their works because they mainly hewed to the conventions of psychological realism in autobiographical formats. Instead Vietnam was the era of journalists, not novelists or scholars, and most of the best-sellers in Japan from the Vietnam conflict consisted of eloquent but nonanalytical war reportage.[64]

Some of the most persistent artistic critics of the Vietnam situation were the musicians associated with the Workers' Music Council (Kinrōsha Ongaku Kyōgikai, known as Rōon) and the workers' choral movement called Utagoe, both of which were tied to labor and leftist parties, especially the Japan Communist Party. Rōon, like its counterpart Rōen in theater, booked inexpensive performances, intended for workers, by Japanese artists as well as foreign visitors, especially from Eastern bloc countries. The national Rōon organization assembled 450 musicians and dancers "to oppose U.S. imperialism" in Vietnam at a Tokyo meeting on May 26, 1965, and it regularly joined with other arts federations sponsored by the JCP to denounce the war as well as the security treaty. Walter Nichols, who served as cultural attaché at the American embassy during much of the war, recalls that at concerts put on by Rōon "the printed programs carried rabid anti-American and antiwar propaganda, even when the concert was classical music or the artists happened to be Americans."[65] Rōon and Utagoe also sponsored several concerts of light music in 1965–1966 that presented songs written by Japanese to protest the Vietnam War, but the largest of them drew just 2,500 people.[66]

The Vietnam conflict fell exactly between theater generations in Japan and had even less effect on drama than on literature or music. From its infancy at the turn of the twentieth century modern theater (Shingeki) has been enveloped in political issues, never more so than during the treaty uproar in 1960. Because Shingeki companies depended so heavily on support from Rōen and the left parties, their members seldom took part in Beheiren meetings, but the companies and their

national federations relentlessly blasted the war as further proof of American imperialism and aggression. Shingeki groups occasionally put on plays about Vietnam by playwrights such as Kurosawa Miyoshi, and other companies adapted Vietnamese materials into road shows, like *Letter from South Vietnam* (*Minami Betonamu kara no tegami*, 1965) by Nakamura Shin'ichi, based on a text by Nguyen Van Choi. By the mid-sixties Shingeki was under attack from an avant-garde theater known as Angura (underground), which rejected both the company system and the heavy-handed ideological theater in which Shingeki was often involved. These youthful playwrights leaped beyond guerrilla theater in the streets to establish a thoroughly postmodern drama in technique, content, and organizational style, one that was largely absorbed in nonpolitical themes retrieved from the ashcans of daily life in the 1920s. Oda Makoto laughingly says "the underground playwrights were probably more revolutionary than we were in Beheiren"[67] in that they had broken through questions of democracy and individualism to discover even newer ways of expressing identity.

Japanese film personalities sometimes protested the war in Vietnam, but the cinema world was plunged so deeply into artistic and financial torpor by the mid-sixties that political movies were an impossibility for almost every director. Such well-known film makers as Imai Tadashi and Kubo Keinosuke devoted many hours to Beheiren, and Yamada Tengo directed an antiwar feature named after the movement, *Peace in Vietnam* (*Betonamu ni heiwa o*). The Daiei studios brought out two documentaries in 1965, *Vietnam in Turmoil* (*Dōran no Betonamu*) and *Blood, Tears, Graves* (*Chi to namida to hakaba*), both of which were criticized for being too pro-American.[68] The sensational young director Ōshima Nagisa traveled around Korea and Vietnam in 1963–1964 making documentaries, but he trained his cameras mostly on social and political problems within Japan and never made an explicitly antiwar film. Official documentaries from the DRV and NLF made their way into Japan and were shown by sympathizers to clubs and civic

groups, and many of Hollywood's features treating the war were screened by the commercial theater chains. Although television camera artists produced some riveting news footage, relatively little of it was turned into documentaries for showing in movie houses.[69]

More visual artists and dancers, as well as pop musicians and a few figures from the traditional Japanese arts, began to speak out as the war deepened. But Oda is probably accurate in saying that few playwrights, painters, choreographers, or musicians stepped out of their hard-won niches to involve themselves in political dissent. As he sees it in retrospect, "there was much less impact from the war on the arts in Japan than in the U.S. There was some influence on literature and much on thought."[70] Nonetheless, even a low level of antiwar activity by arts people, stirred in with all the other protests, made public opinion in Japan even less palatable to the leaders in Washington.

AMERCIAN PIQUE

The United States seemed partly assuaged by Satō's firmer support of its war policies after Lodge and Rostow visited in the spring of 1965. The relatively favorable results of the House of Councillors election in July were a reassurance that conservative rule was solid. When a typhoon moved toward the Western Pacific late that month, the United States informed Japan on July 27 that a fleet of B-52 bombers based in Guam would take temporary refuge at the American airfield at Itazuke in Kyushu. The Japanese government decided that "this was not a matter needing prior consultation under the security treaty."[71] By the same evening the weather in the Ryūkyūs had improved enough to redirect the aircraft from Guam to Okinawa, which the Americans were free to do without consulting anyone. Two days later the United States military command in Saigon announced that thirty B-52s had left Okinawa and attacked Viet Cong concentrations fifty-eight kilo-

meters southeast of Saigon.[72] The storm over this report in Japan once again ruffled relations with the United States.

Asahi revealed on July 31 that while the planes were en route to Vietnam the head of the North American bureau of the foreign ministry had warned the acting United States ambassador, John K. Emmerson, that if they dropped their bombs "this will provoke needless misgivings among the Japanese people."[73] As Beheiren, the Old Left, and many others denounced the bombings launched from territory that was residually Japan's, their government reminded the public that "direct sorties from Okinawa are not a subject for prior consultation," but Foreign Minister Shiina Etsusaburō also let it be known that he had asked the Americans not to use Okinawa for combat operations.[74] He told Washington that "legally there is no problem, but somehow it seems incomprehensible" to use Okinawa to attack Vietnam.[75] Satō too made no attempt to cloak his displeasure, telling the Diet that the B-52s were disturbing and inflammatory.[76]

But the cabinet also tried to be frank with its domestic critics during the uproar. Satō told the Diet that all the parties in the war should sit down and talk without reservation, difficult as this would be to arrange. Shiina repeated the Liberal Democrats' belief that the reason for the war was northern aggression against the GVN. In words that might have been chosen by almost any Japanese diplomat since the 1850s, he cautioned that "public sentiment and the problem of realistic security often clash. We must think as calmly and realistically as we can . . . the two frequently do not agree, in which case it is strictly essential to choose security."[77]

The Japanese government was chagrined by the B-52 episode but unflinching in its agreement with America's overall policy in Indochina. Nonetheless the United States was said to be angry when Shiina expressed regret that the bombers had used Okinawa. The Japanese press reported that some American officials, already vexed by Japan's memorandum trade with China, were now worried that Japan would behave like France under de Gaulle on the Vietnam question.[78] Edwin O.

Reischauer, the American ambassador, was in Washington during the incident and won little sympathy when he told his superiors that they were ignorant of Japanese opinion. Speaking in Boston on August 3, 1965, he argued that the "loss of our close relationship with Japan because of Vietnam would be much more disastrous than anything that might happen in Vietnam itself except a world war."[79] Even so, Reischauer was suspect among the Japanese press because he did not seem to speak loudly enough against the war while he was in the United States. He disappointed the newspapers further when he expressed unswerving support for President Johnson's Vietnam policy at a press conference after he returned to Japan held at the Hotel Okura on August 23.[80] Reischauer evidently took umbrage at suggestions by correspondents and intellectuals that he "would further stoop to indirect criticism of American policy."[81] His feeling insulted that he might not seem to support the war was as remarkable as the wishful thinking of his critics who hoped that he would come out against it.

The reaction to the B–52 operation was understandably sharpest in Okinawa itself. Even the Liberal Democrats in the Ryūkyū legislature joined in a resolution, approved without dissent, repudiating the bombing raid and demanding that such "acts of war" stop immediately. Previously the conservatives in Okinawa had kept their distance from the antibase, proreversion forces, but their support for this resolution and another the previous spring banning Okinawan crews from serving on civilian tugs bound for Vietnam showed how strong the fear of immersion in the war had grown. Satō's trip to Naha on August 19 to promote the restoration of Okinawa to Japanese rule attracted huge throngs, most of them in favor of reversion and Japanese economic aid to the islands, but a number of people in the crowds derided him as "an accomplice in the war."[82]

By the fall of 1965 it was obvious that the United States preferred a military solution in Vietnam, and most Japanese antiwar leaders gave up trying to show the Americans how to end

the conflict. Compared with early 1965 when Saigon was on the verge of collapse, the military situation in South Vietnam seemed to be looking up, the United States command said. After a Japan–United States Security Committee meeting on September 1 both Shiina and Reischauer assailed the doubters in Japan. The ambassador spoke in rather patronizing fashion: "I believe that most Japanese who think about Japan's national interests in relation to the Vietnam situation understand American policy."[83]

A month later Reischauer had his most notorious run-in with the press, an instructive but unfortunate affair that left both parties looking bruised. At a press conference in Osaka on October 5, Reischauer attacked recent stories by Ōmori Minoru in *Mainichi* and Hata Shōryū in *Asahi* for "not providing balanced reports about the Vietnam situation."[84] He called Ōmori a "poor newsman," a "biased reporter," and a "disqualified journalist"[85] for his article in the October 3 issue of his newspaper about the purported bombings of a clearly marked leper hospital at Kin Lap, North Vietnam, by the United States for ten straight days. Pointing out that Ōmori and Hata had filed their dispatches from Hanoi without visiting the village site, Reischauer said that the source for the reports was a propaganda film shown to journalists by the DRV. "Japan's poor newspaper correspondents don't know the difference between propaganda and fact. Japanese newspapers are shameless, and they misrepresent reality."[86] Both men readily agreed that they had seen the movie but not the hospital, although Hata said that neutral diplomats convinced him the film was accurate. Both Hata and Ōmori had visited bombed-out hospitals and schools far from military targets elsewhere in North Vietnam.[87]

This unprecedented intervention by a foreign diplomat caused an even greater sensation than the Ball-MacArthur charges in April 1965 about communists in the newsrooms. Left-wing leaders huffed that Reischauer was reviving the haughty censorship of occupation days. Kyōdō, the wire service, reported on October 6 that Reischauer's views were those

of the state department.[88] NTV showed the controversial film at 2 P.M. that day but scrubbed a reshowing from its 6:55 P.M. international news program after an official at the American embassy called to ask that the station "please be discreet."[89] The broadcaster's excuse for the change in plan was that the footage was four months old and certain scenes appeared to be contrived.

Ōmori was an experienced journalist who had spent a decade reporting from the United States. He and Hata were the first noncommunist journalists to write from North Vietnam that American planes had bombed civilian areas distant from factories, transport facilities, or military bases. Ōmori returned to Japan three days after the blast from Reischauer and rushed out a book explaining his view of the episode. Admitting he had probably been "hasty," Ōmori agreed that he should have been more cautious about the film, that the United States had enough sense not to bomb hospitals, and that its pilots might have mistaken the leper hospital for military barracks. But he was convinced that the facility had been bombed and that it was the Americans who bombed it.[90] When the *Pentagon Papers* came out in 1971, Ōmori published a fuller account of the Reischauer affair. He made it plain that he was forced to leave *Mainichi* a few months after the criticism, although it is also true that he was seriously ill at the time.[91] Ōmori took heart from the admission by the American command in Saigon that the Rolling Thunder campaign had not been antiseptic. He made much of the CIA estimate found in the *Pentagon Papers* that in 1965 about 80 percent of the casualties from the bombings of the north had been civilians.[92]

A day after the Reischauer charges the state department tried to contain the clamor by praising the Japanese press for its independence and confining the criticisms to certain erroneous reports from Vietnam. The heart of the matter to Washington was not poor Japanese journalism but poor American image. The United States was mostly eager to dispel the appearance that it deliberately destroyed hospitals.[93] For their part, the newspapers were aware that their writers had been sloppy

with sources and pledged to provide balanced, independent reporting in the future. Many editors took the Reischauer attack as an attempt to put them on the defensive during debate over the Japan-Korea normalization treaty, which began in parliament the same day.[94]

However intemperate Reischauer's remarks may have been, they were the product of more than just exasperation. The Vietnam War presented him with a new challenge in his carefully cultivated associations with Japanese writers, intellectuals, and leftists. The good will he had developed among his academic colleagues in Japan after the 1960 crisis soon soured as the war escalated. A man who took on each new assignment with zest and self-confidence, Reischauer was not used to being rebutted by fellow intellectuals in scholarly matters, and he reacted stiffly when Japanese started to question him on Vietnam. He increasingly took the dissent to be politically inspired, so he became more and more assertive with the press and the opposition, seeking out television and lecture appearances to put forward the American position. Reischauer admonished the dissenters in Japan for their excessive sentimentalism, faulting them for "concentrating on expressing their concern and disapproval that such a situation" as Vietnam existed instead of analyzing and explaining it to the Japanese public.[95] This more emphatic style turned the ambassador into a highly effective advocate for the United States position on Vietnam.

Compounding Washington's annoyance over the B-52s in July and the newspapers in October were the acrobatics surrounding the normalization of Japanese relations with South Korea during the fall of 1965. The basic treaty, which included $500 million in Japanese economic aid to Seoul and broader fishing rights for Japanese boats, had been worked out in February 1965 and signed in June. Violent demonstrations against the pact in Korea during August were put down with police clubs and martial law, leading Prime Minister Satō to postpone the ratification debate in the Diet until the controversy in Korea calmed down. The United States had encouraged nor-

malized ties between Tokyo and Seoul since 1951; the treaty finally materialized thanks to pressures from America, the Japanese and Korean business communities, and Satō's long-range scheme to retrieve Okinawa.[96]

The opposition parties mustered their full forces against the treaty without much effect. They claimed that the pact amounted to the extension of the Japan–United States security treaty, opening the way for Japanese forces to fight in Korea, as projected in the Three Arrows Study revealed in February 1965. The Left complained that the new arrangement would allow Japanese capitalism to overspread Korea and that normalization was wrong because it did not recognize North Korea. The protesters also saw a link between the treaty and the simultaneous dispatch of 15,000 South Korean troops to South Vietnam in August 1965. As proof of the evils they believed were lurking in closer relations with Seoul, they liked to cite the statement of Kaya Okinori, the right-wing LDP leader, to his party in October 1965: "the essence in the ratification of the Japan–Republic of Korea Treaty lies in confrontation against the world aggression of the communist camp. A red banner flying in Pusan would be no less detrimental to Japan than the Soviet missiles introduced into Cuba were to the United States."[97]

The antinormalization movement generated a new protest group called the Antiwar Youth Committee (Hansen Seinen Iinkai), founded by Sōhyō and the Japan Socialist Party on August 30, 1965. Its purpose was to mobilize young industrial workers to resist the normalization treaty and also the Vietnam War through a relatively egalitarian, decentralized organization in which workers would have much voice. Although Hansen eventually broke with the JSP, in the fall of 1965 it joined in three major demonstrations against the new ties with South Korea, culminating in strikes, meetings, and rallies on November 13. The organizers put the total attendance at 3 million.[98] The massive crowds, and the way Satō rammed the agreement through the lower house by surprise after midnight the previous day, were irksome reminders to the United States

of the crisis in 1960 and worrisome hints that the Vietnam situation or the security treaty might blow up into nasty protests
in the future.

By the end of 1965, despite another $1 million in aid to Sai-
gon voted by the Satō cabinet on October 27, the United
States was once again carping at Japan over the war in Vietnam. Why, the Americans wondered, couldn't Japan see that
China was now a fearsome rival? Why couldn't Japan recognize its own economic strength? Both factors created a persuasive case for greater military spending by Japan, Washington
thought.[99] Pinned down by critics on all sides, President Johnson declared a bombing halt in Vietnam and announced on
December 22 that Vice President Humphrey would visit Japan
as a part of the peace offensive Johnson was launching. To win
Japanese backing for his Vietnam policy, the president declared that for the first time elections could be held for the office of chief executive of the Ryūkyūs—to which Satō responded, according to the *New York Times*, that Japan could
give only its "moral support" for the war.[100]

Perhaps the best sign of the tension and the pique felt by
Washington in late 1965 was the new policy among top American officials of giving no interviews to those Japanese newspapers whose views they resented. The government made an
exception of sorts for Ōmori Minoru, then still with *Mainichi*,
when he asked for an interview with Secretary of State Dean
Rusk. The state department insisted on reading Ōmori's entire
story before publication, and it said that the whole front page
of the newspaper must be devoted to the article on Rusk.
Mainichi naturally refused, and the interview never took
place.[101]

CHAPTER 3

The Silent Partner

"JAPAN has neither the capacity nor intention to undertake military intervention,"[1] Foreign Minister Miki Takeo reassured the Diet in a debate about Vietnam on December 21, 1967. The government insisted again and again that Article IX of the constitution outlawed the use of Japanese troops abroad. During America's eight-year war in Indochina, Japan was a reluctant diplomatic ally but also a tacit economic and military partner of the United States. The Satō government backed Washington's policies toward China and Vietnam, but always with diffidence rather than relish; yet within the limits of Article IX it furnished a great deal of military collaboration and supplied the GI's in Vietnam with everything from lettuce to Sonys. America's great pacifist ally earned several billions of dollars through direct and indirect procurement and advanced into the markets of Southeast Asia because of the war. The Satō cabinet interpreted the security treaty so broadly that the United States had almost unfettered use of its bases in Japan for the fight in Vietnam (atomic weapons and direct combat operations were banned, but neither curb hampered the Americans). The war confirmed that the main purpose of the security treaty was no longer to protect Japan—its Self-Defense Forces could repel a conventional attack—but instead to pursue American strategy in East and Southeast Asia.

REAR ECHELONS FOR THE FIGHT

Tokyo is slightly farther from Saigon than San Francisco is from New York, yet logistically Vietnam was such a jet-age war that the American bases clumped on the Kantō Plain were

84

handy staging areas for dispatching troops and supplies to the war zone. Haneda airport in Tokyo became a key link in the long air route for soldiers bound from Travis air force base in northern California to Tan Son Nhut airfield in Saigon. A dozen big bases and more than 130 other facilities provided by Japan under the security treaty were pressed into use when the United States entered the war with guns blazing in early 1965. U. Alexis Johnson, who served as American ambassador to Japan from November 1966 until July 1969, acknowledged the debt: "Japan was vital to our effort in Vietnam. It provided ports, repair and rebuild facilities, supply dumps, stopover points for aircraft, and hospitals for badly wounded soldiers."[2] Beyond all of this was Okinawa, with its huge air bases and its billets for United States marines. Admiral U. S. Grant Sharp, commander of Pacific forces, put it very plainly on December 10, 1965: "without Okinawa we couldn't continue fighting the Vietnam War."[3]

The number of American troops based in Japan proper hovered around 35–40,000 for most of the war, dipping a bit at the end. Normally about half were air force personnel, a quarter belonged to the army, and the rest served in the navy, marines, coast guard, and auxiliary services. Not included in the figures were sailors from the Seventh Fleet while in port, troops on R & R (rest and relaxation) furloughs from Vietnam, and military dependents (the latter numbered about 40–45,000).[4] The 100,000 or so military-related Americans represented less than a tenth of the figure for the occupation in 1945–1952, yet frictions with civilians near the bases never ceased throughout the postwar period. About 500 Japanese were killed as a result of on-duty and off-duty accidents involving United States forces during 1952–1977, fueling the antibase movement that still smolders today.[5] Nonetheless it is often pointed out that if the troops were Russian rather than American, anti-Soviet feelings would have run very deep.

Until the United States returned certain facilities to the Self-Defense Forces in 1968–1969 in connection with negotiations over Okinawa, it controlled 148 installations in Japan covering

365 million square meters, the residue from nearly four times as much land it held during the occupation. (By comparison the Self-Defense Forces in 1968 were using 836 million square meters, divided into 1,688 installations, for their 234,000 troops.)[6] The Pentagon considered twenty-eight army, six navy, and six air force facilities in Japan as major. Many of these were expanded after 1965 to improve their storage, communication, and medical capacities. Ironically, some of the most important for supporting the war in Vietnam were clustered in the Tokyo region where the antiwar movement was most muscular.

The seventh-century city of Fuchū, lined with gnarled zelkova trees in suburban Tokyo, was headquarters for the United States forces in Japan and home to the Fifth Air Force, with command over Japan, Okinawa, and South Korea. (Later in the war these functions were moved to a nearby base in Yokota.) A large airfield at Tachikawa, just west of Tokyo, was host to the 315th Air Transport Group, the supply headquarters for the American air force in the western Pacific and a central transit point for personnel and materiel. Camp Zama in nearby Kanagawa prefecture was the home of the United States army in Japan, where many thousands of GI's arrived each year for five days' leave from the war zone. A large naval air base in Atsugi included marines and the only complete military shop for repairing jet engines west of Honolulu. It was also the headquarters for naval air forces in the western Pacific. Damaged tanks and other military vehicles from Vietnam were repaired at Sagamihara, also in Kanagawa prefecture. An hour south of Tokyo was the United States naval command for Japan, at the port of Yokosuka, and nearby was the north pier at Yokohama, where the military sea transport service had its offices.

Less noticeable to the Japanese public were other rear echelon facilities that assisted the war in Vietnam: large oil storage depots at Yokohama and Tsurumi, radar and communication centers at Fukaya and Kamisedani in Kanagawa prefecture and at Kashiwa in Chiba prefecture, a procurement office in Yoko-

hama, and military hospitals in Tokyo, Saitama, and Kanagawa. Further west there were air bases at Iwakuni (marines) in Yamaguchi prefecture and Itazuke (air force) in Fukuoka prefecture, and Sasebo in Nagasaki prefecture was a major port for ships from the Seventh Fleet. Bombing ranges and training facilities were sprinkled from Hokkaido to Kyushu, and ammunition dumps, communication stations, and naval anchorages were spread along the Pacific coast. Together with bases in South Korea, Okinawa, Taiwan, Guam, and the Philippines, these installations formed a network coordinated from Hawaii that was quickly activated to support Gen. William C. Westmoreland's military assistance command in Vietnam in early 1965. A report on April 6, 1966, to the military preparedness subcommittee of the Senate, headed by Sen. John C. Stennis, noted how vital the installations in Japan were: "in particular, it would be very difficult to fight the war in Southeast Asia without Yokosuka and Sasebo."[7]

The same could have been said a fortiori of Okinawa. Even before the air campaign in Vietnam began, a squadron of KC-135 tanker planes moved from Guam to Kadena air base. These aircraft were soon used to refuel B-52 bombers during their monotonous westward flights from Guam to targets in Indochina. Okinawa was the jumping-off point for the first 15,000 American combat troops to enter the war, including the 173rd Army Airborne Brigade and elements of the Third Marine Division, beginning in March 1965.[8] Roughly 50,000 United States troops were stationed in the Ryūkyūs during the conflict, staffing ammunition depots, supply warehouses, training grounds, ports, air bases, missile sites, and communication centers. Altogether the military controlled eighty-eight installations, covering three-fifths as much area as its entire facilities in Japan proper and taking up 10 percent of all the land in the Ryūkyūs. The second logistical command, headquartered in Okinawa, handled about three-quarters of the 400,000 tons of goods consumed each month by American forces in Vietnam, mainly through Naha military port and White Beach harbor. The 3,750-meter runways at Kadena air

base averaged a takeoff or landing every three minutes around the clock, totaling more than a million flight operations during 1965–1973.[9] The jungles of Okinawa were training areas for as many as 9,000 United States Army Special Forces (Green Berets) at the peak of the war, and troops from South Vietnam, the Philippines, Thailand, Taiwan, and South Korea also underwent training there. More than 1,000 Japanese Self-Defense Force personnel also were sent to Okinawa each year to observe antiguerrilla techniques.[10] Okinawa was a major storage ground for poison chemicals, a port for American nuclear submarines, and the site of thirty-two nuclear-tipped Mace B missiles in launch shelters beneath the ground.[11] During the Vietnam War the department of defense started calling Okinawa the "keystone of the Pacific"—and even the auto license plates carried the legend.[12]

As the buildup of supplies and the dispatch of troops quickened, many people in Japan grew more irate, even though the threat of Chinese intervention abated after the fall of 1965. Okinawa lay beyond reach, but Beheiren and the opposition parties peppered the Satō government with questions about whether prior consultation was needed before the United States used the bases in Japan proper for certain war-related operations. Under the security treaty and the accompanying agreements, "military combat operations to be undertaken from Japan" and carried out abroad had to be discussed with the Japanese government in advance. In actual fact, the cabinet maintained, no prior consultation was needed so long as the direct combat orders were issued after the troops or bombers had left Japan.[13] Under this generous interpretation, even an airplane based in Tokyo could bomb Vietnam without advance discussion if its orders arrived while airborne.

"Major changes" in American troops, equipment, and the way bases were used also required prior consultation. The Japanese government excluded logistical support from the agenda for prior consultation, and it defined a major change in personnel as the arrival of an army division, a naval task force, or an air division—changes so vast as to be very unlikely. The intro-

duction of nuclear weapons, intermediate and long-range missiles, and new launch sites also demanded advance discussions. Planes, submarines, and carriers capable of housing nuclear weapons could enter Japan without prior consultation so long as they did not actually have such arms aboard. The Japanese government repeatedly took the view that in fact these craft were not carrying nuclear weapons when they reached Japan, inasmuch as the United States did not ask for consultation before they arrived. The Americans said they honored their treaty commitments but also that as a routine of policy they could not confirm or deny the type of weapons their ships and planes carried. This elaborate pas de deux has continued to the present, despite periodic "revelations" by former United States officials that American vessels do not offload their nuclear weapons before visiting Japan.[14] As the Vietnam War showed, the provisions for prior consultation were so vague that the opposition parties naturally denounced them as ineffective. Finally even Prime Minister Satō and President Nixon agreed in November 1969 that prior consultation did not give Japan the veto it once thought it had on how the bases were used, and the war ended without invoking the provisions even once.[15]

Foreign Minsiter Miki was technically correct that Japan could not intervene militarily in the war, but the government stretched the point by quietly helping to recruit civilian seamen through the transportation ministry to staff LST's and other cargo vessels in the war theater. Honda Katsuichi, the well-known *Asahi* correspondent, found that twenty-eight LST's operated entirely by Japanese crews wearing American uniforms were hauling munitions and napalm from harbor to harbor along the South Vietnamese coast early in the war. Twenty other LST's, each rated at 3,660 tons, were staffed by South Korean seamen. Many of the craft were manufactured in Japan; each flew an American flag and was considered part of the United States navy, as had been true during the Korean War when Japanese operated similar ships for the United States. As of January 1967, nearly 1,400 Japanese were work-

ing for the military sea transport service of the United States, in Vietnam and other Pacific locations. Japanese seamen also served on tankers and transport vessels chartered by the United States from Japanese and American shipping companies. Captain Fujiki of a 4,000-ton tanker from Osaka summarized his feelings: "the Americans are using the fuel I'm hauling to bomb the north. It's strictly a business proposition. . . . I'm making ¥100,000 more per month than if I were hauling in Japan."[16]

The first Japanese crew member to die in Vietnam was Saitō Kenzō, who was shot by a South Vietnamese military policeman in Da Nang harbor on November 2, 1964. The Japanese press dubbed the vessels "death carriers": on April 4, 1966, the *Hoku Nihon shinbun* kicked up a stir when it reported that the seamen were guaranteed extra hazard pay if their ships transported nuclear weapons. By September 1966 nine Japanese crew members had been killed running LST's in the war, and more than a hundred had been injured.[17] Already Representative Ishino Hisao had put the Satō government on the defensive by asking on April 1, 1965 whether it sanctioned the voyages. An official from the foreign ministry replied delicately, "it was decided that there existed insufficient danger to warrant the government's intervening to stop crew members who of their own accord wanted to sail."[18] As the peril to seamen rose, the government took pains to defend its laissez-faire attitude. At a lower house budget committee meeting on April 24, 1967, the head of the North American bureau of the foreign ministry, Tōgō Fumihiko, argued that "because the LST crews have no obligations under the [American] draft law or other connections with the U.S. government, it means they are not participating in the war."[19] In short, the LST personnel became a useful metaphor for Japan's role in the war: modest risks for tidy profits, quietly backing the Americans as noncombatants but staying within the rules to hush the protesters.

No Japanese troops served in Vietnam, but indirectly the Self-Defense Forces (SDF) pitched in by taking over certain defense functions in Japan and nearby waters from the Amer-

icans. When he succeeded Edwin O. Reischauer as American ambassador to Tokyo in late 1966, U. Alexis Johnson found that Japan's approach to its own defense was "immature." The *Asahi* journalist Murakami Yoshio believes Japan in the mid-sixties was afflicted by "an emotional weakness" toward the United States characterized by excessive dependence on the Pentagon—what the strategist Momoi Makoto calls Japanese "fatalism" about defense.[20] The war helped to change this outlook by speeding up the cooperation that had started to develop in the late fifties and early sixties between the SDF and the United States military in Japan. According to Congressional Quarterly Service, 15,280 Japanese military personnel received instruction in the United States between 1950 and 1968, more even than the 13,998 from South Vietnam.[21] By 1971 the self-defense agency estimated that 70 percent of its officers had undergone training in the United States.[22]

During the war military leaders from both countries plumped for a closer tie-up in the command structures of the SDF and the United States forces in Japan. Matsuno Raizō, head of the defense agency, told the budget committee of the House of Representatives in March 1966 that "in the future I hope the Maritime Self-Defense Force will hold joint exercises with American nuclear-powered submarines."[23] At that point the SDF consisted of 234,000 uniformed personnel with 200 ships, 900 aircraft, and defensive missles—but no nuclear weapons, then or now. The MSDF took over antisubmarine patrols from the United States Seventh Fleet, and when several dozen American military installations were returned to Japan in 1969 the self-defense agency integrated them smoothly into its network of bases. Ambassador Johnson found that during the war "excellent cooperation at the working level grew up between the SDF and the commanders of United States Forces Japan (USFJ)."[24]

For the first time since World War II, the Japanese sent a flotilla of destroyers through the Straits of Malacca in the summer of 1969, to hold joint maneuvers with warships from Australia and Malaysia. The following year the Satō govern-

ment chose February 11, a holiday with nationalistic over-tones, to send up the first unaided Japanese satellite. With equally bold timing, defense chief Nakasone Yasuhiro an-nounced a five-year military buildup on October 20, 1970, the eve of Sōhyō's annual antiwar day. The plan, contained in the first white paper on defense ever issued in Japan, drew hearty cheers from Washington. It called for doubling outlays for the SDF by spending $16 billion during 1972–1976.[25] Even though the proposal was shrouded in peaceable assurances, it triggered such an outcry among the Japanese public that no white paper on defense was published again until 1976. Still, the spending plan went forward largely intact.

At various points in the war Self-Defense Force personnel went to South Vietnam to observe the American military op-erations. Japanese pilots and officers from other allied nations flew along on combat missions to keep up with the latest tech-niques. When three high officials from the self-defense agency spent a week in South Vietnam in September 1966, the North Vietnamese foreign ministry renewed its bitter attacks against Japanese complicity in the war. The purpose of the visit was to find out how the United States was managing the logistical buildup and to assess the results of the bombings. Both Hanoi and Moscow had protested early in 1965 that Japan was vio-lating the Geneva agreements by serving as a rear echelon for the Americans. Now the North Vietnamese charged that Ja-pan was supplying chemical and biological weapons for the war and that the visiting generals reconfirmed Japan's role as an accomplice of imperialist aggression.[26] Gov. George C. Wallace of Alabama, looking ahead to the 1972 American presidential election, apparently wished the cooperation were even closer: "the war in Vietnam would have been over a long time ago if Japanese troops had joined us."[27]

WINDFALLS FROM THE WAR

The conflict in Indochina cost the United States about $150 billion in direct expenditures, several billion of which ended

up as income to Japanese companies for goods and services provided to American and ARVN forces. Fifteen years earlier, United States procurement for the Korean War had hoisted a flat Japanese economy toward unexpected prosperity. In 1952, the peak year, 63 percent of all Japanese exports were taken by the war. Even after the cease-fire in 1953, payments by the United States in connection with its bases and personnel in Japan averaged nearly $600 million for the rest of the decade, and they still accounted for about 14 percent of Japan's exports as late as 1958–1959. Starting in 1965 the United States suddenly began to place orders with Japan and many other nations for supplies to support its intervention in Vietnam. By then the Japanese economy was six times bigger than in the early fifties, so that the trade generated by the Vietnam War was proportionately much less important than the exports stimulated by the Korean conflict.[28] Still, the extra military business during 1965–1973 earned profits for a diverse mix of Japanese firms and their workers, no matter how often Beheiren denounced them as perpetrators of war on the Vietnamese.

Economists have not agreed on exactly how much money Japan made from the war. Because the Americans reported procurement statistics to the Japanese after 1960 only as a courtesy, the figures were often expressed in general categories and may have understated the actual values. The Japanese ministry of international trade and industry (MITI) kept separate statistics but did not routinely include procurement in its export totals. Because of differing accounting procedures and unclear definitions of cost classifications, even the data relating to the American bases and personnel in Japan are not uniform, much less those for sales overseas to the United States, South Vietnam, and the other countries that supplied them with goods for the war. Even harder to gauge are the indirect war profits Japan earned outside the formal procurement system.

Routine peacetime income to Japan from United States military facilities was known as special procurement (*tokuju*). In 1964 this consisted of $210 million in yen sales (personal consumption by American personnel and their dependents) and

93

$104 million in United States deposits (payroll for Japanese employees on the bases and payments for supplies and services). Setting aside the effects of inflation, most specialists take the 1964 total of $314 million as a constant and attribute the increases in special procurement in the years thereafter entirely to the greater activity at the bases produced by the war. By this reckoning $202 million of the $516 million in special procurement recorded for 1967 can be explained by Vietnam.[29] Some calculations cut the net figure by 15 percent to acknowledge the larger imports into Japan needed to fill the additional American orders. Others include a multiplier effect ($\times 2.0$) to suggest the true impact of the new business on the Japanese economy. Okinawa is omitted from all the estimates; it cost the United States somewhat less to operate its bases there compared with those on the Japanese mainland.

The war also led to direct procurement for Vietnam (*Betonamu tokuju*), which the Bank of Japan defined as sales of goods and services to the United States and South Vietnam for use in the war zone. By assuming that all the growth in Japanese exports to South Vietnam was war-related and that all military requisitions by the United States were actually used in Indochina, the bank concluded that direct Vietnam procurement earned Japan $292 million in 1967, rising to a peak of $467 million three years later.[30] It was widely believed during the war that another $150 million (perhaps twice that sum) in less visible purchases of politically sensitive goods like weapons and chemicals went publicly unrecorded each year.[31] For want of statistics, the Bank of Japan omitted tourism by American soldiers on R & R from its totals.

Hardest to measure but probably most important of all was the indirect procurement brought about by the war: exports of materials, supplies, and components to Korea, Taiwan, and states in Southeast Asia with procurement contracts of their own to fill; exports to consumers in these countries because of general wartime prosperity; and perhaps greatest of all, exports to America to satisfy its boom-time demand for consumer products. Many corporations in the United States could

94

not expand capacity fast enough to manufacture retail items, often because of conversion to war-related output, and as a result the Vietnam War became another lever for Japanese companies to pry open American pocketbooks.

The overheated economy soaked up Japanese color TV's, chemicals, auto parts, electrical cable, and machinery. Even the vaunted American aircraft industry strained under the war, so that a regional United States airline had to order thirty YS-11 passenger planes from Japan. Fuji Heavy Industries exported seven helicopters to Bell Helicopter Corporation, and Boeing relied more and more on Japanese suppliers for parts. On the other hand, Honda scaled down its American sales targets for motorcycles in 1966 because young men were fearful of being drafted and hesitated to buy machines. Banks too were more reluctant to give loans to draft-aged men. Nonetheless by 1967 exports to the United States attributable to the war are thought to have increased by $260 million over the previous year. Overall Japanese exports to America between 1965 and 1972 grew at an average annual rate of 21 percent, partly through normal growth but also because of Vietnam.[32]

The United States used Japanese suppliers early in the war because they were relatively close to the war zone and were famous for speedy deliveries. After 1966 the Pentagon did most of its shopping at home and tried to spread the rest among allies in Southeast Asia, but Japan still benefited indirectly from the resulting demand for imports in those countries. Although the absolute value of direct procurement in Japan for the Vietnam War kept rising until 1970, most corporate and bureaucratic officials think the war had its greatest effect on the Japanese economy in 1966, snapping it out of a minor downturn in the business cycle in 1964–1965 and giving a boost to certain small industries. Unless the war should stop very abruptly, few persons in Japan during the late sixties expressed worries about the loss of procurement contracts when peace came. On the contrary, by 1967 the banks and trading companies were eager to see the war end so that Japan could capitalize on the expected postwar need for its products.[33]

In reaching a final judgment about how much money Japan made from the war, the authorities at MITI were more conservative than economists at the foreign ministry or in the private sector. MITI assumed that a fast rise in nonmilitary trade would have occurred anyway and argued that the war directly and indirectly earned Japan $450 million in 1966 and $600 million the following year (the foreign ministry set the amount at $900 million to $1.1 billion for 1967).[34] In February 1968 the Nomura Research Institute concluded that, after allowing for normal growth in trade, the net tonic of the war on Japan was $73.1 million in 1965, $748.1 million in 1966, and $1,047.1 million in 1967.[35] Working from different assumptions, the Nihon Kangyō Bank estimated the impact at $710 million in 1966 and $870 million the following year. The Sanwa Bank put the figures much higher: $1,200–1,230 million in 1966 and $1,150–1,200 million in 1967.[36] All these calculations assumed that the indirect effects of exports (beyond normal growth) to the United States and Southeast Asia were considerably more beneficial than direct Vietnam procurement itself. Since the latter increased from $292 million in 1967 to $467 million in 1970, while overall trade with the other countries in Southeast Asia as well as with America was also growing, it seems sensible to say that the war allowed Japanese firms to earn at least an extra $1 billion per year, on average, from all sources during 1966–1971.[37]

More important than the actual numbers was the difference these dollars made to the Japanese economy. The consensus is that total direct and indirect procurement did not exceed 7–8 percent of Japan's exports for any year during the conflict, in contrast with the 63 percent reached during the Korean War.[38] But the fresh money was a boon to the young industries with contracts, and it undoubtedly accelerated Japan's recovery from the slump in 1965. The revenues also made a difference to Tokyo's international payments ledger, especially when the bilateral balance of manufacturing trade with the United States turned in Japan's favor after 1965.[39] Possibly the greatest long-term effect was also the most ironic: halfway through the war

Japan replaced the United States as the leading economic power in Southeast Asia, so that one of America's most reluctant allies ended up as the chief beneficiary of the eight-year war to save the Saigon regime.

Vietnam: "An Opportunity, Not a Problem"

Periodically the government faced sharp questions in parliament about how extensively Japan was playing quartermaster behind the scenes to the American forces. The standard official reply was that nobody knew the answer because procurement was a private transaction, because Japanese corporations kept their statistics to themselves, and because the United States had stopped sending detailed figures to MITI after the security treaty was changed in 1960. The revised treaty and status of forces agreement, the government pointed out, did not allow Japan to make its own surveys of American purchasing.[40] The Satō cabinet tried to minimize the matter because procurement was both good diplomacy vis-à-vis the United States and good politics for the Liberal Democrats among their business constituents. As Murakami Yoshio has said, "the Vietnam War to Japanese conservatives was an opportunity, not a problem."[41]

Manufacturers found it easy to deal with the United States army procurement agency because they were always paid on time and only had to deliver goods to the agency's main office in Yokohama or branch in Kobe. At first the orders went to small businesses for combat uniforms, work clothing, sandbags (filled by Vietnamese workers at American bases for a penny a bag), barbed wire, and the symbolic bête noire of Japanese war protesters, jungle boots. After the spring of 1966 procurement shifted to the industrial giants, and trading companies like Mitsui Bussan and Sumitomo Shōji set up departments to handle the requisitions. A year later President Johnson's buy-American policy began to take hold, and Southeast Asian allies began to receive more of the business for textiles and light manufactures. The volume of orders placed with Jap-

anese sources still continued to swell, because only they could produce certain items such as cameras, trucks, diesel engines, locomotives, and two–way radios.[42]

Data from MITI show that Japanese firms supplied most of the materials needed for camps and bases: prefabricated buildings, lumber, cement, cranes, generators, tents, jeeps, and toilet paper. American soldiers drank Kirin beer, chewed Lotte gum, and ate Chiba lettuce. American pilots dropped more than a billion propaganda leaflets, written in Vietnamese and printed in Kanagawa. Some of the injured received transfusions of Japanese blood, and those who died were sent home in polyethyline body bags made in Japan. Many service personnel bought Japanese watches, cameras, and stereos, either while on R & R in some Asian entrepôt or through catalog orders delivered to their bases. Some even purchased miniature rockets, made in Japan, to take home as souvenirs of the war.[43]

Far more controversial was the report first circulated by the New China News Agency (Xinhua) in April 1966 that as much as 92 percent of the napalm used by the United States in Vietnam was made in Japan. Napalm is a jellied gasoline, easily produced from naptha and palm oil, that was poured from low–flying aircraft to ignite the skin of Vietnamese on contact. Suspicion quickly focused on Nippon Yushi Corporation, a leading manufacturer of fats, soaps, and TNT at Taketoyo in Aichi prefecture. The company denied that it produced napalm, but the secretary-general of its plant union said there was no doubt that the chemicals it manufactured could be combined by almost anyone to form the substance.[44] *Mainichi* concluded that "there is no proof that napalm bombs are being manufactured in Japan,"[45] but whether the Americans bought the components for it in Japan remained in doubt. It also turned out that in 1966 the United States suddenly asked the Air Self-Defense Force to return 4,000 napalm "bombs" originally made in America during the Korean War and stored in Kasugai, Aichi prefecture, at an ordnance depot long since returned to Japanese control. If this napalm was subsequently used in Vietnam, it was really no more Japanese than the many

other American products transshipped via bases in Japan en route to the war zone[46]—but the willingness of the ASDF to hand it back rankled many citizens nonetheless.

Japan's exports of arms and ammunition were fairly small during the Vietnam War, but the stepped-up trade in components sold to American military contractors helped to cement the close transpacific relations between the largest defense industries in each country. The munitions manufacturing law of 1953 gave the government basic control over the producers of weapons and ammunition. Prime Minister Ikeda extended this act by putting tight restrictions on the export of arms, a policy that his successor gradually relaxed. The opposition parties charged in 1966 that Japanese firms were selling rifles, machine guns, small rockets, and ammunition to the United States, often laundered through Hong Kong. Foreign Minister Shiina told the lower house in April that the government had no information about procurement from private industry and that in an era of technological warfare it was "difficult to draw a clear cut line between arms and civilian goods." He said the authorities had "no control" over these doubtful cases.[47] In fact, MITI throughout the war forbade the sale of arms to communist states, to countries barred from purchasing weapons by the United Nations, or to countries where conflict was incipient or in progress. Japan was obviously wary of rousing the hostility of its neighbors by selling military equipment, let alone by intervening with its own troops in Indochina. As of August 1969 *Asahi* could discover no exports of Japanese arms to South Vietnam since 1958, and apparently only 50,800 pistols sold to the United States during 1962–1968 appeared on the record.[48] Even the fattest contracts to equip the Self-Defense Forces went to concerns that mainly produced civilian goods: Mitsubishi Heavy Industries and Mitsubishi Electric, which held 38 percent of the business in 1968, earned just 3–4 percent of their gross revenues from arms sales.[49]

Late in the war it became known that Sony manufactured some of the parts used in guiding the smart bombs dropped since 1970 on Vietnam by the United States. On June 28, 1972

the military command in Saigon explained that these weapons, each weighing 340 to 900 kilograms, were guided by laser beams or by TV nose cameras that sent pictures of the terrain back to the bombardier as they were falling. They could usually be steered to within 1.5 meters of the target by remote guidance. An air force colonel named Miller mentioned during the briefing that smart bombs were Sony-equipped, triggering a row among workers at the company headquarters near Gotanda in Tokyo. The following day the Pentagon said the cameras were made by Texas Instruments but the screens were Sonys. President Morita Akio declared that the management had no idea its screens were guiding bombs and sent a statement to the American embassy: "we hope that our products will be used only for peaceful, nonmilitary needs."[50]

Despite the tempest at Gotanda and the periodic protests by big labor, there was very little agitation by workers in the plants supplying the war. One person was fired in July 1965 for distributing the communist party organ, *Akahata*, at Kōkoku Kagaku Kōgyō, the large manufacturer of jungle boots. Employees at a gas factory in Hyōgo prefecture tried to block the sale of their products to the American forces in Vietnam in May 1966, and laborers demonstrated at various times in front of the Tokyo main offices of Mitsubishi Heavy Industries, the largest defense contractor. The following October a small committee of radical students and workers "attacked" the factory of Nittoku Kinzoku Kōgyō in Tanashi, Tokyo, to try to stop the production of machine guns reportedly bound for Vietnam. The same group handed antiwar pamphlets to people arriving for work on November 15, 1966 at Hōwa Kōgyō, an ammunition concern in Nagoya. Six of the demonstrators suddenly rushed inside the gates, where they were soon rounded up by guards and handed over to the police. The authorities clamped down hard on the group, and even though isolated protests were held throughout the war, there was virtually no antiwar sabotage and very little strike activity that could be linked to the Vietnam situation.[51] Like workers in the United States, Japanese employees were prospering from the

war; unlike the American case, no issue of patriotism was at stake, and despite the hectoring from national union leaders, the conflict in Indochina usually seemed too remote for them to run the risks of public dissent.

Other lucrative sources of income from procurement were the repair and maintenance contracts held by Japanese firms to service American ships, aircraft, and vehicles. Several companies maintained squads of mechanics in South Vietnam, but most of the heavy work was done at facilities in Japan. Aircraft maintenance, especially rustproofing and engine overhaul, was the most important service performed in Japan: the value of such contracts rose 146 percent in 1966 over the previous year. Three big concerns did most of the repair work on United States naval vessels and underwent a 378 percent jump in their business during the same period.[52] Near the end of the war the Americans hired Japanese workers to fix damaged trucks, personnel vehicles, and tanks from Vietnam at the army's facility at Sagamihara, Kanagawa prefecture—setting off one of the angriest citizens' protests of the war.

Visiting soldiers on R & R helped to pump up the Japanese hotel and entertainment industries, adding an estimated $13–20 million annually to the Japanese economy. Hong Kong was probably the favorite destination for American troops on furlough, but Japanese newspapers calculated that roughly 40,000 visited Japan during 1966 and nearly 50,000 in 1967. The United States department of defense estimated that the typical soldier spent $53 a day in Tokyo, but others think that $90 is more realistic.[53] Most of the GI's arrived by chartered commercial jet in the dead of night. They were bused from Yokota, Tachikawa, or Haneda to Camp Zama and given $200 along with strict instructions about how to behave during their five-day stay. Several dozen hotels and inns in Tokyo, Yokohama, and Atami had contracts with the United States forces in Japan to put up the visitors, who toured the sights, sought companions, or went shopping in the civilian clothes they were required to rent for the stay. Hundreds of troops each day crowded into the USO center next door to the ele-

gant Kanebō store in Ginza. As with the strips of bars near the navy bases in Yokosuka and Sasebo, the Tokyo establishments drawing soldiers on R & R had to tolerate a good deal of drunkenness and brawling. Yet the greatest concern to most Japanese was that almost nothing was done to screen the troops for cholera, malaria, bubonic plague, or amoebic dysentery when they arrived. The Japanese government, which otherwise observed impeccable standards of public health, quietly allowed GI's to enter unquarantined. Happily no serious outbreaks of infectious diseases resulted.[54]

Japanese universities were usually hostile to the war in Vietnam, and they had few ties to defense contractors and almost none to the military. Even so, they came under suspicion of complicity in the war when the budget committee of the House of Councillors reported on May 19, 1967 that the United States army had awarded about $100,000 a year for the previous nine years to twenty-five Japanese universities and twelve other institutions for research in science, medicine, and engineering. The grant program was no secret among scholars, whose universities were starved for research funds, nor did the research contracts require that the results be classified or even mention that the findings might be used for military purposes. Still the news set off a series of campus disputes, most notably at Keio University, and a government audit in May 1969 revealed that twelve universities had failed to report 279 research projects, worth $283,000, many of which were assumed to be for military purposes. Tokyo University headed the list, with eighty-seven of the unreported "illegally commissioned research items"[55]—some of them modest plums for the professors from the war.

DOING BUSINESS WITH WARTIME VIETNAM

Japan was a low-key partner of United States policies in Southeast Asia during the second half of the sixties through its trade and aid programs with South Vietnam. As John Foster Dulles had hoped in 1954 when he told Japan to look south-

ward for markets, the drive to expand exports there converged with America's anticommunist objectives by providing economic assistance and stability to the region. When the war escalated in 1965, Japanese exports to South Vietnam were running about $35 million per year and imports about $6.5 million. At that point Japan was the GVN's third most important source of imports after the United States and Taiwan. Three years later Japan rose to number one, with $199 million in sales to South Vietnam, and the following year the exports crested at $223 million.[56]

Part of the great leap sprang from American procurement, especially early in the fighting, but most of it was paid for by Saigon's currency reserves accumulated because of wartime prosperity from licit and illicit sources. At first the South Vietnamese bought Japanese trucks, buses, and sewing machines; by 1970 the country was awash with consumer goods of every variety. Radios, tape recorders, television sets, diesel engines, and motorcycles were very widely marketed, legally or otherwise, among the Vietnamese. Relatively few basic materials like steel, cement, or chemical fertilizers were included among the exports to South Vietnam.[57] Japan quickly became known in Saigon for its favorable prices and quick deliveries, until finally in October 1970 the GVN placed heavy duties and taxes on Japanese products to cope with a large trade deficit. Even greater smuggling than usual was the result, making the 1970 official import figure of $146 million in Japanese goods seem very unreliable.[58]

But even in the peak year 1969 South Vietnam was only Japan's seventh most important trading partner in Southeast Asia. The region as a whole took about a fifth of Japan's growing exports that year, and South Vietnam got just 5 percent of that fifth. In a decade when world trade as a whole tripled in value and Japanese exports soared almost six times, the jump in sales to South Vietnam from $35 million when the war heated up in 1965 to $223 million in 1969 was relatively modest, but very welcome.[59] South Vietnam also consumed Japanese products indirectly when it ordered commodities from

other countries. By one estimate, half of South Korea's deliveries to South Vietnam were reexports of Japanese goods, usually as components supplied to South Korean manufacturers. The war also created buying power in other Southeast Asian states because of wages earned thanks to American procurement, leading to bigger orders from Japanese purveyors of consumer goods.[60]

At the same time, South Vietnamese exports to Japan fell from $6.5 million in 1965 to $2.7 million in 1968 because of wartime devastation of production and transport facilities. Timber and raw rubber were among the main items sold. The figures stabilized at about $4 million from 1969 to 1971, then tripled the next year because of a sudden Japanese demand for more timber and especially for frozen shrimp. By 1973–1974 exports had doubled again to about $30 million per year. Even so, the South Vietnamese still incurred a $57 million deficit in their best wartime year for trade with Japan (1973), and during the period 1965–1975 as a whole customs reports showed that Japan earned a net trade surplus of $1.28 billion with South Vietnam.[61] Figures such as these help explain why the Japanese business world expected that the loss of war procurement would be more than offset by the growth in trade and investments in the region once peace came.[62]

Just as 1965 was the kickoff for big Japanese trade profits in South Vietnam, it was also a turning point for the repenetration of Southeast Asia by Japanese capital. Some of the biggest corporations began to multinationalize, although many of the investments were also by small Japanese companies in specific commodity lines. Since nearly 70 percent of Japan's imports from Southeast Asia during the latter half of the sixties were primary products, most investments were intended to assure a steady flow of raw materials. Yet few private Japanese corporations wanted to sink their capital into Indochina while the war was going on. Some were willing to offer South Vietnam long-term credits for purchasing Japanese goods: during 1965–1968 private sources provided $2.7 million for this pur-

pose.[63] By contrast, direct Japanese investments in all of Southeast Asia amounted to $355 million in 1969 alone.[64]

When Japan completed its last reparations payment to South Vietnam in January 1965, it refocused its foreign aid to the whole area on economic development so that the receiving countries could buy Japanese manufactures. Most of the assistance, which ran between $100 and $200 million in the late sixties, went to Burma, Indonesia, Malaysia, the Philippines, and Thailand because their political stability exceeded South Vietnam's. In light of the war, the Satō cabinet limited its help to Indochina mainly to noneconomic programs during 1965–1970. It continued Prime Minister Ikeda's policy of giving medical aid to Saigon, offering $1.1 million in additional supplies in June 1967. The government also sent funds to house refugees, gave X-ray equipment and ambulances, and sent a total of eighty-six surgeons and other medical professionals to a brain surgery unit financed by Japan during 1966–1974.[65] The authorities also provided technical aid by taking on 884 South Vietnamese, 500 Cambodian, and 360 Lao young people for study and training in Japan from 1965 through 1974. During this same time Japan sent 288 technicians to South Vietnam, 287 to Laos, and 293 to Cambodia to assist with agriculture, welfare programs, and other public projects.[66]

The Satō cabinet's most generous financial commitment to Indochina came in 1968 when it announced a $200 million development plan for the region after peace returned. Japan pledged $40 million and asked other countries to contribute the rest. This largess did not satisfy some of the antiwar critics at home, who suspected that the aid was part of an official export policy supporting American aggression in Vietnam. Some persons rejected foreign assistance in principle because of its historic connections with military programs, and others thought Japan should first take care of its domestic welfare and environmental problems.[67] The prolongation of the war, and then the collapse of the Saigon government in April 1975, scotched the development plan, and with it most of the grumbling.

Japanese trade with North Vietnam was small before 1965 and minuscule during the war itself. Six major shipping firms in Japan decided to suspend service to North Vietnam on March 30, 1965 because of the hostilities, forcing suppliers to use third-country vessels. The Japanese government, evidently under pressure from Washington, stepped in to stop the sale of electric cable by Sumitomo Electric Industries and Toshima and Company to North Vietnam in 1966, even though there was no legal basis for this ban. Despite such setbacks, the flow of Hongay anthricite coal to Japan continued at reduced levels until the Easter offensive of 1972, when bombings threw the economy of the north into a tumble. The Japanese also continued to buy pig iron from the DRV; in return they shipped textiles, pharmaceuticals, fertilizers, and iron and steel products. Except for 1969 and 1972, Hanoi ran a surplus with Japan throughout the war, but the actual figures were very modest: exports of $6–7 million and imports of $4–5 million.[68] Only the Soviet Union and China were most important trade partners for North Vietnam, whereas Japan did five times this much business with impoverished North Korea. Important as the Hongay coal and the principle of separating politics from economics were, the trade with North Vietnam was little more than a green apple in the barrel of windfalls that came to Japan from its hushed wartime partnership with the United States.

CHAPTER 4

Steady State

THE FIGHTING in Vietnam settled into a routine of escalation in early 1966, especially after the United States renewed its bombings at the beginning of February (Satō sent Johnson his regrets).[1] For the next year and a half Japan, too, fell into a pattern of incremental engagement with the war. Sales to American forces and normal exports both ballooned; the GI's in the streets seemed younger, more vacant, and more numerous than a year or two before. The government launched another futile round of peace missions but also dug in a bit more staunchly in defense of the thunderous American bombardments. At the same time Japan broadened its involvement with Southeast Asia by joining several international schemes for economic development in the region. Even the antiwar protesters took on regular habits of activity to mobilize people against United States actions in Vietnam. Many ordinary citizens were perplexed by the obstacles to peace during 1966–1967 but continued to return the Liberal Democrats to office. Then in August 1967 an explosion of jet fuel in Shinjuku station and a sobering forum on war crimes alerted the public once again to the hazards of war.

THE GOVERNMENT HOLDS FAST

Soon after Vice President Hubert H. Humphrey visited Tokyo as a part of his whirlwind peace tour at the end of 1965, President Johnson sent the suave diplomat W. Averell Harriman as his personal representative to ask Japan to cooperate in finding a settlement "from America's position of strength."[2] Prime Minister Satō promised to do all he could, but he also reported

to the Diet on January 28, 1966 that Humphrey's proposals in December and Harriman's in January seemed unavailing. A congressional report the following month by Rep. Clement J. Zablocki added: "the Japanese government approves of America's Vietnam policy, but because the media are almost unanimously against it, the government is unable to give its full support to America."[3]

To some degree this finding was a testament to Satō's skill at citing the strong opposition within Japan to foil the entreaties from Washington that Japan back the war more stoutly. But it also reflected the situation that Sen. Wayne Morse had confronted during a visit to Japan the previous fall. He warned the Senate foreign relations committee in February 1966 about the "outright opposition and even hostility" of the Japanese people to the war.[4] During the same hearings the diplomat-historian George F. Kennan testified that the conflict was hurting relations with America's allies: "more unfortunate still, in my opinion, is the damage being done to the feelings entertained for us by the Japanese people; the confidence and the good disposition of the Japanese is the greatest asset we have had and the greatest asset we could have in East Asia."[5] Views like Morse's and Kennan's had little influence in the White House, which sent team after team of senior officials to Tokyo throughout 1966 to try to persuade Satō to aid the American military effort in Vietnam more concretely.

Satō demurred, but he did follow up on the Harriman request by dispatching emissaries around the globe in the first months of 1966 to try to bring the war to an end. Foreign Minister Shiina went to Moscow in January about trade and airline agreements and, like his predecessors before the end of World War II, asked the Soviets to intervene on behalf of peace. Andrei A. Gromyko, the foreign minister, was noncommittal. The vice president of the Liberal Democratic Party, Kawashima Shōjirō, led a delegation to the United Arab Republic and other Mideast countries in February 1966 to discuss solutions to the war, and at the United Nations Ambassador Matsui, who chaired the Security Council that month, devoted much

of his time to promoting a cease-fire. The foreign ministry was miffed when Satō sent a personal representative, Yokoyama Shōkō, on a grand tour of twenty-three countries that spring to drum up support for peace talks. So was the Hanoi government: the day he arrived in Paris the Lao Dong Party organ blasted Yokoyama as "a servant of America's imperialist war of aggression in Vietnam" and a mouthpiece for "Japan's reactionary leadership class."[6]

Even though Yokoyama told reporters in Paris that the Government of Vietnam was a puppet, North Vietnam refused to see him. Like the opposition parties in Japan, Hanoi knew that the trip was a gesture both to the domestic opponents of the war at home and to the United States, which welcomed the appearance of allied support for its peace ideas. Nothing came of these diplomatic forays early in 1966, and apart from lip service paid by Miki Takeo when he succeeded Shiina as foreign minister in December of that year, Japan did little more to bring about a settlement until Satō visited Southeast Asia in the fall of 1967.[7]

Public opinion clearly wanted the government to try to move mountains to end the war. A *Yomiuri* survey in March 1966 discovered that just 21 percent of the respondents throughout Japan believed their country should stick to its present course on the war, whereas 49 percent thought it should be more active in seeking a solution by taking a more independent position. In June the Institute of Statistical Research reported that more citizens found the United States mainly at fault for the Vietnam situation than any other country or group (31 percent, versus 12 percent who blamed all the parties involved and 7 percent who chose the NLF). That same month the press reported that NHK, the public broadcasting network, had hushed up part of a poll of its own in March 1966 because, as Chairman Maeda explained, "it is NHK's ethic not to cause divisiveness or further to intensify issues on which there is political opposition."[8] The offending portion contained the finding that only 27 percent of the public supported

the alliance with the United States and that 42 percent favored nonnuclear armed neutrality.[9]

Satō brushed aside the survey reports as immaterial to Japan's diplomacy, and he also rebuffed the Soviet Union when it complained on February 17, 1966 about the use of "Japanese territory, industry and manpower" to further "the interest of the US aggression."[10] The government replied that it had never given military aid to any belligerent in Vietnam and that its treaty ties to the United States obliged Japan to provide facilities and nonmilitary supplies.[11] The cabinet also offered South Vietnam an additional $190,000 in emergency relief on March 1, to help with the refugees pouring into the cities, and it pledged to increase its medical aid to Saigon for the next fiscal year. Shiina even told the Diet that Japan would be willing to send medical help to Hanoi if necessary, but there is no sign that the government ever did so.[12]

By May the diplomatic offensive had withered, the press was making hay with the recent news that Japanese firms were filling huge procurement orders, and President Johnson was on the verge of authorizing a force level of 431,000 American troops in Vietnam. In the face of sharp questioning, Shiina told the foreign affairs committee of the upper house on May 31 that "Japan is not cooperating positively" with the United States in the war, "but its position is faithfully to honor the Japan–U.S. security treaty." Once again the government was garbing itself in legalistic armor, as it had steadily since the first queries were raised about Southeast Asia and the treaty in 1961. Then, in an unusually candid statement by a government known for its obliqueness, Shiina admitted that "Japan is not neutral" in the war: "Japan is tied to the United States in a defensive security treaty. Japan is not in a neutral position vis-à-vis the United States and North Vietnam."[13] He reiterated the government's familiar contention that "the actions of the American forces in Vietnam are intended to maintain the security of the Far East. Japan has an obligation to furnish facilities and territory for this purpose."[14]

Satō echoed the foreign minister two weeks later when crit-

ics in the House of Representatives excoriated the Americans for recently intensifying their bombings of Vietnam. He said "I can't agree with the opposition to escalation or to bombing the north." Two days later he told the house budget committee, "I'm not defending America, but it is unfortunate if you don't appreciate the sacrifices that America itself is making."[15] Evidently a lot of people in and out of the political system did not appreciate it when the United States extended its air attacks to Hanoi and Haiphong on June 29, 1966. Beheiren held a series of protest meetings, and Sōhyō collaborated with the Japan Communist Party to turn out 32,000 demonstrators four days later in Meiji Park. The riot police dispersed a phalanx of 100 students who were marching to the American embassy in Akasaka.[16]

The Japan Communist Party contended that the latest escalation had lifted the war to a different level. The protest it lodged with the Satō cabinet said: "we strongly request that you immediately cancel your total cooperation and complicity in America's imperialistic aggression in Vietnam."[17] This statement showed once again the gap between the Old Left and the antiwar movement led by Oda Makoto. The JCP assumed that the United States was malevolent and focused its criticism on the true enemy, conservative rule in Japan, badgering the government for backing the Americans. The antiwar leaders, on the other hand, still condemned a specific United States policy more than the country as a whole, and much as they resented Satō for aligning himself with Washington they had no illusions that replacing the Liberal Democrats with an opposition party would bring an improvement. A foreign war, not domestic power, was their chief concern.

By the end of June 1966 even the Fujiyama and Nakasone-Matsumura factions in the LDP, which were anti–Satō in principle, tried to dissociate Japan from the inferno in Vietnam. The maverick Liberal Democratic representative Utsunomiya Tokuma flatly demanded that the government oppose the latest escalation, but naturally the cabinet refused. The foreign ministry on June 30 labeled the bombings "unavoidable in

view of circumstances."[18] Shiina was much bolder. That same day he told the upper chamber, "these bombings are not intended to escalate the war once again; they are intended to bring the dispute to an early conclusion. There is no danger of a wider war. Therefore the government has no intention of asking the Americans to stop bombing Hanoi and Haiphong."[19] A few weeks later Kawashima Shōjirō, the party vice president who had recently returned from peace discussions in the Middle East, declared that "America is fighting for the defense of Japan and all of free Asia by its stand in VietNam."[20] The umbrella put up by the LDP in May 1965 to cover its diverse views of the war was starting to leak because of the bombings, but it managed to hold together well enough to keep Satō and his foreign policies comfortably dry.

Still, the steady support he gave the United States was not enough to please Dean Rusk, the American secretary of state. Speaking at the Kyoto international conference hall in early July 1966, Rusk stressed "North Vietnam's continuing aggression and armed attacks on South Vietnam."[21] He pressed the seven Japanese cabinet ministers who were present to line their country up even more resolutely on the side of the United States. Foreign Minister Shiina replied that "Japan's views and actions on specific issues may not always be the same as those of the United States"[22]—a hard message to get through to either the Americans or the antiwar critics at home, several thousand of whom gathered at the foot of the driveway below the conference hall.

The communication was no smoother between intellectuals and diplomats. The renowned scholar Maruyama Masao recalled that when McGeorge Bundy, the new head of the Ford Foundation, came to Japan in June 1966, "he turned on me in a fury when I told him that never has the prestige of the United States been so low abroad, due to Vietnam."[23] When the hawkish diplomat U. Alexis Johnson was nominated as the new American ambassador to Japan at the end of July, *Asahi* editors later noted, "it seemed obvious that he had been appointed to toughen up the Japan-America dialogue."[24] Soon

after taking office he discouraged Miki Takeo, the new Japanese foreign minister, from making further moves toward peace negotiations and said the war would be settled by military means.[25]

Nonetheless, Japanese diplomacy toward the rest of Southeast Asia moved steadily forward during 1966–1967. The policy of separating economics from politics allowed Satō to sink Japan's trade roots deeper in the region (apart from Indochina) without following the anticommunist line adopted by certain governments there. Japan had already taken part in international organizations affecting Southeast Asia during the past decade. It attended the Economic Commission for Asia and the Far East as a member in 1953, the Colombo Plan meetings in 1954, and the Asian–African conference at Bandung in 1955. Prime Minister Kishi in the late fifties helped to build the base for the Asian Productivity Organization, which was formally inaugurated in 1961. It was only in the mid-sixties that Japan put war reparations safely in the past and turned to a new stage in its relations with the area.

The Satō government took several important steps in 1966 to cooperate more fully with Southeast Asia. In April it convened the first of an annual series of ministerial conferences for economic development in the region. Shiina told the visiting delegates from eight countries that Japan would "develop hereafter a positive foreign policy towards Southeast Asia on the issues of economic development."[26] Japan soon pledged credits to Malaysia and Thailand, set up a consortium of eleven nations to restructure Indonesia's debts, proposed an agricultural development council for Southeast Asia, and promised to raise its global economic aid shortly to 1 percent of GNP. In June Japan attended the first meeting of the Asian and Pacific Council (ASPAC), organized by President Park Chung-hee of South Korea as a political alliance for noncommunist states. Japan was glad to belong but soon called for peaceful coexistence with China, an idea that was a red flag to most of the other members.[27]

Japan shied from the October 1966 meeting at Manila of

113

Vietnam War allies, a lineup that was almost identical to AS-PAC, and made it plain that a stopover in Tokyo broached by President Johnson after the conference was "inconceivable."[28] Johnson's reply expressed his "deep gratitude and appreciation" for Japan's constant support on the Vietnam issue and recognized that "the Japanese posture is as a matter of course somewhat different from that of the nations represented in the conference." Satō immediately closed the exchange by saying he found the president's decision not to visit Japan "extremely thoughtful."[29] A presidential trip to Tokyo would have been unthinkable; protests dwarfing 1960 would almost surely have resulted. Because ASPAC was so tinged with militant anti-communism, Japan kept to the fringes and did not mourn its demise in 1975.

The foreign ministry and particularly the war opponents in Japan were much less suspicious of a second regional organization founded in August 1967, the Association of Southeast Asian Nations (ASEAN). The Satō government welcomed the economic activities of this council, which was mainly intended to protect the independence of Indonesia, Malaysia, the Philippines, Singapore, and Thailand from outside interference by the superpowers. It soon grew clear that ASEAN, unlike ASPAC, had no military agenda, and Japan ended up working closely with the five nations on matters of aid and economic growth.[30]

Probably the most meaningful regional organization Japan joined in the mid-sixties was the Asian Development Bank (ADB), founded in ceremonies at Tokyo in November 1966. The Japanese contributed the first president, Watanabe Takeshi, and $200 million of the bank's initial $1 billion capital. With headquarters in Manila, the ADB was suspect among leftists in Japan and elsewhere as a possible tool of American anticommunist policies, but actually the United States was slow in recognizing the bank at all. Japan was able to help the agency stick to its original purpose, loans for economic development, and the ADB ended up as one link in the chain of international financial institutions that helped East and South-

east Asia gain an edge in many product areas in the seventies.[31] By holding firmly to its measured support for the United States in Vietnam, Japan managed to grow more deeply enmeshed in the rest of Southeast Asia without damaging its small but profitable trade with communist countries. In this sense, the government's political position on the war struck the right chord to mollify nearly all parties abroad—but not opponents of the war at home.

THE PROTESTERS SETTLE IN

While the state was following a steady course on Vietnam during 1966–1967, the resistance to the war in Japan settled into a regular pattern of appeals, demonstrations, letter-writing, and forums for discussing how to get out of the quagmire that Indochina had become. The noisiest early protests gave way to a tireless routine of antiwar work by both the Old and New Left to try to force the United States to switch gears on Vietnam. Marches staged by Sōhyō and the left parties, endemic since the 1950s, were now frequently used to denounce the war. Eventually the ferment led to a huge movement on October 21, 1966 that big labor called the first strike by workers anywhere against the Vietnam War.

Although the protests were quieter after 1965, teach-ins about Southeast Asia were very common during the winter and spring of 1966, mainly on campuses but also in community centers around the country. Most of them were put on by local groups affiliated with Beheiren. The press carried forward with its trenchant reporting and caustic criticism during the first half of the year, both in journals like *Sekai* (which turned radical later in the war) and the daily and weekly fare from the giant publishers. The scuffles between the media and the authorities turned into a tense standoff when the cabinet sent proposals to parliament on April 1, 1966 to revise the broadcast law and the radio law. The changes would give the ministry of posts and telecommunications more supervision over program content. A committee to survey public opinion

about broadcasts was also proposed, but opponents said that its real duty was to censor what could be heard and seen. After a chorus of hoots from many quarters, the plans were withdrawn in June when the government and the LDP could not agree on how to proceed.[32]

TBS, a private Tokyo television station, got into a wrangle with its workers that same month when it tried to send engineers and equipment to South Vietnam to work with CBS on a propaganda film for the United States forces. Finally on June 7 the company president, Imaichi Junzō, dropped the plan on the diaphanous pretext that the "danger such as demonstrations of the Buddhists against the U.S. is increasing at present in Vietnam."[33] After the enormous outcry about the bombings of Hanoi and Haiphong in late June, the press gradually grew preoccupied with the "black mist" scandals enshrouding the Satō regime in the second half of 1966, and apart from occasional events the antiwar movement was not front-page news again until the fall of 1967. One of the exceptions was the singer and peace activist Joan Baez, whose television appearance scheduled for January 16, 1967 was canceled by TBS because her concerts included repartee with the audience, usually about the war. NTV later broadcast one of her performances on January 27, but the announcer-interpreter, Takazaki Ichirō, failed to translate a word. Walter Nichols, who was the cultural attaché at the time, denies that the embassy ever tried to interfere with the contents of concert tours by American antiwar artists, but the press was convinced that the stations had felt pressure from the Central Intelligence Agency via the United States embassy.

A spattering of Vietnam-related paintings appeared in 1966 at the open-submission art shows, and the nineteenth Independent Art Association exhibit in late February of that year was virtually given over to the war. The peace art shows sponsored by antibomb groups each summer at Ueno and Hiroshima also included a few works treating Vietnamese themes. Peace songs by popular American musicians began to be played starting in February 1966, and further antiwar concerts

were held in Osaka, Tokyo, and other cities in 1966–1967, usually before audiences no larger than those for the Rōon and Utagoe events the year before. The government doused plans for a road tour by forty-four members of a North Vietnamese song and dance troupe in May 1966 by refusing to give them visas to enter the country.[34]

Dissident poetry began to appear in February 1966 when the printer-poet Hasegawa Shūji published his first collection of anti-Vietnam works and handed out copies to pedestrians at the Sukiyabashi crossing in Tokyo. This turned out to be a semiannual enterprise, often containing antiwar poems by Beheiren members, with printings of 250–500 copies. Responding to a call for solidarity from several hundred New York poets who gathered on January 14, 1967, at St. Mark's Church in the Bowery, the Conference of Poets (Shijin Kaigi) held a simultaneous meeting that day in Tokyo at which about sixty antiwar poets appeared.[35]

Religious groups were in the front ranks of peace marchers in other countries during the Vietnam conflict, but the priests and congregations in Japan were much less conspicuous. The Japan Buddhist Federation (Zen Nihon Bukkyōkai) sent peace representatives to Vietnam early in the war, but during the Buddhist uprising in Saigon in the spring of 1966 the federation aligned itself with the pro-government faction and continued to support the GVN even after that faction disappeared. The Nihonzan Myōhōji sect, a small Buddhist offshoot, was one of the very few religious organizations willing to take direct nonviolent action against the war. Most clergy who wished to protest did so through published documents, such as the appeal for an unconditional halt to the bombings issued in March 1967 by the heads of Kiyomizu, Enkakuji, Sensōji, and fifty other major temples. On the whole, the Beheiren leader Tsurumi Yoshiyuki recalls, "the Buddhists were very dull and usually supported the conservatives."[36] Certain Japanese Catholics, acting in the peaceful spirit of Paul VI, became politically active for the first time in Japan, joining in Beheiren demonstrations and caring for refugees after the war. Many

117

Protestant denominations sent representatives to antiwar rallies, and a few independent Christian groups helped to shelter American deserters from the armed forces.[37] Still, it is not surprising in a society where social activism by organized religions is so little practiced that the antiwar movement was overwhelmingly secular.

Scientific and scholarly groups pressed on with their opposition to the war, undaunted by the government's steadfast support for the United States. A number of antiwar mathematicians in various cities held roundtable discussions on Vietnam during 1966–1967. About 150 of them gathered at the main gate to Tokyo University for a protest meeting and march on October 11, 1966. They followed this with another demonstration on February 7, 1967. Associations of Japanese life scientists regularly complained to the United States about the effects of Agent Orange, the defoliant that stripped an area of South Vietnam bigger than the island of Shikoku. Three separate petitions signed respectively by 128, 1,200, and 1,439 scientists were transmitted to the United States embassy after it became known that American forces were using herbicides.[38]

Women's leaders joined the antiwar effort with an appeal for peace on May 10, 1966 from officers of civic, temperance, literary, labor, arts, and YWCA groups. When Japanese representatives to an international conference on protecting children returned home on October 11, customs officers at Haneda airport confiscated photographs they had received from the NLF women's federation showing the actions of American soldiers. A number of women's associations raised money for war relief, despite the lack of a tradition of charitable giving in Japan. One of the more successful was a leftist group called Vietnam People's Aid Committee (Betonamu Jinmin Shien Iinkai), which collected nearly $3 million and filled eleven ships with goods for Vietnam during the war.[39]

Some of the arts, religious, scientific, and women's leaders were also active in Beheiren, and yet as of mid-1966 the cumulative effect of all the protest groups on citizens at large was

problematic. A survey taken by *Mainichi* that summer showed that 82 percent of the public criticized American policies in Vietnam, but most of them remained personally uncommitted and very unwilling to resist the war at the polls or in public meetings.[40] Beheiren responded by taking on the self-appointed task of trying to broaden the antiwar movement through mediagenic sideshows.

As the teach-ins continued and contacts with peace leaders in the United States increased, Beheiren laid plans for a lecture tour during June 2–14, 1966 by Howard Zinn, a political scientist at Boston University, and Ralph Featherstone, a field secretary for the Student Nonviolent Coordinating Committee who was later killed in a bomb blast. Zinn and Featherstone met with students, workers, housewives, and others at fifty-four different spots in fourteen cities from Hokkaido to Okinawa. Their visit gave concrete expression to the sense of common purpose the Japanese antiwar movement felt with peace protesters everywhere, and it inspired Beheiren to try nonviolent direct action "to create solidarity with citizens" at large, as Tsurumi Shunsuke put it.[41] Two weeks after Zinn and Featherstone left Japan the American attacks on Hanoi and Haiphong took place, prompting Beheiren to try a sit-in in front of the United States embassy. Although the demonstrators were soon dispersed, the American idea of civil disobedience impressed certain Beheiren people. They sat down in front of Ambassador Reischauer's car and later tried to do the same at Haneda as Prime Minister Satō was preparing to leave Japan. Takabatake Michitoshi explained the impulse to disobey as a rebellion against bureaucratic organization—an attack on "the managed society."[42]

Beheiren also sponsored a Japan–United States People's Conference for Peace in Vietnam, held during August 11–15, 1966, at Sankei Hall in Tokyo. Nine Americans, including the pacifist David Dellinger, and sixty-one Japanese heard Oda Makoto read greetings from Jean-Paul Sartre and joined in long discussions of democracy, individualism, and the authority of the state. Oda vilified the Japanese government's coop-

eration with Washington and led the delegates in signing a "Japan–United States People's Antiwar Peace Treaty," which rejected the use of force in Indochina and reaffirmed the right of each people to determine its own future.[43]

As a result of the Zinn-Featherstone tour and the bi-national conference, Oda reemphasized the importance of individual responsibility and action in establishing democracy in Japan. But he also began to verbalize his growing mistrust of state power, partly under the influence of the American peace movement but partly because the Satō government's steady support for the United States through words and procurements was now much more prominent. Without losing sight of the main goal of peace in Vietnam, Oda and Beheiren gradually added the aim of resisting the state to their list of objectives during 1966–1967. Early in the new year Oda warned his readers:

> Realistically speaking, we are all guilty of complicity in the Vietnam War. We must recognize that each of us is among the perpetrators. In my opinion, this is why we must conduct our opposition movement all the more forcefully. But to put it less practically and more in terms of basic principles, if we don't take a clear position against the war and seek peace here and now, perhaps the hand [holding the gun] will be ours one day. To the extent that we don't firmly nail down our basic principles as individuals, perhaps we will have to fire the bullet on orders from the state.[44]

The state, in other words, is to be resisted in order to insure our individual rights, not just because it is a partner in the Vietnam conflict. We too are guilty of complicity in the war and must oppose it through individual commitment, lest we be co-opted by the state. Oda by early 1967 had grown more impatient and defiant of authority, but he still favored individualism more than antiestablishmentarianism per se. The latter has been a familiar theme in modern Japanese social thought, but Oda's pure individualism, as he sometimes called it, was a

fresh breeze in the tightly structured order of society in the 1960s. Uncowed by the establishment, his closest followers were splenetic about all forms of authority after a TV broadcast of the Sartre-Beauvoir visit on October 16, 1966, was suddenly canceled, to be replaced by "Welcome Home, Peanuts" ("Okaeri nasai Piinatsu").[45]

The spectacle of the season was a gigantic set of strikes and demonstrations staged by Sōhyō and Chūritsu Rōren on October 21, involving 2 million workers (according to the press; Sōhyō counted 5.2 million).[46] The unions claimed that this event was the world's first antiwar strike "to protest the war of aggression in Vietnam" but admitted that other more concrete goals were also in sight: "to establish a minimum wage, to raise wages for public employees, and to oppose the dismissal of miners and rationalization."[47] The famous photojournalist Okamura Akihiko, himself a supporter of the strike, walked among the demonstrators asking their opinions about the Geneva accords, American aggression, and the Viet Cong. He was appalled to find that they answered his questions with "who are the Viet Cong?"[48]

The day ended up far short of the united protest against the war that Sōhyō had in mind when it first planned the rally in June 1966. The Japan Socialist Party was absorbed in attacking corruption in the cabinet by the autumn, and the communists limited their cooperation to reporting plans for the event in *Akahata*. Beheiren showcased its visitors from Paris, the idealist non-Marxist intellectuals Sartre and Beauvoir, and gave short shrift to a strike based on Sōhyō's materialist outlook. The Japan Teachers' Union took part only in a limited way, displeased that Sōhyō had ignored the request of JTU president Miyanohara Sadamitsu to exclude economic matters from the agenda.[49]

In fact they were central and could not possibly be set aside. The strike, which lasted only a few hours in most locations, was played out against a backdrop of labor grievances stretching back to a bitter month-long seamen's strike in late 1965 and early 1966. Because of a recession in 1965, management

offered workers few increases during the prolonged spring wage offensive of 1966. The unions were upset with rising consumer prices and the black mists of scandal swirling about the Satō cabinet. These bread-and-butter issues seem to be the real reasons why big labor could muster the largest turnout since the treaty crisis six years before. Nonetheless, Sōhyō settled into a pattern of regular protests by making October 21 an annual event, known since 1967 as international antiwar day. How well the new label masked the old motives was cast in doubt by the printed banners worn by ralliers in the late sixties: on the front was "America, Hands Off Vietnam" but on the back "We Demand Our Wage Raise."[50] Here was the irony, or possibly the oxymoron, of antiwar protests by workers who were profiting from war production.

MORE STATIC

With the first lower house election in more than three years on the horizon, the Satō cabinet devoted the last weeks of 1966 to cleansing itself of corruption and paid little heed to Vietnam. On New Year's Day 1967 Satō sent irenic greetings to the world and ritually promised that Japan would be happy to mediate the conflict. By then the public mood seemed to match Satō's languor on the war question. By restraining its support for American policy, the government was able to do the maximum feasible to assist the United States without rousing the anger of too many citizens. Back in 1960 people had heard the alert that "Anpo will involve us in war," but it had not.[51] The proportion of Japanese who feared that their country would be dragged into the Vietnam conflict had fallen from 60 percent in August 1965 to 40 percent in November 1966. "Wouldn't it take a real effort," *Asahi jānaru* speculated that month, "to persuade ordinary citizens that the Vietnam War was a central item in the Japanese people's lives, bringing the opposition to the war to the level of the ordinary person?"[52]

Beheiren read the sentiment correctly and decided to add a new approach to its regular schedule of newsletters, speeches,

JANUS: THE TWO FACES OF PROTEST
Trade unionists carrying portable Shinto shrine at May Day rally
in 1965. "Oppose Aggression in Vietnam" by the United States is
the main slogan, but on the side is "Let's Win a Big
Wage Increase." (Photo: Mainichi Shinbunsha)

and monthly rallies. Adopting a tactic used the previous year
by antiwar workers in Okinawa, Beheiren members began
distributing leaflets to American sailors outside the navy base
at Yokosuka on December 1, 1966. The Okinawa protesters
had learned not to alienate the foreigners with slogans like
"Yankee go home" but instead to reach out to those who had
doubts about the war. The Beheiren handouts were titled
"Message from Japan" and told of the polls in Japan opposing
the bombings. The text cited the United States Declaration of
Independence and urged the sailors to consider the dangers of
World War III. At least one American burned the leaflet with
his lighter in disgust.[53] Undeterred, Beheiren representatives

held a series of small demonstrations early on December 8 to mark the moment twenty-five years earlier when Japan attacked Pearl Harbor. The thirty persons present at Shimizu-dani Park in Tokyo heard a tape of the 1941 news broadcast announcing the start of war with Great Britain and the United States. Antiwar leaders carried their pamphleteering to Tachikawa air base in March 1967 and continued to talk with American service people occasionally about resisting the war, leading eventually to the first desertions in Japan the next fall.[54]

The lower house election of January 29, 1967 confirmed that Japanese voters wanted the status quo, despite Vietnam, the black mist scandal, the rise of new parties, and surveys showing that the Satō cabinet was the most unpopular since World War II. Including eight independents who later joined them, the Liberal Democrats won 285 of the 486 seats, a gain of seven compared with the old house. The JSP rapped the scandals, took a leftist line on foreign policy, and ended up with 140 seats, one fewer than before. Both parties lost a few percentage points in the popular vote; most of the gains went to the new party, Kōmeitō. On the other hand, the progressive Minobe Ryōkichi won the governorship of Tokyo in April 1967, and conservatives were chagrined by losses in certain municipal elections that spring, mainly for local reasons unconnected with the static leadership of the national LDP.[55]

Soon after the Diet election Satō unveiled a military spending plan for 1967–1971 that strengthened the Self-Defense Forces in weapons, surface-to-air missiles, FX fighter planes, and helicopters and transport vehicles for ground troops. The new support was less than Washington wanted but more than the opposition parties liked—Japan's Vietnam policy in cameo. Dissident voices inside the LDP carped at Foreign Minister Miki in May 1967, criticizing the government's defense and foreign policies and challenging him: "shouldn't you ask America to stop the bombings?"[56] Also in May the Japan Socialist Party grilled Miki in the foreign affairs committee of the lower house about the scope of the Far East in the security treaty, receiving the standard reply that actions just outside the

area were justified in order to protect the Far East itself. When he learned the next month that Satō would travel to South Vietnam later in the year, the antimainstream leader Fujiyama Aiichirō of the LDP tried in vain to get the prime minister to change his mind.[57] In short, the currents of dissent continued to crackle during the spring and summer of 1967, but Satō held fast to his position on Vietnam, hoping that it would soon pay dividends on the questions of trade and Okinawa.

Asahi led the media in reviving their attacks against United States operations in Indochina in 1967, after a lull the previous winter during the corruption controversy and the elections. The newspaper ran a series on villages in battle that sparked a good deal of correspondence from readers. Mori Kyōzō, a senior editor of *Asahi*, told a conference of seven leading world newspapers held at Kyoto in May that "the American side must recognize that in essence the Vietnam War is a colonial liberation movement and national independence move-ment,"[58] a view he was not free to put so baldly in the editorial columns. Television remained far more cautious: when TBS planned to show an interview with Kugai Saburō, a Japanese delegate to the Stockholm war crimes panel in January, the Marui department store chain asked that Vietnam not be taken up, lest the huge audience of housewives for the 10 A.M. pro-gram be put off by such a controversial topic. TBS cut a sec-tion of the interview and finally broadcast it a month late, on June 26, 1967. Marui pulled out as a sponsor in July, and the program folded two months thereafter.[59]

With the Vietnam controversy still bubbling and possible revision of the security treaty only three years off, the govern-ment set up the Japan Information Center (Nihon Kōhō Sentā) on June 27, 1967 to fortify its policies by giving official views on public issues and supplying information to the press. This step was promptly jeered as propagandistic by nearly every-one the center was meant to persuade. Satō also invited cen-sure from his critics by traveling to South Korea for the inau-guration of President Park on June 30, the first Japanese premier to visit that country since World War II. While he was

there, Satō softened up Vice President Humphrey for the forthcoming talks in November 1967 in Washington on the Ogasawara and Ryūkyū Islands.[60] An opinion poll in early July confirmed the prime minister's judgment that the warfare in Vietnam was disturbing but not galvanizing to most citizens. In a poll of 3,024 young and middle-aged people, the political scientist Mita Munesuke found that 11.4 percent listed the Vietnam War when asked what issue angered them the most, well behind political corruption (28.6 percent) and inflation (22 percent).[61]

Two events in August 1967 brought the war back into the headlines. On August 8 a freight train collided with tank cars filled with jet fuel for the United States air force in Shinjuku station, the world's busiest terminal. The resulting fire burned

FUELING THE PROTESTS   Firefighters hosing down
a burning tank car after a freight train derailment in Shinjuku
station, Tokyo, on August 8, 1967. The tankers were filled with
aviation fuel bound for U.S. air bases in western Tokyo.
(Photo: Mainichi Shinbunsha)

for hours and reminded people of the hazard posed by trans-
porting 4.84 million liters of aviation fuel each day through the
center of Tokyo, traveling on the Yamate and Chūō lines to
Tachikawa, and sometimes onward via the Ōme line to Yokota. Several times this amount was hauled daily on the suburban Nanbu line from Kawasaki to Fuchū and Tachikawa. The
conflagration at Shinjuku was one of the first problems that
brought the nascent environmental movement together with
the antiwar protesters.

Ever since a similar fire at Tachikawa station burned nearby
stores in 1964, citizens in western Tokyo had been worried
about the shipments, and residents had often protested to the
Japan National Railways about the thirteen unattended grade
crossings on the Chūō line west of Mitaka and the thirty-four
on the Nanbu line.[62] To quell the anxieties, the Americans in
early 1967 had stopped painting "caution inflammable jet
fuel'" on the sixteen-car trains, but after the Shinjuku fire it
was impossible for commuters not to think of warplanes as
they watched the slow processions of black palanquins bearing
their daily tribute to the United States.

The second spectacle that month was the war crimes "trial"
held in Chiyoda Kōkaidō, Tokyo, on August 28–30, 1967, by
a committee closely tied to the Japan Communist Party. The
Stockholm tribunal on Vietnam War crimes, convened the
previous January by the British philosopher Bertrand Russell,
had found Japan and five other countries guilty of the crime of
aggression as accomplices of United States policy in Indochina.[63] The Tokyo panel was clearly intended to embarrass
the Japanese government more than to denounce the Americans. The twenty-eight "justices," including the Marxist historian Hani Gorō, acted more like prosecutors than judges; no
defendants or lawyers were present. Sartre, Russell, and the
Japan Socialist Party sent messages, but Beheiren recognized
the trial as a media stunt to promote a political party, not to
end the war, and decided to stay away.[64]

Suekawa Hiroshi, the head of Ritsumeikan University, presided over long hours of testimony from two groups of Japa-

nese scientists, scholars, technicians, and workers who had visited North Vietnam to investigate American actions. The DRV, which apparently held high hopes for the publicity value of the trial, cooperated with enthusiasm. It suppled photos, films, and documents, as did the thirty-six Japanese witnesses belonging to the two groups that testified. The unsurprising verdict was that the United States was guilty of aggression and of using illegal and immoral weapons. Moreover, the summary judgment continued, "the Japanese government and Japanese monopoly capital are guilty of actively conspiring and cooperating in America's aggression and war crimes in Vietnam, and in international law they are accomplices of the Americans."[65]

Beyond all the ideology and jargon was the somber record of Indochinese destruction and Japanese entanglement. Even those who knew the panel was a mouthpiece for Hanoi and the JCP found it hard to ignore the hundreds of pages of evidence, some of it previously unreported in the Japanese press. The organizing committee brought out separate volumes on the role of the United States, as first detailed at Stockholm, and the part played by Japan as collaborator in the war.[66] The documents on Japan dealt with eight subjects:

1) the government's "failure" to regain Okinawa and the Ogasawaras, which were instruments of American aggression
2) reparations and other early assistance to the GVN
3) the use of United States bases in Japan to support the war
4) arms sales to the Americans
5) government assistance in recruiting LST crews
6) the expansion of the Self-Defense Forces
7) cooperation with South Korea, allowing Seoul to send nearly 50,000 troops to Vietnam
8) government propaganda to the Japanese people saying it was in their best interest for the Viet Cong to be suppressed[67]

For both Satō's supporters and opponents, no matter what their foreign policy views, the tribunal produced the most systematic and thorough evidence yet of how deeply involved in Vietnam Japan had become. The report showed that Satō, like Lyndon B. Johnson, had quietly let his country grow more deeply enmeshed in war abroad while boldly pursuing economic prosperity at home. The press covered the August 1967 event with detached thoroughness, well aware that it was even more obviously a political trial than the allied war crimes tribunal in Tokyo right after World War II. The allied military trials were somewhat closer to true judicial proceedings, but both courts were seasoned with a spicy dose of victor's justice. As the Tokyo panel on Vietnam and the press accounts of its testimony foreshadowed, Japanese-American relations faced a rocky path ahead in the fall of 1967 after nearly two years of steadiness and predictability. Some of the biggest stones were outcroppings of the war.

Choppy Waters

THE FALL, winter, and spring of 1967–1968 decided the fate of the Johnson presidency, raised stubborn questions about the American strategy in Vietnam, and brought a near-freeze on escalations, a partial halt to the bombings, and the first attempt at peace talks in Paris during May 1968. These same months were the stormiest of the war thus far for Japanese-American relations, bringing ferocious pressures on Prime Minister Satō to change course or perhaps even step down. He made two controversial trips to Southeast Asia in the early fall of 1967 and then flew to Washington for a summit with Johnson that made little headway on the return of Okinawa. New groups joined the debate about Japanese foreign policy during angry protests against his departures from Haneda airport, and the desertion of four American sailors from the carrier *Intrepid* in October brought much greater publicity to Beheiren, which arranged their safe passage to Sweden via the Soviet Union. Then a series of squabbles over United States bases, ships, planes, and military hospitals made the Japanese public acutely aware of the irritation that resulted from hosting huge military installations at the height of a vicious war. When Satō began his Southeast Asian journeys in September 1967, active opposition to the war in Japan was still limited, but by the next summer it had begun to ripple out to people who had never lifted a finger or a voice before.

FRICTION OVER SATŌ'S TRAVELS

The prime minister's voyages to Southeast Asia in September and October 1967 were closely connected with Japan's new

economic presence in the area, through procurements and regional organizations like the Asian Development Bank. The visits also burnished his credentials as an expert on Asian problems for his forthcoming meeting with President Johnson in November. Satō's forays took place amid another outbreak of public criticism of the United States. That summer the leftist governors Minobe Ryōkichi of Tokyo and Ninagawa Torazō of Kyoto called for an end to the shooting and the start of peace talks without delay—the first time any heads of prefectural governments had spoken out. (Satō had been apprehensive when Minobe was elected the previous April with support from the JSP and JCP because he was afraid Minobe would not use the police to protect adequately against demonstrators; in fact Minobe called them out regularly. Ninagawa developed close ties with the communists after 1966.) The governors' views may have affected the public outlook on the United States sampled by *Asahi* in September, but the intensified bombing during the summer was the main reason why America's popularity slumped. Only 26 percent of those surveyed said they liked the United States, down from 31 percent in a similar *Yomiuri* poll taken in October 1965, and 19 percent said they disliked America, up from just 5 percent.[1] Eventually Satō's firm support for United States policies in Vietnam threatened to become a political liability.

Despite the public uneasiness about America and the war, Satō deliberately moved closer to the United States in the fall of 1967, as he had in May 1965, because of the benefits he thought would accrue to Japan on trade and Okinawa. A team of Liberal Democrats joined representatives from other anticommunist nations to observe the presidential election in South Vietnam on September 3, 1967, pronouncing the voting "fair" even though they visited only certain polling places selected by the GVN.[2] At the same time Satō made a ceremonial visit to Taiwan during early September. Then during a ten-day trip to Burma, Malaysia, Singapore, Thailand, and Laos at the end of the month Satō was greeted warmly as the likely dispenser of economic aid. He chose Bangkok, where the

Thais were nervous that the war might spread westward, to declare that ending the bombings would not bring peace. Such forthright support for the American air strategy pleased both Washington and the Thais, but back in Japan it angered the antiwar leaders, opposition parties, and even the Asian-African group in the LDP.[3] Satō's announcement in Bangkok helped to mobilize some noisy resistance in Japan to his follow-up tour of Southeast Asia, scheduled for October 8–22, 1967.

The second trip was controversial because the prime minister planned to visit South Vietnam as well as Indonesia, Australia, New Zealand, and the Philippines. Satō told a press conference before departing that he would discuss peace everywhere he went because it was the key to prosperity for both Southeast Asia and Japan: "herein lies the importance of my visits to Southeast Asia."[4] He also made it plain that he would have more credibility with Johnson if he had seen South Vietnam in person—a bold move for the premier of a nonbelligerent, since none other had set foot in Saigon during the war, but a risky one for Satō at home. The prime minister had staked his political future on reacquiring Okinawa; he reasoned that visiting Taipei and Saigon would help him persuade Johnson to return the Ogasawaras at once and the Ryūkyūs very shortly.[5] The public wanted Okinawa back immediately, but Satō knew that in the midst of war the United States would ask for more time. That time could be purchased with the electorate only by securing the smaller Ogasawaras, whose reversion his trip to Saigon would presumably assure.

The political trade-off for adopting this tack was a gale of protest throughout Japan against the prime minister's scheduled visit to South Vietnam. A group of scholars led by the physicist Yukawa Hideki pleaded with Satō to change his mind, arguing that his presence would help to legitimize the Saigon government. Beheiren took up the issue at its regular meetings and said the trip would prolong the war. The parties out of power, as well as anti-Satō Liberal Democrats like Fujiyama Aiichirō, ridiculed the foreign ministry's contention that skipping a Southeast Asian country with which Japan had

diplomatic relations would be a snub.[6] Most portentously of all, about 2,500 students and workers held a bloody clash with riot police near Haneda airport as the prime minister departed on October 8, the first violent moment in a vast chain of rallies and demonstrations over foreign policy that drew 18,730,000 participants during the next two and a half years.[7]

The students appeared that morning at Haginaka Park near Haneda wearing helmets and carrying staves for the first time. Not even in the fractious street demonstrations of 1960, which altogether involved about 15.8 million protesters, were such implements used, nor were there injuries to Diet members or the police. From the fall of 1967 on, as the Beheiren leader Iida Momo observed, students traveled to demonstrations bearing staves. By decorating these with flags or placards, the students turned them into political symbols and immunized themselves from arrest.[8] The students at Haneda on October 8 belonged to factions or sects of the national federation of student self-government associations (Zengakuren) that opposed the influence wielded by the Japan Communist Party over Zengakuren through its own faction, Minsei. The dissident sects, including Shagakudō, Shaseidō, Chūkakuha, and the more independent Kakumaruha, ended up battling Minsei and nonaligned groups for control of university campuses in 1968–1969, but their motive as the prime minister winged to Southeast Asia was antiwar, not political advantage within Zengakuren. One statement on September 26 said, "Prime Minister Satō's official visit is clearly intended to encourage the war of slaughter against the Vietnamese and to win the approval of international society."[9] Even though the eventual campus struggles had little to do with Vietnam, much later one Tokyo University student recalled that the Haneda battle had been decisive for him: "October 8 is when I realized it was no good if you only advocated themes; first you have to give rise to concrete actions, then carry them out to completion."[10] Oda Makoto, who was not at Haneda, might have said the same.

Unable to block Satō's departure for Jakarta that morning, the demonstrators threw rocks, set police vehicles on fire, and

injured hundreds of riot police, who were protected only with helmet visors and small hand shields. After a three-hour battle, the protesters were subdued with tear gas and water cannon. More than 300 were arrested, and twenty-four were eventually convicted of various offenses. Several hundred demonstrators were injured, and one lost his life during the melee. Yamazaki Hiroaki, a nineteen-year-old student at Kyoto University, apparently died either because of a beating from the police (as demonstrators alleged) or because he was run over by a police vehicle commandeered by students (as police claimed). Yamazaki was the first person killed in a political demonstration in Japan since Kanba Michiko, an undergraduate at Tokyo Univeristy, was trampled or strangled to death on June 15, 1960.[11] During the midday uproar while the anti-JCP student sects were fighting the police near Haneda, 80,000 Minsei members were enjoying a picnic at Lake Tama sponsored by the communist party organ *Akahata*.

The protest against Satō's trip to South Vietnam was a turning point in the resistance to the Vietnam War because it brought both the violent students and the youth antiwar committee, Hansen, actively into the protest movement for the first time. Hansen began as a committee of young workers in Sōhyō to oppose the Japan-South Korea treaty normalizing relations in the fall of 1965. It became an *onigo* (wayward child) when it defied the Japan Socialist Party and Sōhyō in May 1967, joining the dispute against expanding Tachikawa air base into the community of Sunagawa nearby. In the fall of 1967 Hansen's leaders began to speak of internationalism, in contrast with the highly national character of the Old Left, and they stressed the principles of independence, originality, and unity with other antiwar groups. After joining in the October 8 fracas, Hansen used the slogan "from the peace movement to the antiwar struggle" to complete its ideological break with Sōhyō, and henceforth the committee shared many objectives and platforms with Beheiren. But its youthful membership was much drawn to the violent student radicals on campuses

134

in 1968–1969, leading many of its 20,000 followers into extremism and alienating both Beheiren and the public at large.[12]

Prime Minister Satō's second circuit around Southeast Asia ended with Saigon on October 21, 1967, where he spent an hour conferring with President Nguyen Van Thieu and fifty minutes with Vice President Nguyen Cao Ky. Until his recent trip to Thailand, Satō had accepted the American bombardments of Vietnam as unavoidable; this time he told the leaders he met that stopping the air war would be useless "until the North Vietnamese indicate they will make some corresponding response."[13] Satō gambled on seeming slavishly pro-American in the short run so that he could nail down the return of the Ogasawaras, calculating that the public would be so happy to have the islands back that it would forget, or forgive, his coziness with Washington on Vietnam. In reality his backing for the bombings in October earned more attention in the United States (the president was apparently very pleased) than in the Japanese press. William Bundy noted that the Japanese government, like Great Britain's, "accepted our recent bombings with much less outcry than I, frankly, would have anticipated."[14] Satō's stopover in Saigon was fortuitously cut to fewer than four hours by the death of his mentor, former Prime Minister Yoshida Shigeru, a development that pushed his token appearance in South Vietnam into the background.[15]

As Satō rushed home on October 21 for the funeral, the first international antiwar day was being held the same afternoon by Sōhyō throughout Japan. Unlike the strike in October 1966, the demonstrations were entirely devoted to the war and involved just 255,000 workers, not the 2 million who had turned out the year before (police estimates; Sōhyō counted 5.2 million in 1966 and 1.5 million in 1967).[16] Separating a war protest from economic issues reduced the attendance drastically, but it also fostered demonstrations the same day by groups that normally had nothing to do with big labor. While Sōhyō and Chūritsu Rōren assembled 60,000 people at meetings in Meiji Park, about a thousand anti-JCP student radicals marched on Aoyama Dōri until they were herded up Kira

Dōri toward Shinjuku by the police. Beheiren and thirty civic groups rallied in front of the American embassy. Antiwar day probably represented the peak of cooperation between the Old Left and new groups opposed to the Vietnam War, even though the memory of penalties assessed the year before kept many unionists on the sidelines. Although it held no picnics that day, the Japan Communist Party warned Minsei away from the protests and offered Sōhyō only a minimum of moral support.[17]

ROUGH SAILING IN WASHINGTON

As Satō prepared for his trip across the Pacific, the country was taken aback by the self-immolation of a seventy-three-year-old peace worker, Yui Tadanoshin, who fatally burned himself on November 11, 1967, in front of the prime minster's official residence in Nagatachō. Yui wrote in his suicide letter to Satō that he had learned loyalty and patriotism during the Russo-Japanese War of 1904–1905 but now saw the United States repeating in Vietnam the mistakes Japan had made in China during World War II. He said he was writing "in hopes of ending the suffering of the Vietnamese people as soon as possible."[18] He asked Satō to press Johnson for an end to the bombings and the start of peace negotiations.

Yui died in a Tokyo hospital shortly before 4 P.M. the next day, five minutes before the prime minister's jet took off from Haneda for Washington. The riot police took no chances for this departure, ringing the airport with 7,000 officers carrying large duralumin shields and quantities of tear gas. Twenty police boats patrolled nearby rivers, canals, and sections of Tokyo Bay, and helicopters were deployed overhead. The Liberal Democrats assembled 1,600 youths wearing blue ribbons and waving small Japanese flags to bid Satō farewell from the roof of the terminal building. Near the airport about 3,000 students from the anti-JCP factions of Zengakuren fought the police with stones and staves near Ōtorii station, resulting in more than 500 injuries and 300 arrests. Outside the main en-

trance to the airport another 7,000 representatives from Beheiren, Hansen, the Socialist Party, and other groups demonstrated peacefully against the support for American policies in
Vietnam they assumed the prime minister would reaffirm
when he met President Johnson the following day. The press
unanimously condemned the radicals' violent tactics at Ōtorii,
calling the Haneda episodes of October 8 and November 12
dark smirches on the heretofore impeccably arrayed antiwar
movement.[19]

By the time he traveled to the United States Satō had assumed such a high posture on the reversion of Okinawa that it

SHIELDS AND STAVES   Riot police battling
student demonstrators at Ōtorii station, Tokyo, during the
second Haneda incident on November 12, 1967. Later that afternoon
Prime Minister Satō departed from Haneda airport for a
summit meeting in Washington with President Johnson on
Okinawa and the Vietnam War. (Photo: Kyōdō Tsūshinsha)

137

was politically imperative for him to make progress toward that goal during the summit. He told Johnson of his "support for the United States position in the search for an appropriate and just solution" to the Vietnam War. He said he was waiting for Hanoi to take actions that would justify a stop to the bombings and, in terms reminiscent of his "red imperialism" speech in May 1965, he offered his unqualified endorsement of America's efforts to curb the expansion of communism in Asia.[20]

Satō told the National Press Club on November 15 that "in the recent round of trips to the Asian countries, I have keenly felt that this U.S. endeavor in Vietnam is well understood and is duly appreciated."[21] Separately he said that during his tours he had found "widespread support" for "free-world efforts to cope with communist intervention and infiltration."[22] These words showed a subtle but significant rise in the threshold of support for the war from a leader whose demure backing of American policies had vexed William Bundy, Walt Rostow, Dean Rusk, and the president himself for more than two years. It is no wonder, according to a *Yomiuri* dispatch on November 17, that Johnson told the prime minister he had seen eighty-seven heads of state or government during the past year but none had been more direct or helpful than Satō himself.[23] After this encounter Satō was often known in Japan as Lyndon Johnson's favorite prime minister.

Still, the mission to the White House went far from smoothly. On the critical question of Okinawa, the United States at first proposed language that would commit it merely to returning the islands "at the earliest possible date,"[24] but the Japanese objected that such vague timing represented no real advance since the January 1965 communiqué acknowledging Japan's desire to reclaim the Ryūkyū Islands. The Satō-Johnson agreement of November 15, 1967, contained three main points: 1) concerning the Ryūkyūs, "the United States military bases on those islands continue to play a vital role in assuring the security of Japan and other free nations in the Far East"; 2) "an agreement should be reached between the two

governments within a few years on a date satisfactory to them for reversion of these islands"; and 3) steps would be taken at once to restore the Ogasawaras to Japanese control (formally accomplished on June 26, 1968).[25]

The Japanese delegation had assumed all along that the Ogasawaras would be returned and was disappointed that the date for retrieving Okinawa was not specified more exactly in the communiqué. Instead a tripartite consultative organ on the reunification of Japan and the Ryūkyūs was established, with American, Japanese, and Okinawan representatives. This committee was expected to discuss a timetable for reversion, but Satō unilaterally tried to speed it along by telling a news conference on his way home to Tokyo that Okinawa would return to Japan "within two or three years."[26]

The prime minister arrived back in the capital determined to placate the Americans by carrying out reversion without removing either the American bases or nuclear weapons from Okinawa, but the domestic political climate forced him to put the bases on an equal footing with those in Japan proper (*hondo nami*), without nuclear weapons, when the Ryūkyūs were finally returned in May 1972. He also urged Presidents Maeda of NHK and Morita of Sony to cooperate in a Lyndon Johnson project to spread educational TV throughout remote villages in South Vietnam. NHK had earlier expanded its Vietnamese-language news broadcasts because "the Vietnamese people have not been receiving impartial news. Now they can objectively determine their viewpoints for themselves."[27] This propagandistic television scheme fell through when the Tet offensive showed how fragile Saigon's control over the countryside had become.

The stronger backing for American war policies expressed during Satō's three foreign trips in the fall of 1967 apparently raised no new anxieties among the public that Japan would be drawn into the fighting. A Kyōdō poll taken in December showed that for the first time since the United States escalated the war in early 1965, fewer people agreed than disagreed that "there is a danger Japan will be involved in war" (35.4 percent

139

versus 37.3 percent).[28] Everyone welcomed the agreement to return the Ogasawaras, but only the mainstream factions within the LDP professed satisfaction with the modest outcome of the summit concerning Okinawa. Most of Satō's political opponents believed that he traded too much hearty support on Vietnam for too few concessions in return. They complained that Japan would soon regret any shift in foreign policy away from Ikeda's emphasis on getting along well with all neighbors. The socialists and communists added that the results of the Satō-Johnson conference seemed to tie the reversion of Okinawa too closely to the automatic extension of the security treaty in 1970.[29]

Apart from economic affairs, regaining Okinawa was the centerpiece of Satō's foreign policy. It is incongruous that he had to move substantially closer to Johnson in word, if not deed, in order to regain the greater autonomy for Japan that reversion signified. Satō's newly staunch support for American policy in Vietnam was synchronized with fresh talk about Japanese self-reliance in defense and hints of an adjustment in relations with the United States to give Japan more initiative in its foreign policy.[30] Having a strong leftist opposition and active antiwar movement at home helped Japan avoid getting too close with the United States by making it impossible to send more than TV's and medicines by way of practical assistance to South Vietnam. Washington knew that if it pressured Satō into backing up his new declarations of support with material or military aid, the opposition and public would be furious. The prime minister also cleverly used the existence of a powerful Left to justify both a small defense budget and the demand for restoring Okinawa, implicitly telling the Americans that if they objected too strenuously, the security treaty would be jeopardized and a cabinet might even topple, as in 1960.[31] In this way the opposition parties, antiwar movement, and public opinion limited how concretely Satō could help the Americans in Vietnam and boosted his efforts to win greater freedom of action for Japan in foreign affairs.

In the most proximate sense, the prime minister's carefully

orchestrated tours of Southeast Asia and endorsements of the American bombings failed to win him the main goal at Washington, a definite schedule for regaining Okinawa. But maneuvering closer to Johnson, however dismaying to his inveterate critics, evidently cost Satō little additional support at home beyond what had long since eroded because of his earlier, more qualified approval of the war. Nonetheless he was now more closely identified with Johnson than ever, a source of acute discomfit when the president abdicated the following spring.

JUMPING SHIP IN JAPAN

Satō Eisaku was chagrined to learn after arriving in Washington that an organization tied to Beheiren had announced on November 13, 1967 that four American naval airmen had deserted ship in Japan and made their way to the Soviet Union. About sixty people desert the United States armed forces every day in peacetime, and more than twice that number deserted during the Vietnam War—although rarely in a war zone or a staging area.[32] Beheiren said it supported the sailors not as romantic outlaws but as individuals who dared to place their human rights above the claims of the state. Oda and Beheiren saw the act of desertion as "the retrieval of personal freedom" from the oppressive power of the state that forced people to fight against their will.[33]

No event transformed Beheiren more greatly than the desertion of the four airmen from the aircraft carrier *Intrepid* on October 17, 1967. Up to then, Douglas Lummis notes, the antiwar movement was plugging along without much public notice apart from occasional rallies; but when it found deserters on its hands, Beheiren attracted so much attention that it grew into a sizable national organization.[34] The four sailors asked representatives of Beheiren for help in reaching safety in a third country. In a statement filmed on November 1, the four called themselves "patriotic deserters" who opposed the escalation of the war "because in our opinion the murder and

needless slaughter of civilians through the systematic bombing of an agricultural, poverty stricken country by a technological society is criminal." They said they renounced the war "as true Americans, not affiliated with any political party. . . . It is our fervent hope that our actions will move you, wherever you are, whoever you are, to do whatever you can to bring peace to Vietnam."[35] When Oda, Tsurumi Shunsuke, and Yoshikawa Yūichi showed this film to the press on November 13 at Gakushi Kaikan, it created the kind of sensation that only the Japanese weeklies can fully exploit. Despite their claims that Beheiren enticed the men into deserting in order to publicize its cause, the weeklies' assertions have been shown to be untrue by everyone connected with the episode.[36]

Beheiren members counseled the deserters, provided safe houses, and raised funds to send them to Sweden by way of Siberia and Moscow. An American student in Tokyo apparently arranged with the Soviet embassy at Mamiana for four boarding passes on a regular Russian passenger ship from Yokohama to Nakhodka. The United States navy confirmed the desertions on November 14, and three days later the four men appeared on television in Moscow. By January 1968 they were settled in Sweden, where as of mid-1985 Richard D. Bailey worked in an electronics firm and Michael A. Lindner was a carpenter. The other two, John M. Barilla and Craig W. Anderson, apparently left the country in the interval.[37]

The Beheiren affiliate that worked most closely with American service people after the *Intrepid* incident was the Japan Technical Committee for Assistance to Antiwar U.S. Deserters (JATEC). "I always explained that we weren't communists, that we were just opposed to this war, especially to the bombings," says the chief JATEC counselor, Tsurumi Yoshiyuki. "I told them there was no truly safe place for them to take refuge anywhere in the world."[38] JATEC representatives pointed out that it was not illegal for Japanese citizens to assist deserters but that the status of forces agreement allowed the United States to ask the Japanese police to obtain court orders and seek out deserters for return to the military authorities.

Further, once they left the armed forces the Americans could be charged as illegal entrants or residents under the immigration control law.[39] Japan in 1967 scarcely recognized the concept of political asylum, and deserters knew they would have to move on to a more hospitable country if they wanted to avoid perpetual tangles with the authorities.

By early 1968 JATEC encouraged antiwar soldiers and sailors to write Washington, protest in their barracks, join public demonstrations, register as conscientious objectors, and consider deserting. The second number of a serial pamphlet called "A Message to American Soldiers" said of desertion: "we do not ask that you undertake it lightly without considering exactly what might happen. But we hope you will consider it. It could have a powerful effect in building up pressure against the war."[40] JATEC had trouble finding escape routes for deserters to Europe after the Soviet Union stopped cooperating in the summer of 1968. "They told us henceforth to send only officers or else crew from nuclear subs," according to Yoshikawa Yūichi.[41] Presumably Moscow backed out because it did not want to antagonize the United States needlessly over deserters from a war in which the Soviet Union had little strategic interest.[42] Altogether JATEC managed to help about thirty American deserters to find exile in northern Europe, through contacts in Cuba, Poland, Czechoslovakia, and China. Not all deserters worked through Beheiren, nor did all leave Japan promptly. A few of them were rounded up by the Japanese police. It is thought that at least fifty-one service personnel had deserted in Japan by 1969, when pressure from the police and a decision to work directly with the antiwar resistance movement on bases led JATEC to cease sending deserters abroad. By then Tsurumi Yoshiyuki and his colleagues had earned a wry accolade from the Senate armed services committee as "the most active and effective" of twenty-three organizations in seven countries working with American deserters.[43]

"I could sympathize easily with the young American draftees," Oda recalls, "because I had been in the United States. I

saw the draftees as victims of their own government as well as aggressors against the Vietnamese." After two and one-half years of denouncing the war in general, "working with deserters gave us a way to get involved more directly with Vietnam." He thinks Japanese young people who were the same age as the draftees sympathized with the deserters: "there was a lot of public support for what we were doing with deserters," Oda remembers. Referring to the terrorist campaign against Japanese candy makers in 1984–1985, he says, "it was very similar to the current wave of sympathy for 'the man with twenty-one faces' in the Glico-Morinaga conspiracy."[44] By this Oda meant that the public sentimentally admired the men as Yoshitsune-like underdogs defying authority, even though Beheiren leaders saw them instead as the flowering of democratic individualism.

"It was this issue," according to Oda, "that gave ordinary people a starting point for direct contact with individual Americans." A few shopkeepers and barbers who twenty years earlier had been in awe of the GI's came forward to Oda offering shelter to the deserters, aware that they were not august soldiers but scared young Americans with no place to turn.[45] "Beneath the continuous prosperity of Japan during the Vietnam War," adds Tsurumi Yoshiyuki, "were some ordinary, salt-of-the-earth Japanese for whom the war was an opportunity to help the American soldiers. These were adults with regular occupations who had to work during the day but gave their spare time, not students with plenty of time."[46] Yoshikawa Yūichi, the secretary-general of Beheiren, concurs:

> The biggest effect of the Vietnam War was that the Japanese started to criticize the U.S., not just learn from it. From 1945 to 1965, the flow of culture was one-sided, from the U.S. to Japan. During the Vietnam War, the Japanese learned from actual experience that the Americans were ordinary people just like themselves. . . . It was a real discovery to find out that American soldiers were or-

144

dinary people with fears and weaknesses just like us. They lived with Japanese families for days, weeks, sometimes six months at a time. This conversion of Japanese was based on actual experience, not just a theoretical realization.[47]

Just as the desertions had no effect on America's ability to fight in Vietnam, the activities of JATEC did not reach beyond a few thousand citizens at most, but they led Beheiren to discover a certain reservoir of support beyond those who surfaced at its regular rallies and protest meetings.

The *Enterprise* Drama

The Japanese press lit into Prime Minister Satō during the last weeks of 1967 for supporting the Americans so loudly on Vietnam and coming home from Washington with so little to show for it. *Asahi* began the new year with a grandiloquent swipe at the United States for misunderstanding the history of Asia and said that "we hope for a solution to the Vietnam War as quickly as possible," because fellow Asians were suffering and because the newspaper had "misgivings lest the war in Vietnam trigger a major international crisis."[48] President Johnson by then was dealing with a fresh problem in addition to the war: a $3.5 billion payments deficit for the United States during 1967. He sent Walt Rostow to explain some new dollar defense measures to the Japanese government, including a curb on American investments overseas and restrictions on military procurement outside the United States. The American embassy informed Satō of the impending visit on New Year's Eve and gave him just thirty-six hours to prepare. The prime minister interrupted his private holiday to receive Rostow at this Kamakura villa on January 2, 1968.[49] This abrupt conference and the frosty tidings it brought were omens of the stormy half-year ahead for Japan and America. By June 1968 the two countries reached the acme of frictions over military bases, thanks to a series of untoward events partly arising from

145

the war. The first of these was a port call by the nuclear-powered aircraft carrier *Enterprise* at Sasebo on January 19.

The United States informed Japan that it might be necessary for the ship to visit as early as November 1965 when it joined the Seventh Fleet to launch bombers against North Vietnam and the Viet Cong. American nuclear-powered submarines had first entered Japan on November 12, 1964, when the 2,360-ton *Sea Dragon* called at Sasebo amid loud demonstrations mounted by the Old Left. The main objection to the subs was that they might be carrying nuclear weapons, although the Japanese government said it assumed they did not and the United States commanders said, "we honor the treaty." By the end of 1966 the antisubmarine protests had quieted; the visits continued almost without incident, and by the mid-1980s a nuclear-powered submarine was putting into Sasebo or Yokosuka almost weekly. Conventionally powered aircraft carriers capable of carrying nuclear weapons visited Sasebo regularly during the Vietnam War without major opposition.[50] What was different about the *Enterprise* was the synergy of its gigantic size, its nuclear fuel, its pivotal function in the war, and the timing of its arrival in port.

Responding to questions in parliament, Satō stated on February 14, 1966 that the government had no objection to port calls by nuclear-powered carriers if they contained no nuclear arms and posed no radiation hazard. Both Japan and the United States said that prior consultation was unnecessary because the visits were temporary, to allow for provisioning and shore leave for the crews. The security treaty and accompanying agreements did not specifically bar the introduction of nuclear weapons to Japan, but to be politic the United States respected public feelings by keeping them out, according to the senior diplomat Richard L. Sneider.[51] Knowing this, the Japanese government assumed that the Americans would ask for advance discussions before bringing nuclear weapons in. When no request came from the captain of the *Enterprise*, the government blithely told the public that there must be no such arms aboard. But Foreign Minister Miki conceded that no one

could enter the ship to find out, and for security reasons the Americans would not discuss their weaponry. When the acting chargé d'affaires at the United States embassy informed the foreign ministry on September 7, 1967 that the *Enterprise* needed to dock for fresh supplies, the official reason given for making the notification was mere courtesy.[52] In reality it was an instance of de facto prior consultation.

The cabinet that same day approved a visit at some point in the near future, after consulting with the Japanese Atomic Energy Commission and reassuring itself about the safety of the ship. Then the port call was put off until after Satō's trips to Southeast Asia and Washington, in order to skirt controversy during the Okinawa negotiations. The United States ambassador to Japan, U. Alexis Johnson, later wrote that he saw an enormous protest brewing over the visit and gave the Japanese "every opportunity to change their minds, but they did not."[53] Satō welcomed the port call, in line with his outspoken support for America's Vietnam policies and his campaign to reacquire Okinawa, and he evidently thought that having the *Enterprise* arrive would "help overcome the nuclear allergy of his people."[54] Instead the move backfired, and Satō later admitted the visit had set back his plans to raise the public's "defense consciousness."[55]

The *Enterprise* affair was a moment of high theater in the antiwar movement, a week-long drama that is remembered more vividly in Japan two decades later than any other Vietnam protest. The *Enterprise* was the first nuclear-powered carrier to call in Japan, even though the oil-fueled *Ticonderoga*, an identical 75,500-ton carrier that was a veteran of the Gulf of Tonkin incident, had tied up nine days earlier in Sasebo without a stir. The *Enpura*, as the ship was known to its opponents, became a target of frustrations felt thoughout the Japanese Left: despair over the endless war, helplessness at stopping the government's new coziness with Washington over the bombings, and anger that the prime minister was ramming port calls by huge, battle-tested warships with reactors and possibly nuclear weapons aboard down the nation's throat as a prelude to

extending the security treaty two years later. The *Enterprise* offended the sensibilities of many Japanese who did not like having the United States and Japanese governments deliberately irritate their innate nuclear allergy. Few of them enjoyed being forcibly awakened from the nonnuclear idyll they had created for themselves since Hiroshima and Nagasaki.

Nearly every group in the political rainbow appeared in Sasebo to greet the *Enterprise*. The Liberal Democrats mobilized the extreme Right to wave American flags from sound trucks and called a public meeting to show films about the carrier, but the event was canceled when only three children appeared. Every opposition party sent representatives to speak out against the ship because of its link with nuclear weapons, and all except the Democratic Socialists saw the visit as an attempt to deepen Japan's involvement in Vietnam. Sasebo's famous gangsters demonstrated side by side with anti-JCP radical students, a thousand of whom were from Tokyo and commuted each evening from Sasebo to dormitories at Kyushu University in Fukuoka. As sound trucks blared the *Star-Spangled Banner*, other protesters sang the *Internationale*. Prostitutes with red and blonde hair lined up at Sasebo bridge to greet the 3,200 sailors, who mostly spent their five days of R & R on the base at dockside. No American was injured during the week of demonstrations. [56]

The first clash occurred on January 17, 1968, when unarmed radical students encountered taunts from right-wingers and tear gas from the police, who arrested twenty-seven demonstrators and inflicted more than 100 injuries. [57] The largest rally drew 50,000 people to a civic baseball stadium on January 18, the date the *Enterprise* was due to arrive. Labor leaders, rightist groups, and members of Hansen all shouted their slogans while Beheiren followers held a small rally nearby in Matsuura Park. Mayor Tsuji, who admired the United States navy and "lobbied hard to let his city have the honor of this great ship's visit,"[58] arranged for a youth chorus to sing in front of Sasebo station.

There was further violence the next day when the ship fi-

BRIDGE OF SIGHS   Riot police (left) confront
helmeted radical students protesting a port call by the
nuclear-powered U.S. aircraft carrier *Enterprise*, Hirase bridge,
Sasebo, January 17, 1968. (Photo: Mainichi Shinbunsha)

nally entered port. Local unionists put on a protest of their
own, and members of both Gensuikin and Gensuikyō shouted
ban-the-bomb messages reminding the American sailors they
were now in Nagasaki prefecture. Demonstrators from Old
Left organizations danced in zigzag formation in the streets
while confused fighting was breaking out at various intersec-
tions. A follow-up rally by the JSP and JCP on January 21
drew 20,000 protesters and hundreds of police; 160 persons
were injured in the battle.[59]

The rumpus at Sasebo brought the demonstrators much
sympathy and helped to restore the peaceful image of the antiwar movement. People all over Japan watched the daily cov-

erage on television and were aghast at the ruthlessness of the police against the defenseless protesters. As Ishida Takeshi has written, "in the face of a well-equipped and extensive police machine, the avoidance of violence strategy is sensible and effective in that one can attain a stronger moral position *vis-à-vis* police brutality and hence increase one's public support."[60] This support ebbed when student radicals began carrying staves on campus later in 1968, but the antiwar movement itself stayed free of violence for the most part until the early 1970s.

Local residents in Sasebo collected $2,000 to help the students after the January 17 imbroglio and hurled both epithets and rocks at their own police the next day out of disgust. After the beatings they suffered on January 19, demonstrators passed the hat and took in about $2,800 from the crowd. Whether or not they were angry with the police, many Sasebo citizens worried about nuclear carriers in their port and turned out for both the mass rally at the ball park and the subsequent meeting called by the JSP and JSP.[61] Parallel demonstrations broke out all over Japan as people saw the gray hulk at its berth and the confrontations outside the base on television. Student protesters in front of the foreign ministry in Tokyo fought with the police, resulting in eighty-nine arrests; discussions were held outside commuter stations and letters that month to *Asahi* quadrupled (2,516 of them dealt with the *Enterprise*).[62] Even though its representatives were dwarfed by the other demonstrators at Sasebo, Beheiren benefited from the renewed media attention paid to the war. It is said that nearly half of the local Beheiren units that sprang up during the Vietnam War were formed because of the publicity given to the American deserters in November 1967 and the *Enterprise* protests two months later.[63] Incensed by the sympathy that welled up for the demonstrators, the ministry of posts and telecommunications rebuked the television companies for their coverage of the episode. Although he privately admitted the *Enterprise* visit had boomeranged, Satō said in public that the port

calls would continue. In fact no nuclear-powered carrier entered port again in Japan until March 1983.[64]

TET IN JAPAN

The *Enterprise* sailed from Sasebo on January 23, 1968, for Vietnam but was quickly diverted to Korea when North Korean gunboats seized an American spy ship, the *Pueblo*, in international waters that same day in the Sea of Japan. The media treatment of the crisis reminded the Japanese public that their ports were intimately connected through the United States navy to the Cold War just off the horizon to their northwest. Prime Minister Satō chose this moment of tension to reassure the public, and also recoup his credibility as an advocate of peace, by proclaiming Japan's three nonnuclear principles— key watchwords of the defense debate in Japan ever since.

In a parliamentary speech on January 27, he declared that the government would allow neither the manufacture, possession, nor introduction of nuclear weapons in Japan. Actually the state had been observing these principles ever since a United States marine barge filled with atomic bombs was discovered offshore in the Inland Sea in 1958, causing a sensation. By formally embracing the nonnuclear guidelines in the chill political atmosphere of January 1968, Satō hoped to calm public fears over the *Enterprise* and *Pueblo* and build fresh support for his pro-American views of the Vietnam War. Just as he had stepped closer to Johnson in November 1967 in order to get away from him, Satō now adopted a forthright nonnuclear policy so as to win acceptance of a stronger, more autonomous defense as well as the retention of nuclear weapons on Okinawa after reversion. His critics thought the prime minister cynical and showy for enshrouding himself in a ten-year-old nonnuclear mantle, and they attacked him for dragging his feet on the nuclear nonproliferation treaty then under discussion by most of the major nations. (Japan finally signed the agreement in February 1970, the ninety-fifth country to do so.) His opponents and supporters were both dumbfounded when

151

Satō was awarded a Nobel peace prize in 1974 for his stance against nuclear weapons. The more serendipitous told themselves that the award was really intended for the Japanese people because of their firm belief in peace.[65]

The Tet offensive took place in January and February 1968 when Viet Cong and North Vietnamese forces simultaneously attacked the American embassy compound in Saigon, other major cities such as Hue, and three dozen provincial capitals throughout South Vietnam. Although the American-ARVN counterattack set the communists back militarily, the offensive permanently flattened the morale of United States troops in Vietnam. Seeing their own embassy under siege on television made skeptics of many persons in the United States who had not seriously questioned their country's policy before. The result was a big growth in the American peace movement, the retirement of President Johnson from public life, and a modest shift in military strategy in Vietnam.[66]

In Tokyo the flow of vehicles at the gate of the American embassy and the movements of ships and planes at nearby bases showed how serious a crisis Tet was. Japanese television crews covered the offensive thoroughly, and the newspapers were blanketed with the story. Each medium sent extra writers and photographers to report the month-long attack, many of whom stayed on in Vietnam to provide fuller coverage than had been available before Tet. Tokuoka Takao, the *Mainichi* reporter who was the first Japanese to visit Hue after United States marines recaptured the city in early February, says he was able to travel freely and never encountered suspicions of him as a Japanese traceable to his government's strong support of American policies.[67]

The greater presence of Japanese journalists after Tet brought much more attention to life in wartime Saigon in the media back home. Because the United States command was aware of the critical public view of the war in Japan, it "provided all sorts of conveniences for the Japanese press corps in Saigon."[68] Nonetheless readers and viewers learned that plastic war toys made in Japan were sold at street stalls as Christ-

mas presents for Vietnamese children and that full-color ads for Japanese consumer products were shown in movie theaters before the feature came on. During 1968 South Vietnam became the number two foreign market after the United States for Honda motorcycles. By the end of the year the population of Japanese in the south numbered about 350, including business people, journalists, diplomats, spouses of Vietnamese from marriages during World War II, medical experts, volunteers working with refugees, and after-service technicians for Japanese products.[69] Not enumerated were the crews serving on LST's along the Vietnamese coast.

Learning about the Japanese physician (Dr. Watanabe), the Japanese restaurant, and the growing Japanese presence in Saigon after Tet made the public back home much more aware of how deeply their country was involved in the war. So did the sudden disclosure that eighteen B-52s had been moved to Okinawa from Guam on February 5, 1968, as a direct result of the *Pueblo* incident and the Tet offensive. The United States had spent $16.5 million to improve its air facilities in Okinawa during 1966–1967, including longer runways at Kadena air base. Now that nerves were drawn taut in both Northeast and Southeast Asia, the time was opportune to move the giant bombers closer to both trouble spots. The Americans immediately began bombing Vietnam from Okinawa, which was 1,300 kilometers and $25,000 closer to Saigon than was Guam. During the ten-week siege of Khe Sanh ending in April, B-52s pounded the hills surrounding the marine enclave with 10,000 tons of high explosives a week, dropped at midpoint in their twelve-hour round-trip flight from Kadena.[70] As with the temporary refuge taken by B-52s in July 1965, this stunning development kicked up a huge fuss in Okinawa and Japan.

The Ryūkyūan legislature unanimously asked United States High Commissioner Ferdinand Ungar to remove the aircraft, and residents of the islands staged daily protests against the black-winged bombers. Amid a cacophany from the press and opposition parties, the foreign ministry made an offical protest to the United States on February 12:

The stationing of B-52s on Okinawa is no doubt to serve as a deterrent force in view of recent developments. On the other hand, it is a fact that the B-52s are creating a sense of uneasiness among the people of Okinawa. We believe this situation is not desirable to the United States. Thus we would like consideration to be given to removing the uneasiness among the people.[71]

Ambassador Johnson replied that the planes would be taken away when the turmoil in the Far East subsided. The foreign ministry dropped the matter, and by 1970 virtually all the B-52 raids were being conducted from Thailand, reportedly cutting the cost from $50,000 to $5,000 per run.[72]

Antiwar leaders in both Japan and Okinawa scoffed at the government's protest as too timid and kept up their call for removing the bombers. Gensuikyō led a big rally outside the Kadena runways on February 18, and the opposition badgered Foreign Minister Miki until he revealed on February 26 that the United States had assured him that Okinawa would not become a permanent B-52 base. Early the next month a poll of Okinawans showed that 86 percent of them were anxious about the planes,[73] and after President Johnson announced a partial halt to the bombardments on March 31 the pressure to get rid of the aircraft intensified, but to no immediate avail.

Satō toned down the note of protest to the Americans on February 12 and refused to ask them to withdraw the B-52s because negotiations over the future status of the Ryūkyūs were at a delicate stage. The largest crowd ever to appear at a rally in Okinawa turned out on April 28, 1968, to support immediate reversion, and four days later American soldiers battled a group of demonstrators seeking the removal of the bombers outside Kadena air base. The issue flared up again on November 19 when a B-52 crashed on takeoff from Kadena, burst into flames, and burned Yara elementary school with the loss of five lives. Once again Ryūkyūan legislators unanimously resolved to abolish the bombers, as did all the opposition parties in the Diet. The struggle continued throughout 1969 until

CHOPPY WATERS

Prime Minister Satō and President Nixon agreed late in the year on a formal date for reversion.[74] Soon after their summit most of the B-52s were redeployed to Thailand.

Just as it is impossible to distinguish antiwar from antibase and pro-reversion sentiments in the Okinawa protests, it was the combination of the *Enterprise* and *Pueblo* episodes, the Tet offensive, the B-52s, and the simmering question of Okinawan autonomy that put great pressures on the government in the winter and early spring of 1968 to modify its foreign policies. Satō stuck to his guns because he needed American good will on both trade and Okinawa, knowing that his political base was still firm despite the continual public uproar since October 1967.

Ōji and the Second Johnson Shock

The prime minister's Job-like demeanor was pained by a fresh set of frictions over the war on March 18, 1968, when the United States abruptly opened a military hospital for wounded Vietnam veterans at Ōji, in northern Tokyo. Nearly two years earlier the United States army Far Eastern map service had moved from an installation in Ōji to Hawaii, and the Americans announced in June 1966 that the Seventh Field Hospital at Johnson air base in Saitama prefecture would be relocated in Ōji. As casualties increased in Vietnam, the army rushed the conversion of the map center in December 1967 and opened the 400-bed facility the following March without telling anyone.[75]

Because the Japanese government believed that the security treaty allowed the Americans to use the facility as they pleased, it did not object to the move. This stance gave the antiwar movement a clear instance of governmental complicity and a highly visible inner-city target. Housewives in white aprons appeared outside the gates to plead for the safety of their neighborhood. A series of demonstrations led by the anti-JCP student factions, by Hansen, and by Beheiren during March and April led to more than 600 arrests and 1,500 inju-

155

ries. In a bloody scuffle between students and police officers on April 1, a patrol car was burned and a bystander was killed by a flying stone—the first death in a protest since October 8, 1967, at Haneda.[76] Governor Minobe of Tokyo implored the United States military headquarters at Fuchū to move the hospital; finally when the violence got out of hand the Tokyo district court forbade any further demonstrations at the site.

A flyer distributed by Beheiren during the uproar asked, "why has a field hospital been built at Ōji? Because the Japanese government, under the security treaty, is cooperating with America's war in Vietnam. . . . The Vietnamese people and the citizens of Ōji are both victims of war."[77] Actually most of the demonstrators at Ōji were irate residents without strong views on Vietnam who were angry at the clatter of helicopters—the aural symbol of the war—and fearful that communicable diseases might spread from the hospital to the neighborhood. Because it was a unity of opposition, the alliance of shopkeepers, local laborers, housewives, and antiwar leaders was temporary and very unstable, accounting for the unsystematic nature of their protests and the periodic violence that burst forth. Still, the Sasebo and Ōji episodes of citizen cooperation with the antiwar movement were worrisome to the government, which agreed by late March that something had to be done to relocate the hospital, even though Satō refused to ask the Americans to do so directly. The United States, which had never been sure that Ōji was a wise choice, immediately agreed to begin looking for a suitable place to move the facility.[78]

Soon after the demonstrations subsided amid promises to move the hospital when feasible, the United States forces in Japan announced in June that there were six malaria patients at Ōji and more in two other field hospitals. Even so, the Ōji issue had no discernible effect on electoral behavior in the district, either in voting for the Kita ward assembly or in the national polls for the House of Councillors in the summer of 1968. After laying plans in early 1969 to move the facility to an army golf course along the Tama River in Inagichō, the

United States forces decided on November 7, 1969 to abandon the scheme and simply close the Ōji hospital because five others were available and American casualties were diminishing under the policy of Vietnamizing the war.[79] Thus the American headquarters in Japan plucked this large thorn from Satō's flank, one he chose to carry with him for a year and a half rather than extract, lest he upset the delicate negotiations over Okinawa and the security treaty that culminated two weeks later in the triumphal summit in Washington.

Beset with furors over the *Enterprise* in January, bombers in February, and Ōji in March, Satō was totally unprepared for Lyndon Johnson's weary announcement on March 31, 1968 that he would not seek reelection the following November. Politically the prime minister was even more shaken by this second shock from Johnson than he had been three years earlier when the United States began bombing North Vietnam without warning. By now he was so closely identified with the president and his Vietnam policy that when Johnson announced his retirement the first serious suggestions were heard that Satō too should resign.

Satō learned only minutes in advance about the president's decision, which was broadcast shortly before noon Tokyo time on April 1. He felt personally betrayed and immediately got ready to face demands from the opposition that he quit to accept responsibility for backing a failed policy that many Japanese believed the United States would now renounce.[80] An editorialist wrote that "Sato should admit his own mistakes with the same courage as the President and retire from the Prime Ministership."[81] Members of the Fukuda and Miki factions of the LDP, as well as the Asian-African group, tried to maneuver Satō into withdrawing because of his poor handling of the Sasebo and Ōji incidents. Many Liberal Democrats felt humiliated by Johnson's departure after they had fruitlessly supported him on Vietnam for three years and their prime minister had made unnecessary avowals to him in October and November 1967.[82] Satō rode out the squall, which soon subsided; he felt chastened by the developments in Washington

but determined to keep his foreign policy on course because thus far Japan's close identification with American mistakes in Southeast Asia had cost its own diplomacy almost nothing.

Outside the political system the reactions to Tet and the Johnson withdrawal were more guarded. Many reporters called the Tokyo Beheiren office after the president's speech, congratulating the group for years of hard work and asking when it would dissolve. Oda told them that Beheiren would continue its efforts until the war was over and that its objectives had not yet been met.[83] Like the American media, the press in Japan welcomed the speech as a major turning point in United States policy and called it a decisive step toward peace (in fact it was neither). The newspapers also euphorically predicted that all factions in Japan would unite to promote a change in policy toward China, although this did not happen until four years later. Public opinion continued to list the war as a top item of concern, second only to inflation, although by now hardly anyone cared very much which side, if any, won. In what was probably the classic example of Japanese political relativism and situational judgment during the entire war, a *Yomiuri* poll in mid-1968 asked people how they would like the conflict to end. Just 2.8 percent said in favor of the United States and the GVN, and 5.7 percent said in favor of the communists. Another 30.1 percent replied that it "doesn't matter, so long as it ends," and a remarkable 44.5 percent said they hoped the war ended "so neither side loses face."[84]

BASE IRRITATIONS

Two days after the Johnson bombshell and the fatal brawl at Ōji, a cry arose in parliament over the use of Haneda airport as a takeoff point for American soldiers headed for Vietnam. *Asahi* had first reported statistics on charter flights in April 1967, most of which were one-hour stopovers for food and fuel, with landing fees and customs formalities waived under the status of forces agreement. The chartered aircraft of Flying Tiger, Northwest, and Pan American routinely arrived over

Tokyo without advance warning for security reasons, to the dismay of controllers in the tower and civilian pilots in commercial and general aviation. The Boeing 707s, each jammed with 165 soldiers, landed at Haneda because the air bases at Yokota and Tachikawa were too clogged with supplies and other military traffic. The Haneda Tōkyū Hotel soon began to resemble a military barracks.[85]

In the first year of major troop commitments to Vietnam, nearly 100,000 American service personnel are thought to have been passed through Haneda on their way to the war zone. The number of arriving military flights averaged nearly 100 per month in 1966 and 1967. Many citizens were displeased to learn that as many as thirteen Japanese flight attendants served meals on certain charters and that Northwest, starting in late 1965, gave priority to military passengers on its regular commercial flights.[86]

When the press first highlighted the issue in April 1967, a group of legislators went out to the airport for a look. They prevailed on the foreign ministry to raise questions at the next meeting of the Japan–United States joint committee on the status of forces, which blandly declared on April 13 that the military air transport service had no intention of increasing its daily flights. There the matter rested until April 3, 1968, when a socialist member of the upper house, Maekawa Tan, cited fresh figures showing that 2,226 military charters took off or landed at Haneda in 1967 and that just as many were expected in 1968.[87] Maekawa revived the matter partly to nettle the cabinet while Satō was under fire to resign, partly to show concern over the possible military use of a new airport the government was planning at Narita, and partly to keep up the pressure on the security treaty issue. He asked if prior consultation was needed before Haneda could be used for combat purposes, since the airport was not a base and was not covered by the treaty. The government's answer was both no and yes. One legal expert said that civilian airfields were outside the scope of the treaty, but Foreign Minister Miki said the use of Haneda for direct combat operations, inconceivable as it was,

certainly would need prior consultation.[88] Both officials impassively assumed that the Americans using Haneda en route to Vietnam were not headed for direct combat because they had not yet received their precise battle commands. The soldiers who had infantry orders knew better.

Although less connected with Vietnam than the *Enterprise*, the B-52s, Ōji, or Haneda, the discovery of unusual levels of radioactivity in the waters of Sasebo harbor 100 meters from the nuclear-powered attack submarine *Swordfish* on May 6, 1968, became a headline story for nearly a month, confounding defense relations between Japan and the United States still further. Shortly after the Gulf of Tonkin incident in 1964, Prime Minister Ikeda changed his mind and authorized port calls by American nuclear-powered submarines, despite strong public fears about radioactive pollution. Satō shrugged off the criticism that poured down on him when the *Sea Dragon* made the first such visit on November 12, 1964 at Sasebo, three days after he took office. When Narita Tomomi, the secretary-general of the JSP, asked the new prime minister what would happen if a leak occurred at Sasebo, Satō said, "not only is the population there small, but we don't even think about such things."[89]

By 1968 nuclear-powered subs had made two dozen calls at Sasebo and Yokosuka (the latter starting in May 1966), with only one suspected incident of abnormally high radiation in the environment. Nerves in Sasebo were still raw from the *Enterprise* visit in January, so naturally citizens were up in arms when ten times the normal amount of cobalt 60 was found in the harbor while the *Swordfish* was in port during early May. Experts from the science and technology agency tested the waters repeatedly, found no further unusual radioactivity, and declared that it was impossible to pinpoint the source of the anomalous reading on May 6. The agency also revealed its suspicion that the *Swordfish* was the cause but admitted that it lacked proof.[90] The Americans denied that a single drop of radioactive coolant had been discharged and brought in three technicians to verify it with extensive water sampling.

The *Swordfish* episode was more a media event than a public protest, but it grew awkward for the government when the press learned that there were secret agreements with the United States about disposing of primary reactor coolants and measuring radioactivity. The science and technology agency refused to release data on the subject, provoking charges of a cover-up. Instead it handed out soothing leaflets to the fisher-people in nearby ports, who were terrified by the radioactive threat to their livelihoods. The United States took a rigid position throughout, refusing to waive its rights in an emergency to discharge coolants within internationally recognized limits. But the navy also suspended calls at Sasebo by nuclear-powered submarines for the next eighteen months.[91]

Just as the waves from the *Swordfish* were subsiding, the government ran into trouble when an American RF-4C Phantom plane from Itazuke air base in Fukuoka crashed into an unoccupied research laboratory at Kyushu Univeristy barely thirty meters from a cache of cobalt 60. Although no radioactivity spewed into the environment, citizens were annoyed at this latest accident involving the American air base, which had recently been reopened in the wake of the *Pueblo* affair after a long campaign to close the urban airfield had finally succeeded in 1965. The Phantom crash, which was the 109th since 1945 at Itazuke, so enraged students at the university that they would not let the authorities remove the wreckage or repair the building for many months. The mayor of the city and the governor of Fukuoka prefecture, both Liberal Democrats, were forced by local protesters, including some LDP politicians, religious leaders, and PTA officers, to visit Prime Minister Satō and the American embassy to demand that the base be reclosed.[92] Eventually Itazuke joined a long list of facilities the United States proposed to return to Japan in a document transmitted the following December.

One more source of almost incessant chafing was the chronic dispute over lengthening the runways at Tachikawa air base by taking away housing from Japanese civilians in Sunagawa. Ever since May 1955 local citizens had resisted the

racket made by American planes and the periodic proposals to extend the runways into residential neighborhoods north of the base. The quarrel rekindled early in 1967 as the Vietnam War escalated. Residents grew more aware of the vital role the base played as a supply headquarters for troops in Vietnam, especially when anti-JCP students from Zengakuren and the Santama unit of Hansen stepped in to lead antiwar protests. A large demonstration on May 28, 1967 resulted in altercations with the riot police and a number of injuries. Another major clash took place on July 9 as 2,500 young people shouted: "don't send planes to Vietnam!"[93]

By then Tachikawa averaged 2,300 takeoffs and landings a month, a constant source of enervation to the people living nearby. As the demonstrations drew more and more crowds in 1967 and 1968, the proportion who turned out because of noise pollution, threats to their housing, or generalized anti-base sentiment grew as well. Still, the Sunagawa protests did not shed their antiwar character. The students and Hansen members persuaded Tanaka Kiichirō to let them use his land just outside the fence at the end of a runway to erect a memorial tower that was finished on December 16, 1968. (Later it was extended to a height of thirty meters to obstruct landings.) On December 19 the United States command announced that is was canceling its plans to extend the runways.

The protesters nonetheless dug antiwar trenches around the base, and even when the news came on October 3, 1969 that the Americans would consolidate their logistical operations at Yokota and return Tachikawa to the self-defense agency, the student leader Miyamoto Masao replied stonily, "the danger that Japan will be enveloped in war has not been reduced in the slightest."[94] Hoshi Noriaki later directed two semidocumentary films on Sunagawa, *Zango* and *Zoku zango* (both 1971), that brought out the militance of the struggle.[95] Although Tachikawa remained an important Air Self-Defense Force base after 1969, it was never seriously considered as an alternative to Narita for locating the new Tokyo international airport. The stated reason was that it impinged on air corridors re-

served under the security treaty for military use; no doubt another was the bureaucratic rivalry between the transport ministry and the self-defense agency.

It was clear by mid-1968 that American bases had become unwelcome to a majority of Japanese because of their connection with a bogged-down war in Vietnam, their record of local frictions from Sasebo to Sunagawa, and their affront to national pride. Douglas H. Mendel, Jr., found that year that only 14 percent of those polled wanted to retain the bases, whereas 61 percent favored removing them.[96] The government knew that this was not a realistic view of national security, but it also recognized the need to talk with the Americans about the bases, like Ōji hospital, in a way that would assuage the public without roiling the Okinawa negotiations. Satō met with the commander of United States forces in Japan on July 18, 1968 to ask for an accommodation on the base problem. Soon both the American military brass and the embassy staff agreed that about one-third of the installations in Japan should be returned or relocated, an achievement for which Ambassador U. Alexis Johnson accepted credit.[97]

The United States plan, announced on December 23, 1968, after the ninth meeting of the Japan–United States security consultative committee, called for restoring thirty-two facilities and relocating twenty-one others. When the changes were completed, the United States still had ninety-eight installations with the same troop levels, better efficiency, and a completely undiminished capacity to support the Vietnam War. By cutting back on night flights, returning a few of the most controversial and least vital bases, and surrendering golf links and expansive American-style housing, the United States helped to insure that agitation over the bases would not impede the automatic extension of the security treaty in June 1970.[98] These arrangements effectively oiled the choppy waters around the base issue, but they did little to propitiate the growing numbers of antiwar protesters who demonstrated in public during 1968 and 1969.

163

Waves of Dissent

JAPAN was swept by the flood of antiwar and antiestablishment sentiments that engulfed nearly all the advanced industrial countries during 1968 and 1969. A good deal of the youthful ferment around the globe was culturally innovative but politically irrelevant, at least in the short run. The new views of self, community, and authority proclaimed in speech and song in the late sixties stirred a whole generation to question the corporate and bureaucratic leviathans that dominated society and impinged on individual freedoms. Yet when the revolt of the sixties receded, it was far from clear how much it had changed the nature of politics or helped to shorten the Vietnam War.

In Japan, as elsewhere, critics of the war increasingly regarded it as a symptom of the oppressive rigidity of vast political and economic institutions. The antiwar movement became enmeshed, but not submerged, in the broader tide of antagonism to authority that washed across the nation at the end of the decade. The scale of protests expanded almost continuously from June 1968 to the fall of 1969, eventually surpassing the turnout for the security treaty demonstrations of 1960. At the same time the scope of the opposition grew much wider, taking in the resistance to extending the security treaty beyond 1970 and the demand for regaining a nonnuclear Okinawa as well as the movement against the Vietnam War, especially once President Nixon assured the world in 1969 that the conflict was "winding down." In addition, many radical students who had made their debuts as activists in the antiwar struggles of 1967 now began to tackle on-campus issues of university governance, but their fondness for violence even-

tually did them in. By late 1969, as agitation by the young against established forms of power began to subside in France, Germany, and elsewhere, student activism in Japan was likewise in rout. But the broader protest movement was in full flower: by the time Prime Minister Satō flew off to retrieve Okinawa from the Americans in November 1969, every sector of opposition in and out of the formal political system was mobilized against some key component of his diplomatic policy toward the United States.

FROM PEACEFUL PROTEST TO DESTRUCTIVE RIOTING

Shortly after the tragic confrontation at Ōji on April 1, 1968, leaders of Beheiren decided to capitalize on the initiative shown by ordinary citizens at Sasebo and Ōji by planning a month-long antiwar movement known as the June Action. The aim was to draw all sorts of peaceable civic groups into one concerted effort to stop the war through activities too sustained for governments on either side of the Pacific to ignore. By bringing hundreds of local Beheiren units together with federations of musicians, photographers, mathematicians, tree-planters, old people, children, and the like, Beheiren hoped to surmount the violence and sectarianism of the radical students who had begun turning up at antiwar demonstrations during the previous half-year.

In mapping out the June Action, Oda Makoto plucked a leaf from the American peace movement. On April 26 he and four other leaders called for a nonviolent national anti–Vietnam War action month during May 19–June 19, 1968. In a direct mailing to more than a thousand civic and cultural groups, they declared:

> The Vietnam War faces a turning point. We must not overlook this turning point or remain mere spectators. People throughout the world are demanding that America immediately and totally cease its war in Vietnam and

that the right of the Vietnamese people to independence and self–determination be fully established. . . . We also demand that the Satō government take responsibility for carrying out its policy of cooperating with the United States in the war.[1]

All groups and individuals who shared these goals were invited to join in the daily series of events that comprised the June Action. More than 225 organizations responded, uniting with Beheiren to stage the most important set of purely antiwar rallies of the Vietnam era in Japan.[2] The first international antiwar day on October 21, 1967, was the high–water mark of cooperation between Beheiren and the Old Left; the June Action correspondingly represented the first significant joint effort by groups of nonviolent, politically unaffiliated citizens whose only bond was that they opposed the war.

Of all the Japanese demonstrations against the Indochina conflict, the rally on June 15, 1968 most nearly resembled the October 1969 moratorium in the United States as a respectable middle–class gathering of concerned citizens. Operating on a budget of about $550, Beheiren managed to draw people to Tokyo from all over the country through word of mouth. Nearly 11,000 of them jammed the open–air amphitheater in Hibiya Park for speeches and then marched to Sukiyabashi, where they held a peaceful sit–in. As grandmothers walked along with infants strapped to their backs, about 10,000 colored leaflets and artificial flowers tossed from nearby buildings fluttered to the streets below.[3]

Small as the crowds for the June Action were compared with the peace movement in other countries, Oda and the rest of the antiwar leaders were gratified that thousands of people who had never attended a demonstration before the American military desertions in October 1967 or the *Enterprise* visit in January 1968 were now willing to step forward to denounce the war. Hidaka Rokurō, a left–wing sociologist and co-organizer of the June Action, took heart from a survey conducted the same month which showed that only 11.9 percent

LONG MARCH "Stop Killing the Vietnamese People"
was the theme of a demonstration at Sukiyabashi, Tokyo,
led by Beheiren on June 15, 1968. Other rallies
were held that same day in Osaka and elsewhere as a
part of Beheiren's June Action.
(Photo: Mainichi Shinbunsha)

of the public thought "the current foreign policy of our government fully reflects the opinions of the citizens," whereas 63.7 percent thought it did not. "This is the first time since 1945," he wrote in the August 1968 *Sekai*, "that the gap between support inside and outside the Diet has been so great."[4] Still, as Hidaka admitted, elections in Japan are poor mechanisms for reflecting public opinion on foreign affairs, and it was no surprise that the Liberal Democrats retained control of the upper house in the national balloting on July 7, 1968. The party lost just two seats and actually improved its percentage of the popular vote compared with the previous poll.[5]

Pleased with the spirit of cooperation that sprang forth in the June Action, Beheiren held an international convention at Kyoto in mid-August 1968 to talk about "resisting the war and transforming society." More than 200 Japanese joined thirty-seven delegates from abroad in round-table discussions of Vietnam, conscription, deserters, and exiles. They also dealt with the Okinawa and security treaty questions, which had been left aside during the June Action. Just as the Japan–United States people's conference two years earlier had reflected the agenda of the American peace movement at the time, the Kyoto convention buzzed with talk of "fundamental social change" (*henkaku*) that some critics mistook for a newfound antiestablishmentarianism on the part of Beheiren.[6]

Actually what Oda meant was that citizens should take matters into their own hands, through the same nonviolent direct action that Beheiren had first attempted after the Zinn–Featherstone visit in June 1966. Now the emphasis was on what Oda called "restoring our humanity"[7] by liberating Okinawa and opposing the treaty as well as by pursuing the main goal of ending the Vietnam War. Henceforth the tactics included unannounced demonstrations and sudden sit-downs in busy roads, outside military bases, and along the tracks carrying aviation fuel to American aircraft. *Henkaku* did not mean basic change in the structure of society but just an added set of tactics, clearly sanctioned for the first time at the Kyoto convention, to accompany the advertisements, teach-ins, petitions,

and rallies that reached their pinnacle in the June Action. It is very clear that Oda and his colleagues deplored violence and did not encourage student or labor radicals to use it. Yet it is also easy to see how persons fond of rough play might interpret his ideas about changing society as license to take matters into their own hands by force.[8]

Despite Oda's insistence on peaceful civil disobedience, one of the most violent moments of the antiwar movement in Japan came on October 21, 1968, when radical students trashed Shinjuku station, set cars ablaze in the nearby streets, and burned down a police box with a Molotov cocktail. This second annual international antiwar day started as a joint demonstration by both the Old Left and what journalists were beginning to call the New Left, including Beheiren and other nonviolent civic groups as well as Hansen and the anti-JCP student sects. But the harmonious spirit that prevailed a year earlier quickly paled in the face of unyielding police power and ceaseless student truculence spilling over from the campuses. Before the fighting broke out, Oda warned his listeners outside the east exit of the station that the afternoon was growing more ominous:

> Ladies and gentlemen, we are opposed to the American war in Vietnam. This is a demonstration to demand that the Japanese government end its complicity in the Vietnam War. There are women and children in this demonstration. We are marching along holding placards and flowers. Take a look at the riot police. They are holding truncheons for beating people and are surrounding us. Is this the face of Japan, a supposedly peaceful country?[9]

Later that day Sōhyō and Chūritsu Rōren assembled 50,000 workers at Meiji Park, the largest of 270 rallies supported by labor, the JSP, and even the JCP throughout the country. The police estimated the total nationwide attendance at 170,000, down from 255,000 the year before.[10]

The fighting in Tokyo broke out when approximately a thousand young people left the Sōhyō rally and headed for

169

Shinjuku, where roughly the same number of Hansen followers, bearing the flags of their local chapters, held down the
main street from Isetan department store to the east exit of the
station. Another 6,000 anti-JCP members of Zengakuren
were milling about near the side of the station to try to block a
freight train with aviation fuel headed for Yokota air base.
When the police moved in to clear the students, they fled into
the labyrinthine station and overran both the commuter and
freight tracks, stopping rail traffic for the rest of the evening.
Outside the station more than 60,000 commuters stood by as
the riot police stormed the barricades and finally subdued the
radicals after midnight with hoses and tear gas.[11]

The Tokyo metropolitan police department mustered
25,000 officers for antiwar day, half of whom were deployed
at Shinjuku once the melee got under way. Other groups of
protesters battled the police at Ginza, Yaesu, the education
ministry at Toranomon, and the self-defense agency at Roppongi. More than 200 people were arrested in the fray at Roppongi, and another 500 were apprehended in the main battle at
Shinjuku, where the police finally invoked the crime of riot
against those who turned the interior of the station to rubble.
It was the first and only time since 1952 that the Japanese authorities have ever declared a riot. The criminal proceedings
against the top suspects dragged on for sixteen years until the
supreme court finally ruled on Christmas Eve 1984 that there
had been "a common intention to riot"[12] among the radical
student groups who occupied the station.

The postmortems in the press mistook the anarchy at Shinjuku as a protest against United States bases more than against
the war, but the critics agreed that its real cause was sectarian
conflict on the campuses.[13] The national railways canceled 714
trains normally carrying 350,000 passengers; the Odakyū and
Keiō department stores above the station in Shinjuku and
many other merchants around town closed down during the
disorders. Including the bill for police protection, damage to
the station, and lost revenues to railways, taxis, stores, and
restaurants, the uproar may have cost nearly $18 million.[14] Iida

RUMBLE AT ROPPONGI Student protesters attempt to
ram the front gate of the self-defense agency headquarters in Tokyo
during international antiwar day, October 21, 1968.
(Photo: Kyōdō Tsūshinsha)

Momo, the veteran Beheiren leader, was not fooled by the
radical students: "we knew that what was happening was a revolt and not a revolution."[15] It was Beheiren's task, he said, to
transform Japan's foreign policy through nonviolent direct action in the year ahead.

Even though the public abhorred the violence of the student
activists, the government knew that antiwar sentiment had
grown much more widespread in the year since Satō's trip to
Washington in late 1967. When President Johnson announced
an unconditional halt to the bombings of Vietnam just before
the American presidential election, the cabinet responded on
November 1, 1968 that "the Japanese government warmly
welcomes the latest American step to stop bombing the north

completely" and called on both sides to discuss peace more seriously.[16] A fresh survey of 2,445 voters taken the following
month showed that only 14 percent of those polled wanted the
United States tọ defend the GVN and that 56 percent wanted
the Americans to withdraw, up from 38 percent in late 1966.
No segment of Japanese opinion, young or old, liberal or conservative, wanted foreign troops to stay in Vietnam any
longer. This same sample favored retaining the security treaty
but also wanted to remove the United States bases from Japan.[17] Luckily for Satō, the return of one-third of the military
installations in late December 1968 helped to defuse the antibase sentiment, but it did little to blunt the criticism of his unflinching support for the Americans in Vietnam.

BEHEIREN DIVERSIFIES

With Richard M. Nixon as the new American president, 1969
was the year of Vietnamization. This new tack, originally chosen by President Johnson, was partly a public relations gesture
to silence domestic critics of the war in the United States. Under this program, more and more South Vietnamese were
drafted for military service and equipped with vast quantities
of munitions from the United States while American ground
troops were gradually withdrawn. Vietnamization also meant
a diplomatic stalemate at Paris and an intensified air war, soon
spilling over into Laos and Cambodia. Even the political war
turned nasty: the program of eliminating hostile village leaders, known as Operation Phoenix, was a far bloodier version
of the revolutionary development schemes carried out during
Johnson's presidency.

As in the United States and Europe, the Japanese antiwar
movement reacted cautiously to the new American leader during the spring of 1969, uncertain whether he would end the
war as he had promised or prolong it under the veil of turning
it over to the South Vietnamese. Both Beheiren and the Satō
cabinet were unsure about how to size up the new American
ambassador, a career Middle East specialist named Armin H.

Meyer, when Nixon promoted U. Alexis Johnson to under-secretary of state for political affairs in January.[18] Like peace advocates everywhere, Oda and the others in Beheiren were disappointed that President Johnson's withdrawal from politics in April, the Paris peace talks starting in May, and the bombing pause before the election in November had not produced a cease-fire. At the same time the Japanese antiwar leaders began to feel an impelling need to speak out against the extension of the security treaty, scheduled for June 1970.

Beheiren held a two-day conference in February 1969 at the Nihon Seinenkan building in Meiji Park to chart future strategies for resisting the war. About 120 representatives came from fifty-one affiliates throughout the country for free-form discussions, without keynote speeches or lengthy reports from the top leaders, dealing with the issues that local groups thought were the most urgent. One was that Beheiren should reach out beyond students to involve far more ordinary citizens than before. The movement had never been primarily based on the campuses, even though teach-ins and university chapters of Beheiren were common, but now the delegates thought it would be wise to diversify in light of the campus violence that culminated when the police recaptured Yasuda auditorium at Tokyo University on January 19.[19] Tsurumi Shunsuke also advocated reaching out to a wider audience through more writings. By June Beheiren had started publishing *Shūkan anpo*, which Oda called "a tool whereby each individual can spring into action and fashion the movement."[20]

The conference formally agreed to add a fourth goal, stopping the security treaty, to the original aims of peace in Vietnam, self-determination for the Vietnamese, and an end to Japan's complicity in the war. From this point onward the antiwar movement was firmly yoked to the resistance against the treaty, but Beheiren never surrendered its organizational independence to the chief opponents of the pact, the established unions and opposition parties. Oda and the other antiwar leaders always distrusted the ulterior political motives harbored by the Old Left; they agreed to cooperate on the

treaty issue because it was the rationale for the government's involvement in the Vietnam conflict. They decided that adopting this fourth objective was a way of continuing Beheiren's struggle against the war by other means.

After the conference the antiwar leaders decided to start holding mini-demonstrations every day in the major cities, sometimes marching in French style holding hands, sometimes dancing or skipping along, sometimes sitting down on streets or plazas in direct civil disobedience. Beheiren also agreed for the first time to show solidarity with the opponents of the new Narita airport, who had battled the government and its highhanded bureaucratism in defense of local farmers since 1966. In addition, the spring of 1969 was when JATEC turned from helping American deserters find havens abroad to working directly with antiwar soldiers and sailors on the bases. Beheiren people began helping dissenters within the Self-Defense Forces as well. The most famous was Air Staff Sergeant Konishi Makoto, who was arrested for handing out antiwar leaflets to fellow airmen at Sado in October 1969, forced out of the service, and finally acquitted in February 1975 by the Niigata district court when the self-defense agency refused a court order to submit fourteen of forty subpoenaed documents.[21]

The antiwar leaders once again encouraged artists to shed their predilection for pure art and to involve themselves more thoroughly in resisting the war. The Artists' Peace Conference (Bijutsuka Heiwa Kaigi) gathered 600 signatures of painters "opposed to American aggression in Vietnam" and tried to pump more life into the peace art show held each year in Tokyo. Haryū Ichirō, the critic and Beheiren member who had organized a big "antiwar and liberation" exhibit in July 1968, continued to raise funds with works donated by artists critical of the war, using the proceeds to send medical supplies to Vietnam in 1969. Public attitudes were running strongly against the American presence in Indochina by 1968–1969, but Haryū recalls that political paintings and activities by artists still "did

not show such strong anti-American sentiment" even though they expressed implacable opposition to the war.[22]

Otherwise the left-wing musical organizations remained the most vocal artistic critics of the conflict. After being denied visas several times, a scaled-down song and dance troupe from Hanoi put on twenty-three performances at the end of 1968 with the backing of the workers' music federation Rōon. The Tokyo Rōon sponsored concerts by antiwar composers of popular music in early 1969, and Utagoe marshaled hundreds of singers and dancers for stage extravaganzas against the war. In Osaka the Kansai chorus, a central component of Utagoe, held orchestral and ballet programs from 1969 through 1972 to encourage the public to aid the people of Vietnam.[23] Although these musical organizations retained their close links with the Old Left, by 1969 Beheiren and other civic groups had fewer qualms than before about publicizing and supporting such antiwar concerts.

Several important feature movies that depicted the harshness of the conflict began to appear in the theaters during 1968 and 1969. One was Horikawa Hiromichi's *Farewell to the Gang in Moscow* (*Saraba Mosukuwa gurentai*, 1968), in which a Japanese jazz pianist taught a black GI on R & R from Vietnam how to play better—a reversal of the usual roles. Another was *The Okinawa Islands* (*Okinawa rettō*, 1968), directed by Higashi Yoichi, which showed the oppression of local residents by American forces at the height of the fighting in Southeast Asia. The blockbuster production of the midwar period was Yamamoto Satsuo's *Vietnam* (*Betonamu*, 1969), which was produced by a committee that collected money from more than eighty groups and several thousand individuals. This bitterly antiwar documentary included footage supplied by the North Vietnamese government and was immediately denounced as propaganda by those who did not choose to believe the sad face of war it portrayed.[24] In spite of these examples from film, music, and the visual arts, Beheiren continued to run into a stone wall of artistic pride and professional detachment when

175

it tried to reach out to painters, sculptors, print makers, and performers in the stage and studio arts.

People in the antiwar movement also took a direct hand in the Ryūkyū question by joining the raucous Okinawa Day demonstrations that attracted 130,000 people to central Tokyo on April 28, 1969. Even though the Beheiren leaders had always supported the idea of reclaiming the islands, before 1969 they had not joined very vigorously in the public call for reversion because they feared that once Okinawa was restored, many Japanese would wash their hands of the war its bases supported and deceive themselves into thinking that they had stopped Japan's complicity, if not the fighting itself. But now Beheiren and other antiwar organizations saw that Okinawa had to be confronted because it was corollary to the upcoming treaty issue.[25]

In addition, Prime Minister Satō proposed to the Diet in March 1969 that the bases on Okinawa be governed by the same nonnuclear rules as those elsewhere in Japan after reversion, a retreat from his position after the Washington summit in November 1967. This principle, called *hondo nami*, had first been broached in public by Foreign Minister Miki the previous October. Of course the war critics in Japan wanted the Ryūkyūs to be free of atomic weapons, but they joined in the reversion demonstrations starting in April 1969 because they feared that Satō would make unwise concessions to the United States in return for *hondo nami*, including field training on Okinawa for South Korean, Thai, and South Vietnamese troops and continuing the air war from Kadena with B-52s. Finally, the Okinawa question was pivotal to some of the anti-JCP student sects, other campus groups, and the young workers in Hansen whose cooperation Beheiren very much needed in order to press on with the struggle against a war that many Japanese, like many Americans, thought was almost over.

Okinawa Day turned into a fiasco. The government refused a rally permit to an alliance of student factions, even though other left organizations were allowed to demonstrate. While labor, the communists, and Beheiren all held peaceful meetings in civic parks, as many as 8,800 radicals from the anti-JCP

Zengakuren sects joined with helmeted workers from Hansen for a spree of violence and virtual anarchy in central Tokyo.[26] Altogether 1,030 persons were arrested during the pandemonium. The protesters took over the tracks at Tokyo station, stopping all railway traffic on the highline, and threw rocks from the roadbed at riot police below. Moving to the back streets of Ginza, they erected barricades and called the area from Yaesu to Sukiyabashi the Ginza liberated zone, after the Latin Quarter in Paris the year before. Other factions briefly took over parts of Kasumigaseki and Kanda (near the universities) and declared them liberated as well. Beheiren representatives at the Nishi Ginza subway station finally talked the radicals into leaving peacefully about 9:30 P.M., and after the tear gas drifted away the police heard much criticism of the decision to deny the students permission to demonstrate.[27]

The leaders of Sōhyō were appalled to see Hansen youths wearing helmets and carrying lumber to bash the police and the pro-JCP demonstrators, exactly like the radical students from the anti-JCP factions. The Japan Socialist Party tried to conciliate the tiff between Hansen and the parent union with platitudes; the communists denounced the violent young workers as "fascist-style Trotskyites"—a remarkable epithet even for the JCP.[28] Beheiren was sheepish but undaunted after the chaos of Okinawa Day. Tsurumi Yoshiyuki later tried to put a good face on the new developments by celebrating Beheiren's new association with radicalism as a logical consequence of the effort to spend less time in meetings and more in the streets. He rather grandly said Beheiren, Hansen, and the student movement were "manifestations of an ongoing cultural revolution in Japan" that rejected dogmatism and group standards in favor of self-assertiveness and spontaneous action. The result of existential free choice, he concluded, was that individuals were no longer "passive functionaries" but instead believed that "when you advocate something, you must be the first to do it."[29] Acting in concert with radical students, workers, and airport protesters was a new approach for Beheiren, but the principles of nonviolence and individual commitment through concrete action endured from the beginning

177

CHAPTER 6

AFTER THE BANQUET   Helmets signifying various
anti-JCP sects litter the tracks at Shinbashi station, Tokyo,
after a feast of violence by radical students on Okinawa Day,
April 28, 1969. (Photo: Kyōdō Tsūshinsha)

of the movement in April 1965 until it dissolved in 1974. Although Beheiren never condoned the rough tactics of the student sects and constantly labored to bring in more ordinary citizens, Tsurumi Yoshiyuki correctly saw that the antiwar movement shared a radicalism of spontaneous action, not ideological principle, with the students and workers.

THE CROWDS OF SUMMER

"Beheiren and groups like it are like flies" that pester the authorities and keep coming back when you drive them away,

the peevish head of the national public safety committee told
the cabinet a few days before the largest New Left demonstration of the Vietnam War era in Japan took place in Tokyo on
June 15, 1969. Although the police expected 15,000 people to
appear at Hibiya Park for the Beheiren rally that day, afterward they admitted that twice as many had shown up, and
most others put the figure at 60–70,000.[30] The slogan of the
day was "oppose the war, oppose the treaty, return Okinawa." This marked the first time that every anti-JCP group
joined together to hold a peaceful rally, helping to erase the

THE MAGNET   Oda Makoto addressing an antiwar demonstration
in Tokyo that drew as many as 70,000 people to Hibiya Park,
including helmeted protesters from Beheiren and Hansen.
(Photo: Yoshikawa Yūichi)

179

bad memories of Okinawa Day in April. Far more antiwar laborers and students attended the event than the June 1968 demonstration at Hibiya, which was much smaller (11,000) and almost exclusively middle-class. Beheiren's energy and its skill in preventing violence at this gigantic meeting jolted the Old Left and forced it to reconsider its strategy for united action to topple the security treaty in June 1970.

The date of the New Left demonstration was chosen to mark the ninth anniversary of the antitreaty protests at the Diet building when Kanba Michiko was killed. Someone carried her portrait as the crowd filed out of Hibiya Park toward the Diet building, then doubled back to Shinbashi, Ginza, and Yaesu. When the column reached Tokyo station at the end of the five-kilometer route, the last protesters were still waiting to leave the park. All the newspapers called the day a success and showed surprise that so many people had turned out, even at the risk of being tarred by violence. Actually the adults and other peaceable demonstrators set an example of decorum that made it shameful to be seen with rocks, staves, or helmets. Nearly all of the 170 persons detained by the police that day were radicals from splinter factions who were seized at smaller gatherings elsewhere in Tokyo.[31]

Pleased that no one found any flies on him after the June 15 rally, Oda Makoto set off five days later on an antiwar caravan around Hokkaido, arranged by the Beheiren unit in Sapporo. En route he dashed off a retrospective for the August issue of *Sekai*, in which he declared that "something is starting—a whirlpool of humanity beginning with June 15."[32] Oda meant that the antiwar activists were at the center of a widening vortex, drawing more and more citizens in from the edges as it built momentum for individual self-awareness and personal commitment to stopping the war. Even the Japan Communist Party grudgingly recognized after the Hibiya demonstration that "henceforth the struggle will not just be carried on by the JCP and JSP acting jointly" but by other groups as well.[33] The press and the socialists both agreed that the New Left, led by Beheiren, was now strong enough to stand on its own and that

FRENCH-STYLE DEMONSTRATION   Beheiren members
holding hands as they march through Sukiyabashi, Tokyo, after
the largest New Left rally of the war era on June 15, 1969.
(Photo: Kyōdō Tsūshinsha)

the possiblity of a truly united front in 1970 against the treaty,
a goal long cherished by the Old Left, had actually diminished
because of the June 15 rally. Tsurumi Yoshiyuki gave what
was probably the *coup de grâce* to the matter when he wrote that
unity consisted not of a policy agreement on fine points but "a
guarantee on the principles of diversity of action and spontaneity of participation. This means that as far as we are concerned, it is more nearly a matter of faith and personal disposition than a problem of ideology."[34]

June 1969 was also when the Aliens' Peace for Vietnam

181

Committee was formed by foreign residents of Japan who opposed the war. Long before then foreigners had started petitioning the American embassy, writing letters to editors, and holding protest marches. One of the largest of these was an eighty-person procession of well-dressed foreigners to the United States embassy on June 26, 1968, each of them carrying an American flag or a placard denouncing the war and wearing a small lapel pin with the Japanese characters for peace. The new committee was headed by Ronald A. McLean, an American teacher of English in Tokyo whose suit against the justice minister for permission to stay in Japan beyond 1970 was finally turned down by the supreme court in October 1978. The justices found that even though foreigners enjoyed many rights of political expression in Japan, the justice minister had broad discretion over immigration matters.[35]

Almost immediately after the aliens' peace committee was established the government refused to let three American pacifists, including the well-known Buddhist priest Brian Victoria, reenter Japan after sailing their antiwar yacht *Phoenix* to China and back. Victoria was eventually allowed to stay in Japan, where he had lived for ten years, but the authorities rounded up a number of other outspoken critics of the war on visa-related technicalities, including dissenters from Vietnam, South Korea, and Taiwan.[36] The plight of the Vietnamese living in Japan came into view when about forty of them sat in at the Government of Vietnam embassy in June 1969 to protest the forthcoming Nixon-Thieu talks at Guam. Altogether about 130 Vietnamese, mainly students from the south, had been caught in Japan when the war heated up in early 1965. Those from South Vietnam who sat in at the embassy in June 1969 soon found that the flow of money to them from their families back home was cut off by the Saigon government, and several of the protest leaders were drafted by the ARVN. One was convicted in absentia by a South Vietnamese military court when he failed to report for induction.[37]

Another crackdown occurred in July 1969 when the police put an end to the Sunday afternoon gatherings of young peo-

ple who came to sing war protest songs on the mosaic tile plaza at the west exit of Shinjuku station. Ever since February of that year Beheiren had sponsored the informal events, known as folk guerrilla, which were patterned after the sing-along concerts organized in the underground Umeda station in Osaka by a Christian minister, Kimura Taku, in the fall of 1967. Starting in May 1969 the Shinjuku police periodically cleared away the crowds on the pretext that they were blocking pedestrian traffic. Then on July 5 the folk guerrillas tried to stop radical students with metal pipes from smashing a nearby police box during a concert, but the booth was destroyed and these folk-singing events were permanently banned. At their height they drew as many as 7,000 participants, making them collectively the most widely attended activities sponsored by Beheiren during the war. The protest song that was probably as well known among Japanese as *Blowin' in the Wind* became to Americans was *Friends (Tomo yo)*, which began: "Friends, in the darkness before the dawn, Friends, let's light the flames of struggle, The dawn is near."[38]

The day after the folk concerts were officially abolished, President Nixon announced his Guam doctrine at a press conference on July 25, 1969. The antiwar leaders in Japan were relieved to learn that the United States would not henceforth intervene directly in Asian wars and that it expected its allies in the region to undertake their own defense by conventional means. On the other hand, America would continue to keep its treaty commitments by providing air, naval, and material support. Gratified though they were at this formula, the Japanese newspapers mostly interpreted Nixon's policy as a 180-degree turnabout, ignoring the fact that it was really a reversion to the policies of Truman, MacArthur, and Eisenhower.[39]

The Satō cabinet worried about any future withdrawal of United States forces from South Korea but correctly calculated that no sudden change in the American bases in Japan would take place. Among the public at large, the controversial Far East clause of the security treaty seemed a bit less menacing after the Guam announcement—until the press revealed in Au-

gust 1970 that Undersecretary of State Johnson had told a Senate subcommittee the previous winter that the bases in Japan existed entirely to defend the Far East: "we have no forces, either ground or air, in Japan that are directly related to direct conventional defense of Japan."[40] Overall Nixon's program helped to mollify antiwar critics in Japan by forecasting a more discriminating American role in Asia in the future, and Satō too was pleased that the Guam doctrine was consistent with Japan's plans to regain Okinawa.

The stickiest moment of the summer for the antiwar movement came when the Osaka Beheiren unit held a counterculture exposition on August 7–11, 1969, on the grounds of Osaka castle. Young people in southern Osaka had been busy for more than a year with poetry readings, folk concerts, art shows, and films opposing the war, and they convinced the Beheiren conference in February 1969 to support an antiwar show that summer, named Hanbaku, to combat the "commercialism and big-power nationalism" of the world's fair planned for 1970 in Osaka, known as Banpaku. The theme of Hanbaku was "peace and liberation for mankind," in contrast to the official "progress and harmony" slogan of Expo '70.[41]

The event was controversial because it seemed diversionary to many Beheiren people, however much they agreed that a free-flowing, existential movement like theirs should be able to shift issues and tactics without losing character. Haryū Ichirō questioned whether a counter-exposition was the best way to reform either foreign policy or art.[42] The local organizers, who had drawn large crowds to their antiwar art festivals in central Osaka, were disappointed that only 6,000 people showed up for Hanbaku, nearly all of them workers and students connected with the movement against the war. Takabatake Michitoshi criticized the Hanbaku group for selling books at a profit and measuring their success in numbers of visitors, exactly like a real exposition.[43] The show contained a lot of stale antiwar posters but few weapons or other objects from the battlefield. Perhaps most unsettling were its antiestablishment overtones, which even the antiwar leaders who

184

were most leery of state power thought could only hurt their efforts.

THE RADICALS MOVE OFF CAMPUS

Attacking the university, corporate, and political establishments was the essence of the Japanese student movement in the late sixties. For this reason, as well as the penchant of certain factions for violence, Beheiren tried to keep a tight rein on campus groups that joined its demonstrations once the students and antiwar organizations began to cooperate in late 1968. The results were dappled: disasters at Shinjuku in October 1968 and Ginza the next April, equable rallies at Hibiya in June and September, and then a fearsome rampage by the militant sects on October 21, 1969.

Most student self-government associations at Japanese universities had pledged allegiance to the Japan Communist Party, and the majority of politically active undergraduates belonged to their campus branch of Minsei, a national organization of students sponsored by the JCP. The radical anti-JCP factions such as Chūkakuha, Shagakudō, Shaseidō, and Kakumaruha regarded all the established political parties as much too intertwined with the business and bureaucratic scaffolding of Japanese society. The anti-JCP sects were represented on only a minority of campuses and controlled about 15 percent of the student governments. Minsei and the anti-JCP factions collectively formed Zengakuren, the national federation of student self-government associations. Other radical students in the late sixties—especially graduate students, interns, and young researchers—who rejected both the JCP and the sects began to form independent joint struggle councils (Zengaku Kyōtō Kaigi, or Zenkyōtō) on their own campuses, unconnected with any party or national student group. Conservative students had organizations as well, and many others had neither the time nor the interest to involve themselves in the disputes that wracked 152 of Japan's 377 four-year universities by 1969.[44]

Radicals in the anti-JCP factions and the individual Zenkyōtō councils took the lead in nearly all the campus conflicts during the late sixties. The issues varied from one university to the next, but they usually clustered into one of three subsets, in order of frequency: on-campus problems (tuition increases, aloof professors, university governance), domestic political and economic policy (the industrial-bureaucratic-political elite), or Japan's relationship to the outside world (Vietnam, Okinawa, the security treaty, China). One index of the overcrowding and poor quality of higher education was the population of Nihon University, Japan's largest, where 83,000 were studying—more than the entire enrollment at all four-year universities in 1937.[45] The problems were genuine and the concern was real; it would be a mistake to dismiss the overall student movement as a self-indulgent ego trip, even though many radicals were self-absorbed and insensitive to others.

The anti-JCP sects and the Zenkyōtō councils rejected the dogmatism of the Old Left and usually preferred sentience to logic. Followers of Trotsky, Mao, and Togliatti were sprinkled here and there, but most radicals spurned doctrinal reasoning in favor of subjective self-expression and individual self-determination. They often stressed their unique nature as human beings in defiance of the mechanical culture, rationalism, and progress imposed by the ruling oligarchy since Meiji. Some were self-styled hippies; the back-to-nature impulse was strong, especially among those who admired the self-sufficiency of the Edo-era masterless samurai.

In the late 1967 one radical student said of his faction: "most of us join Sanpa for personal reasons rather than out of pure political conviction." When he entered college, "I was experiencing freedom for the first time. . . . Soon after I joined the movement. I enjoyed the activity and *demos* [demonstrations] gave me satisfaction."[46] The students were especially ineffective politically because of this degree of emotional preoccupation. As the *Asahi* writer Fukashiro Junrō noted, "the New Left is less political than existentialist in its ideological content."[47] It is easy to see why Oda's ideas of democratic individ-

ualism and self-generated action appealed to the campus radicals, even though the sects imposed more discipline than Beheiren or other civic groups.

The anti-JCP factions often referred to demonstrations by students affiliated with Minsei as quiet incense-burning ceremonies (*oshōkō demo*). Instead many radicals aped the samurai life-style of purity, sincerity, and simplicity—and helmets and weapons as well. The writer Usami Shō believes that many undergraduates secretly admired the activists for their brio and swagger: "the average student says 'I cannot follow their lead,'" yet "a great many students feel 'they are doing things which we ourselves want to, but cannot do.'"[48] The radicals scoffed at established authority and reviled the universities for uncritically serving as a training ground for big business. They urged fellow students to rebel against the establishment (*zōhan*), rejecting privilege and bourgeois morality in favor of an existential selfhood known as *jiritsu*. The philosopher Yoshimoto Ryūmei first popularized this idea in 1964, describing it as a nonpolitical sense of human autonomy based on acting as well as knowing.[49] Such views were very close to both Oda Makoto's thinking and the search for personal authentication in the indigenous commoner tradition found during the 1960s in the pop art of Yokoo Tadanori and the underground theater of Kara Jūrō.

The campus radicals, like the Beheiren leaders, argued that protesters should recognize themselves as victimizers rather than victims, although they more often referred to middle-class capitalism than to the Vietnam War as the ground of exploitation. Seeing themselves as beneficiaries of affluence and privilege, the radicals preached at length about engaging in self-negation and identifying with the poor and the outcast—casualties of the economic system their universities helped to perpetuate. The Zenkyōtō councils were much taken with the notion of participatory democracy, which meant a bigger share of power on campus and much more involvement with public issues through direct action, now that parliamentary

democracy had been co-opted into supporting the war, in defiance of public opinion.[50]

Attractive as such ideas were to many students, the radicals fell into an elitism of their own that eventually alienated most of the public. Their tactics of berating professors in kangaroo courts and battling police in the streets showed little of the self-denial they urged in quieter moments. At the height of the unrest Marius B. Jansen wrote of the student protesters: "with a fine elite consciousness and scorn for the lower orders of class and morality which they disturb by their actions, they meet a mixture of tolerance, amusement and respect on the part of their fellow Japanese that has so far made them immune to discipline or reproof."[51] Prime Minister Satō waited until the public tired of the uprisings, then pushed through a universities control bill on August 19, 1969, that allowed the education minister to close a campus if a dispute went on too long.[52]

Oda also was cautious about the student activists because he thought their self-absorption made it hard for them to see how the war in Southeast Asia affected Japan: "I was astonished to read some university student movement handbills which proclaimed that students were somehow assisting the people of Vietnam by struggling against tuition rises."[53] Although Beheiren had been active on campuses from the start, only in the Shinjuku fracas of October 1968 did the militant sects join in an antiwar demonstration side by side with Oda and his followers. The best Oda could say after the catastrophe was that it had at least been effective in shutting down the station.[54] As the squabbles between factions grew and more universities were deluged with fighting, nonviolent students began to drift over to outdoor coffeehouses set up on campus by Beheiren and ended up attending its demonstrations downtown.

Because the Zenkyōtō councils shared many points of style with the antiwar movement and because they were less hierarchical than the anti-JCP sects, many of their members who rejected violence found themselves joining in Beheiren activities as well, since neither was exclusive about who took part.[55] Beheiren cheered the national alliance of Zenkyōtō councils

when it was officially established at a meeting held in Hibiya Park on September 5, 1969 of 30,000 radicals from forty-six universities.[56] Actually the meeting was anticlimatic; it turned out to be not a new beginning but instead the last chapter of peaceful cooperation between the antiwar and student movements.

Early the next month the press reported that 20,000 Self-Defense Force soldiers in the Tokyo area and more than 50,000 elsewhere in Japan could be mobilized for riot duty if necessary to combat the violent demonstrations expected that autumn. Although the troops were never pressed into service, the radical workers and students were completely unintimidated by the announcement. On October 10 the new federation of Zenkyōtō councils held a rare series of demonstrations jointly with Hansen and several of the anti-JCP sects of Zengakuren in fifty-three places around the country to oppose Satō's forthcoming trip to Washington and the extension of the security treaty. The Vietnam War was a secondary issue that day, which ended in strife with the police and so much friction among the sponsors that no such concerted action by New Left groups was attempted again.[57] The next morning the police inexplicably raided the Tokyo Beheiren office and seized about 100 pamphlets, account books, and other items that a court later found "completely irrelevant" to the case of a demonstrator from Waseda arrested the night before.[58]

Possibly the most violent episode in the entire Japanese antiwar movement came on October 21, 1969, when at least 467,000 Old and New Left protesters turned out nationwide, according to the police (Beheiren claimed 860,000). The day was cold and rainy in Tokyo, where shopkeepers turned the commercial districts near commuter stations into ghost towns because they feared a rerun of the previous year's international antiwar day. Actually the carnage was even worse this time. While the JSP and JCP drew 60,000 demonstrators to Yoyogi Park for an occasion they saw as "the key struggle auguring the success or failure" of the antitreaty effort in 1970, Beheiren attracted another 10,000 or more to its favorite venue, Shimi-

189

zudani Park.[59] Otherwise the protests were led by radical students and ended in a complete debacle.

Except for Beheiren, none of the New Left groups received permits to demonstrate, so they took to the streets instead. During the day a crowd of about 10,000 gathered silently at Shinjuku station, anticipating the battle that began about 6:30 P.M. at the east exit when 3,000 radicals fought with at least that many police. No longer could the protesters hurl rocks from the train tracks, because the roadbeds had all been tarred over. The brawl continued for nearly four hours, while other demonstrators flooded into the station, halted traffic on all the lines, and clashed with riot police along the street between the west exit and Ōme Kaidō, a main thoroughfare.[60]

A few kilometers to the north, the avenue from Takadanobaba to Waseda was in a state of siege. Hansen and other radical groups also carried out scattered guerrilla raids on police outposts all over town. They showed what they thought of a united front with the Old Left by burning a sound truck belonging to one of the unions. A group of university students grabbed some construction materials and tried to set up a liberated zone near Iidabashi station, until they were routed by the police. Someone threw a Molotov cocktail into the headquarters of the Seventh Riot Police Detachment, one of twenty-three police booths and stations attacked during the fracas. Similar skirmishes took place in Osaka and other big cities, overshadowing the generally peaceful rallies sponsored that day by labor, the opposition parties, or Beheiren in about 600 places nationwide.[61]

The 1969 antiwar day was the biggest and most violent set of demonstrations about foreign policy in Japan since the Vietnam War started, even though a good part of the reason for the crowds was the prime minister's impending flight to the United States to discuss Okinawa and the treaty as well as the war. Although the property damage was more widespread than during the previous year's riot, injuries were held down by the presence of 25,000 police in Tokyo and 50,000 more throughout the rest of the country—the greatest show of force

since the end of the occupation, easily eclipsing the 51,400 officers on duty nationwide during the protests in 1960. Altogether 1,505 persons were arrested, 1,221 of them in the capital, a new record that stood for barely three weeks before renewed fighting at Haneda toppled it.[62]

October 21 was a sorry spectacle in a year of unprecedented violence by radical youths. The authorities calculated that 2,460 street battles took place in 1969, leading to 14,748 arrests—but not a single fatality. Only a small fraction of the clashes can be attributed specifically to antiwar activity; most were prompted by the same antiestablishment sentiments and sectarian violence that threw the campuses into an uproar. The Old Left castigated the radical students for their absolute individualism and lack of organization, leading them into the fruitless trap of anarchy. Tsurumi Yoshiyuki of Beheiren likewise denied that violence had any redeeming value, even a symbolic one; he chided the young activists for their selfish, playboyish behavior and reminded them to show concern for solidarity and human liberation.[63] The upshot of the 1969 antiwar day was that student radicalism was thoroughly disgraced and all pretense of unity among the leftist forces evaporated. Yet the accumulating waves of dissent, now buoyed by concern about the Okinawa and treaty issues, posed Prime Minister Satō an unavoidable challenge as he planned the cardinal achievement of his foreign policy: the return of Okinawa with no loss of security.

CHAPTER 7

The Protests Peak

SATŌ EISAKU faced the decisive passage of his long prime ministership during the same seven months that Richard Nixon confronted his first big crisis over the Vietnam War. Nixon chose November 3, 1969 for a polemical televised speech on how he planned to end the war, hoping to draw the sting from a huge nationwide demonstration planned for the middle of the month. A few days later came the news that a company of American soldiers had massacred hundreds of Vietnamese civilians in March 1968 at the village of My Lai. The shocking report and revolting photographs of the slaughter helped produce the largest one-day turnout for political gatherings in American history at the peace rallies held on November 15.

Within a few months it became known that, under the guise of "winding the war down," the administration had been secretly bombing Cambodia for a year. When Nixon announced on April 30, 1970 that he had sent American ground troops into Cambodia as well, hundreds of campuses erupted in unprecedented anger across the United States. News of the invasion also touched off the greatest campaign of citizen lobbying in the history of the Congress, finally prompting the legislators to cut off any further funds for United States troops in Cambodia once they were withdrawn at the end of June.[1]

Satō left Japan on November 17, 1969 for his summit with Nixon amid tumultuous demonstrations at Haneda and reached Washington less than forty-eight hours after 250,000 protesters had thronged the capital, where police ringed the White House with buses and the president watched football on television while the marchers shouted their opposition to the war. Satō returned home in triumph the following week with

a firm agreement that Okinawa would revert to Japan in 1972. He immediately called an election for the lower house, in which the Liberal Democrats gained an astounding thirty-two seats, and he also set about slacking the tension over the security treaty. Even though three-quarters of a million people showed up on June 23, 1970 at rallies around the country to denounce the automatic renewal of the pact—far more than on any single day in 1960—still Satō's successful diplomacy and shrewd management of domestic politics helped the government elude a real showdown over the treaty. At the same time the prime minister kept on supporting American policy in Vietnam while saying he hoped peace would come soon. November 1969–June 1970 was a period of crisis for Nixon but one of catharsis for Satō, who faced far less opposition to his policies on Vietnam, Okinawa, or the treaty once the wave of protest crested on June 23.

OKINAWA, THE WAR, AND THE TREATY

"There was no overwhelming pressure in Japan or Okinawa for reversion," the senior American diplomat Richard L. Sneider has written. "The argument for reversion, which eventually prevailed, was that it was necessary to act before the pressures for reversion became so great as to endanger the total U.S. relationship with Japan."[2] Another veteran of the American embassy in Tokyo, Edwin O. Reischauer, took a different view of the matter. In an interview published in August 1969, he said that "we have a colony of one million Japanese" in Okinawa, even though the United States "wouldn't have a colony of one million Englishmen or Italians."[3] In fact nearly all Okinawans, and the great majority of Japanese, thought the case for reversion was compelling by the late sixties, thanks partly to Prime Minister Satō's bold leadership on the issue since August 1965 but also to the Vietnam War, which helped bring the question to a boil.

Seeing the American bombers depart for Vietnam each morning made it impossible for residents of Okinawa to for-

get the key part their islands played in the war. Vietnam presented them with a dilemma, since more than a quarter of the GNP of the Ryūkyūs was generated directly by the United States bases. Whereas most persons on the Japanese mainland who criticized the war also opposed the presence of the bases, anti–Vietnam War sentiment was much stronger than antibase feelings among a people so dependent on the military for their livelihoods. After Okinawa was officially returned in 1972, a top leader of the reversion movement said in retrospect: "Okinawa was in the position of being an assailant of the Vietnamese people because it provided bases and labor for the Vietnam War. While seeking peace and opposing the war, people had to earn their livings by working on the bases. People on Okinawa worried about this contradiction."[4]

The reversion issue had festered ever since the San Francisco peace conference in 1951 made more lenient provisions for residents of Japan proper than for the people living in the Ryūkyūs. The umbrella organization for the reversion movement, Fukkikyō, consisted of three leftist parties in the Okinawan legislature and various labor, women's, teachers', and student groups. Even though many islanders believed that Japanese on the mainland had treated them in the past like poor cousins, the demand for reversion grew loud after the Vietnam War escalated in early 1965. During the second half of that year a number of reversionist candidates were successful in legislative and municipal elections. As base facilities were expanded in 1966 and 1967 to support the war, farmers formed alliances with antiwar groups to resist land condemnation and held regular demonstrations near the United States headquarters. Zengunrō, the main union representing base workers, held an enormous rally on April 28, 1968 to support merger with the mainland and to attack the no-strike ordinance that it believed hurt the ability of workers to gain better benefits. The momentum toward reversion was speeded up greatly by the periodic protests against the B-52s when their daily bombing runs to Vietnam started in February of that year.[5]

A seasoned progressive in the Okinawa legislature, Yara

Chōbyō, was elected as the first chief executive of the Ryūkyūan government on November 10, 1968, with backing
from a coalition of leftist parties. Even though conservatives
won eighteen of the thirty-two seats in the legislature that day,
and despite a lack of real power in the office itself, Yara immediately became the central figure in the reversion movement throughout the islands. To avert a potentially disastrous
general strike set for February 5, 1969, he sought concessions
from the United States high commissioner and also traveled to
Tokyo to pry loose assurances from the government that it
would do what it could to have the B-52s removed.

Kimura Toshio, the deputy chief cabinet secretary, told him
that the bombers would probably be gone by midsummer,
and the strike was canceled. Yara lost both face and influence
when the aircraft were not withdrawn on schedule but instead
continued to bomb Indochina for another year. He also
worked hard on getting the Americans to take away the 13,000
tons of chemical warfare agents stored on Okinawa after the
Wall Street Journal reported on July 19, 1969 that a leak of poison gas had injured twenty-five United States troops. Shortly
after the Nixon-Satō summit in November, Washington announced that the substance would be removed. When the last
trailer of poison gas eventually departed in September 1971,
officials of the Ryūkyūan government spread salt with their
own hands to purify the soil.[6]

The insistence on regaining Okinawa was almost universal
in Japan proper by the fall of 1969, notwithstanding a Gallup
poll in September showing that the American public opposed
giving the islands up by a margin of 62 to 24 percent.[7] But the
entire Japanese Left was worried about the conditions under
which reversion would take place. Some groups clamored to
have the American bases removed as a sine qua non for reacquiring the Ryūkyūs; nearly all were skeptical about whether
nuclear weapons would really be removed, as promised by the
prime minister since March 1969. To quell the rumbles, the
government let it be known in early November that it had
once again offered to act as a "responsible intermediary" be-

tween North Vietnam and the United States.[8] The cabinet was relieved that a *Mainichi* survey published the same month reported steadily dropping anxiety among the general public about being drawn into the Vietnam War through the security relationshp with the United States. The proportion who believed that Japan (including Okinawa) was not in danger of being attacked in the near future or directly involved in war rose to 54 percent, compared with 37 percent in a similar poll in December 1967.[9] Then the press began to report the My Lai massacre less than two weeks before Satō's trip to Washington, adding to the fervor of the opposition to his departure on November 17.[10]

Altogether the five days of demonstrations during November 13–17, 1969 involved fewer protesters than the international antiwar day three weeks earlier but led to even more arrests. Sōhyō led off with a series of strikes on November 13, while Beheiren drew a crowd of 5,000 to an evening rally at Shinjuku to denounce any plan for reversion that would let the United States continue to use Okinawa as a rear echelon for the war. That same evening 325 anti-JCP radicals were arrested after making guerrilla attacks around Ginza and injuring sixteen passers-by.[11] Strikes and meetings continued for the next two days, setting the scene for a series of demonstrations in 832 places throughout the country on November 16. The police put the total attendance that day at 121,000, about a quarter of the turnout, by their estimate, on international antiwar day.[12] Indecisiveness by the Japan Socialist Party and the labor unions, together with the tightest security ever imposed on a postwar political demonstration in Japan, apparently accounted for the dropoff.

Antiwar groups driving up the Tōmei expressway in vans were pulled over at police roadblocks and questioned. Body pat-downs were carried out at the Tokyo interchange, and the riot police also intercepted radicals traveling by train before they could get near the airport. A number of potential demonstrators were photographed in advance by the authorities.[13] The precautions were so stringent that not even Beheiren

could get permission to hold a rally on November 16, yet nearly 15,000 persons turned up at Hibiya Park anyway for an illegal but peaceful meeting. Violence broke out in nearby streets afterward, led by radical students who had attended the gathering in the park, without the concern for comportment they had felt at similar Beheiren events the year before.[14] The JSP confined its protests to a big meeting in central Tokyo but sent a few demonstrators to Haneda.

Hansen members and radical students began throwing Molotov cocktails about 4 P.M. at a railway terminal near the airport. Soon there was "a sea of fire in front of Kamata station," *Asahi* reported the next morning. The riot police looked on as teams of local vigilantes wearing yellow hats and armbands began to strike back at the protesters with poles and baseball bats—a comedown from the rapport between citizens and demonstrators the previous year at Sasebo and Ōji. The police confined the battle to the Kamata area while other officers stared down the crowd keeping a peaceful vigil outside the airport itself.

Other disruptions broke out at Tokyo station and the west side of Shinagawa. The radicals' objective was apparently to control Kamata overnight and create such an uproar that the prime minister's departure the next morning would have to be canceled. But the riot police uncovered most of the weapons the protesters had stashed in advance near Kamata, and the fighting was under control soon after 7 P.M. Deploying 25,000 officers in Tokyo and at least 50,000 elsewhere, the authorities seized 1,689 persons in the capital and another 168 in other locations for a total of 1,857 arrests, compared with 1,221 in Tokyo and 1,505 nationwide on October 21. The number booked on November 16 set a new record for political demonstrations since 1952 that has not been equaled since.[15]

Satō's DC-8 took off in heavy rain shortly after 10 A.M. on November 17, while radicals continued their violence in Tokyo and other cities. The police arrested another 288 demonstrators that day and said they had confiscated more than a thousand Molotov cocktails during the previous week in To-

197

kyo alone. As with the antiwar day skirmishes three weeks earlier, the number of injuries was greatly reduced by adequate riot gear and the sheer numbers of police on hand. No firearms were used, no riots were declared, nor did any fatalities occur despite the arson at Kamata.[16]

In retrospect the five-day outpouring of violence accomplished nothing by way of generating more opposition to Satō's diplomacy. Instead it cost the antiwar movement dearly to have radical activists paralyze the suburban train system and burn cars to embarrass the prime minister as he headed off to reclaim Okinawa. Now that Beheiren and other civic groups were tightly interwoven with the antitreaty and reversion protests, the acrid odor of violence inevitably clung despite their insistence on peaceful dissent. The public, as Mutō Ichiyō of Beheiren pointed out after November 16, was far more tolerant of massive police power after two years of campus and street battles than it had been at Sasebo when officers clubbed unarmed demonstrators to the pavement. By the end of 1969 the riot police had developed much greater sophistication at the crowd management, "patiently encircling a demonstration and slowly contracting, arresting the last holdouts at the center," according to Haryū Ichirō.[17]

Others in the antiwar movement, discouraged that the promise of the June Action of 1968 and the joint June rally in 1969 had now been dashed, blamed their frustration on the authoritarian power of the state. Iida Momo said of the effort to stop Satō's trip: "as far as I was concerned that was the decisive battle, which would determine whether we could build up a successful movement to prevent the renewal of the Mutual Security Treaty. But we lost. The power of the police was simply too great, and we were militarily defeated."[18] Few of the dissenters wanted to admit the most important element of all: the prime minister brought back a highly popular present from Washington that swelled the nation's pride and made it easier to overlook his firm support of the unpleasant war in Vietnam.

OKINAWA: A BARGAIN?

When Prime Minister Satō arrived at the Japanese embassy in Washington on November 17, 1969, Oda Makoto was presiding over speeches and antiwar skits before an audience of 150 people at Dupont Circle, about half a kilometer from the embassy gate.[19] Undeterred, the prime minister plowed through a grinding three-day schedule of conferences, tête-à-têtes with President Nixon, and official dinners with dignitaries. At the end of the talks he kept a return engagement at the National Press Club on November 21, where he spoke confidently of the "new Pacific age" ahead and used a haunting term from the 1930s to describe it: "a new order will be created by Japan and the United States."[20]

Continuing the security treaty so as to protect East and Southeast Asia under the recent Guam Doctrine was the top American goal in the negotiations, and Nixon was willing to pay the price of Okinawa to keep the treaty intact. He apparently recognized that the United States had little choice in the matter, because of the reversionist sentiment in both Japan and Okinawa and Satō's commitment to reacquiring the Ryūkyūs as soon as possible. The Americans feared a replay of the 1960 treaty crisis more than the Japanese did by the time the two sides began discussing the nature of their future defense relationship beyond June 1970, when the pact could be altered or scrapped on one year's notice. Satō was confident that the violent protests of 1968–1969 would abate once he pinned the United States to a definite date for reversion. On the other hand, the Americans knew that the prime minister had his heart set on regaining Okinawa and demanded a high price in return—but not so stiff as to threaten the treaty itself.

The long Satō-Nixon communiqué of November 21, 1969 promised that Okinawa would be returned in 1972 and that the United States bases there would be governed by the same provisions as those in the rest of Japan. This meant that nuclear weapons would be removed and that the Americans would consult in advance if they wanted to reintroduce them, as they

had secretly done on the Japanese mainland without consultation in 1955–1958.[21] The nonnuclear stipulation represented a victory for the new Japanese foreign minister, Aichi Kiichi, who had replaced Miki Takeo in November 1968. Both U. Alexis Johnson and Dean Rusk had agreed with Aichi because of Japanese sensitivities and because there was a large stockpile of nuclear weapons available in South Korea.[22]

But the reversion agreement failed to incorporate the principle of *hondo nami* ("same as the mainland") in a tangential but important sense. Technically the term referred to denuclearization (*kaku nuki hondo nami*), but it was widely used to mean that the bases on Okinawa should have identical status

Who Won? Prime Minister Satō (left) and President Nixon after the Washington summit on November 21, 1969. Japan agreed to the extension of the bilateral security treaty; the U.S. promised to return Okinawa. (Photo: Mainichi Shinbunsha)

with those on the mainland. The fourth point in the Satō-Nixon communiqué dealt with the Vietnam conflict in explicit terms:

> The president and the prime minister expressed the strong hope that the war in Vietnam would be concluded before return of the administration rights over Okinawa to Japan. In this connection they agreed that, should peace in Vietnam not have been realized by the time reversion of Okinawa is scheduled to take place, the two governments would fully consult with each other in the light of the situation at that time so that reversion would be accomplished without affecting the United States' efforts to assure the South Vietnamese people the opportunity to determine their own political future without outside interference.[23]

Critics of the agreement immediately noted that full consultation at the time of reversion might call for continuing the bombing of Indochina from Okinawa, something that would have been unthinkable from bases in Japan proper. Others complained that Japan had been browbeaten by the American negotiating team when they learned that their government would pay the United States $320 million for facilities to be handed over when reversion occurred.[24]

In agreeing to continue the Japan–United States mutual security treaty, the two governments explicitly acknowledged for the first time that "the security of the Republic of Korea is essential to Japan's own security" and that "the maintenance of peace and security in the Taiwan area is also a most important factor for the security of Japan."[25] Both statements seemed baleful to proponents of closer ties between Tokyo and Beijing. The communiqué also redefined prior consultation to remove the presumption that Japan would use it to veto American actions involving bases in Japan. The *New York Times* quoted Satō the following day: "the security of Japan could not be adequately maintained without international peace and security in the Far East."[26] The Americans were happy with

the Satō-Nixon agreement because it established a common defense interest in the Far East between Japan and the United States, implying what Undersecretary Johnson's testimony to Congress two months later made explicit: the purpose of the treaty was now not at all to protect Japan but entirely to assure the stability of the region.[27] Although Nakasone Yasuhiro, the director-general of the self-defense agency, had suggested a month before the summit that the security treaty be replaced by 1975, Satō and Aichi preferred to retain the military alliance as the cornerstone of their foreign policy. Some of the Cold War assumptions on which it was based continued to guide Nakasone's diplomacy while he served as prime minister in the mid-1980s.[28]

In the wake of President Nixon's announcement at Guam the previous summer that the United States would play a more selective role in Asia, the November communiqué reassured the smaller states in the area that America expected to continue its military presence. The agreement also said that Japan would contribute to the economic rehabilitation of Indochina once peace returned, in line with Washington's long-term goal of having the Japanese take over some of its responsibilities in Asia. Satō reinforced this commitment, which he had voiced at various times since taking office in 1964, during a long speech to the National Press Club on November 21. He not only talked of a "new order" in the Pacific under Japanese and American leadership but also said his country could be expected to follow "a more independent" policy on defense.[29] The People's Republic of China attacked the reversion agreement as "an utter swindle," and the next April Zhou Enlai, the Chinese premier, and Kim Il-sung, the prime minister of North Korea, jointly warned that "Japanese militarism is vainly trying to realize its old dream of a 'Greater East Asia Co-prosperity Sphere' and has openly embarked on the road of aggression against the people of Asia."[30] In fact not until Tanaka Kakuei took over as prime minister in July 1972 did Japan try to put Satō's ideas about a more forthright policy in Southeast Asia into practice.

To obtain a nuclear-free Okinawa and an uninterrupted se-

curity treaty, Satō was willing to acknowledge the regional scope of the military alliance, pay $320 million for American facilities on Okinawa, and agree to an aid program for Southeast Asia that big business in Japan wholeheartedly applauded. He accepted the Guam doctorine but also left the United States a small escape from the *hondo nami* principle, should the Vietnam War still be going on and the bases still be needed when the Ryūkyūs were restored in 1972.

The prime minister made one more concession that cost his more than all the rest: he secretly agreed to restrain Japan's flourishing exports of synthetic fibers to the United States, because the Nixon cabinet was under pressure from American textile manufacturers to cut foreign competition. When it turned out he could not deliver on this promise, the two allies sank into a dismal dispute that ended only when the Americans strong-armed Satō embarrassingly in late 1971—a Pyrrhic victory, Richard J. Barnet has pointed out, because Japanese textiles soon grew too expensive for almost any market except their own domestic consumers.[31]

Without knowing about the secret arrangement, the Japan Socialist party thought Satō had already paid too high a price for Okinawa, whose reversion the JSP called "the first step toward realizing the long-held dreams of the Japanese." The socialists expressed fears that the Vietnam conflict would delay reversion beyond 1972 and that their government would take the United States at its word about removing nuclear weapons, without actually verifying that they were gone.[32] The communists blasted the communiqué for tying Japan's security to South Korea, Taiwan, and South Vietnam. They agreed that the public was anxious about whether the government would insist on removing nuclear arms and forbidding direct combat operations from bases in Japan, including Okinawa.[33] Both Kōmeitō and the Democratic Socialist party welcomed the reversion agreement but said the status of nuclear weapons on the islands would need to be clarified.[34]

The public at large was delighted at the prospect of regaining Okinawa and thought the result had been well worth the cost. Satō immediately set a general election for December 27,

203

1969, and when the LDP scored a huge gain of thirty-two seats in the House of Representatives he crowed that the outcome was a ringing endorsement of the treaty. By then a majority of voters favored keeping the treaty, according to opinion surveys, even though many skeptics still worried that it might involve Japan in an unwanted war.[35] Still, the main reason for the LDP's success was undoubtedly the agreement on Okinawa.

Nonetheless, the election results were far from a mandate for the domestic or foreign policies of the conservatives. The rate of voter participation was the second lowest since 1945, a sign of indifference toward politics rather than enthusiasm for the treaty or the LDP. The party actually slipped from 48.8 to 47.6 percent of the popular vote compared with the previous election; only a disastrous showing by the polarized JSP allowed the Liberal Democrats to snap up so many additional seats. Referring to the clever timing of the election and the massive publicity given to Okinawa, Mutō Ichiyō dismissed the outcome as a "victory of political tactics," not a landslide for the conservatives.[36] Yet even if the reversion agreement did not quite generate a stampede in favor of the LDP, at least it resolved the Okinawa dilemma and allowed most citizens to put the issue behind them. The vast majority faced the new year with refurbished pride in their nation and fresh confidence in the prime minister. They even expressed somewhat greater favor of the United States: the proportion who liked America rose 3 percent in 1969 and 2 percent in 1970 compared with 1968, and the proportion showing dislike for American fell 3 percent in both years.[37] Most significantly, the voting handed Satō an ample majority in the lower house and reduced the chances of a serious challenge to either his Vietnam or treaty policies.

THE ENIGMA OF JUNE 1970

As Japan entered the new year nearly everyone agreed there would be no crisis over the security treaty in 1970. Both the Old and New Left conceded that the momentum against the

treaty, the war, and the terms of Okinawan reversion had been dissipated in the chaotic street fighting and the disconnected efforts of various antiwar groups the previous autumn. But the protest movement was far from hushed during the early months of 1970. Tsurumi Yoshiyuki unceasingly reminded his readers, "the Vietnam War is not a fire across a distant shore; it is a war that necessarily affects all Japanese in one way or another."[38]

The base workers' union in Okinawa, Zengunrō, certainly agreed: it led 35,000 employees out on strike for five days in January to support two large groups of workers who had just been dismissed as well as to protest the possible use of bases to continue the fighting in Southeast Asia after reversion. On April 28, 1970, Hansen and the New Left sects fought with riot police while the JSP and JCP held a combined rally in Yoyogi Park on what was labeled the "first annual Okinawa humiliation day." Although the organizers were upset about the terms of the reversion agreement, the goals of the demonstration were murky and the event turned out to be even more disorganized, and the radicals even more obstreperous, than during the Okinawa Day fiasco the year before.[39]

As elsewhere, the news of the American invasion and bombardment of Cambodia at the end of April instantly revived people's anxieties and reignited support for the antiwar movement in Japan. The press raised a huge cry, and even Satō reverted to language he had not used for the past three years: he gamely defined the American operation as "an unavoidable action" while loudly calling for bombing halts, further troop reductions, and more vigorous peace talks. Most citizens were shocked by this most recent expansion of a war they thought was fading away. A survey taken by the United States Information Agency in June 1970 found that among nine countries around the world, Japan tied Sweden for the highest percentage of residents whose confidence in America was diminished by the invasion (58 percent, versus 3 percent whose confidence was increased).[40] Just as Cambodia was the last straw to thousands of Americans who deluged their representatives in Congress during May of that year, the attack undoubtedly helped

to swell the crowds who turned out for the daily demonstrations sponsored by Beheiren and other civic groups during the June Action of 1970.

"A *demo* a day" was the motto of the protests that month against the treaty and the war. At first the gatherings at Shimizudani Park consisted of 150 or 200 persons, who usually marched afterward through Akasaka and Toranomon to Shinbashi. By the middle of the month demonstrators had grown to 3–4,000 each day at Beheiren meetings, and other groups held sporadic protests elsewhere in Tokyo and other cities as well. Oda and the June Action committee sponsored a large joint rally with the anti-JCP students and Hansen on June 14 at Yoyogi Park to denounce Satō's foreign policy, to mark the tenth anniversary of Kanba Michiko's death, and to revive the spirit of peaceful cooperation from the New Left rally of June 15, 1969. The police estimated that 35,000 people appeared for the event; Beheiren put the figure at 72,000, larger than any of its previous meetings.[41]

Once again the joint demonstration was peaceful, partly because the riot police rounded up more than a hundred radicals belonging to the Marx-Lenin faction of Zengakuren who stormed past Harajuku station brandishing Molotov cocktails just before the rally began. But the main reason the assembly was calm was that violent tactics were in complete disrepute after the disasters of October and November 1969. Instead, *Asahi jānaru* detected "a certain sense of liberation and new youthful energy spreadings its wings" among the crowd at Yoyogi, as though the New Left had learned to accept the security treaty and decided to allow each individual to choose the best way to resist its untoward consequences, such as entanglement in Vietnam.[42] Ōe Kenzaburō, the young novelist and Beheiren member, was more pessimistic. Writing a few days later in *Mainichi*, he lamented that despite huge protests like the one on June 14, "the power of the state is predominant" through the greater precision and sophistication of the riot police compared with five or ten years earlier.[43]

The greatest single set of political demonstrations since Ja-

pan regained autonomy in 1952 took place on June 23, 1970, the date when the security treaty was automatically extended. At first glance this was an improbable occasion for a turnout that police estimated at 774,000 nationwide and *Mainichi* put a 1.5 million—well above the official one-day peak of 555,000 in June 1960.[44] A huge protest seemed unlikely because there was no *crise de système* within the Japanese polity in June 1970. Unlike the battles over the security issue ten years earlier, there was no threat to the survival of the Satō cabinet, let alone to the parliamentary process. In contrast to their predecessors in 1960, radicals shared little consciousness of reordering the political system, only an ill-defined frustration with established forms of power and a strong alienation from organized politics. Whereas Kishi had flaunted his arrogance and abused democratic procedures in ramming the treaty through the Diet, Satō wisely stayed out of sight and quietly persuaded the United States to continue the alliance unchanged. This allowed the treaty to renew itself automatically, as provided for in the 1960 agreement, without any need for parliamentary debate. Satō insured that the opposition would have no forum for catcalls by winding up the special postelection session of the Diet by mid-May. He also soothed the anti-Americanism of people living near military bases by increasing the government's payments to impacted areas by 31 percent in the budget for fiscal year 1970.[45]

Another reason why June 1970 seemed inauspicious for a huge protest movement had to do with how the public perceived its relationship with the outside world. Japan was much more prosperous and comfortable in 1970 than ten years before; per capita income had tripled in the interval, far surpassing Prime Minister Ikeda's dreams when he took office in 1960. Satō appealed to citizens' pride by talking vaguely of a more "self-reliant" defense within the treaty system. Most people were convinced that the military alliance with the United States had paid off: it had saved the country billions of dollars in defense spending and had not dragged Japan into war with its neighbors, despite the grim fears aroused by the

Vietnam War. Even though Japanese of various backgrounds had a more realistic (and less laudatory) impression of the United States by 1970 compared with five years earlier, the most irritating frictions in the relationship had apparently been eased by the promised reversion of Okinawa, the return of a number of military bases in Japan, and the election of a new American president with plans for ending the war. Popular feelings about the United States were undoubtedly more complicated, ambivalent, and diverse among different social strata than before the conflict in Indochina, but people generally seemed persuaded that continuing the treaty was a better idea than any other option for Japan's foreign relations. Still, their uncertainty showed in an *Asahi* poll conducted on June 4–5, 1970. Only 51 percent could say definitely whether the pact was contributing to the safety of Japan (37 percent said yes and 14 percent no).[46] This suggested that even if the public at large harbored misgivings about the treaty, only a small minority would actively oppose its renewal. The vast majority were fundamentally conservative and reasonably satisfied with LDP rule.

A blowup over the treaty in June 1970 also seemed doubtful because of the near-collapse of the radical student movement by the end of 1969. Not only had the public grown impatient to the point of exhaustion with the young activists, but the universities control bill of August 1969 had also made administrators far more bold about calling the police in to put down disturbances on their campuses. As a result, many of the Zengakuren sects lost their home bases, and a hard core of about 700 radicals was still in jail while the June Action of 1970 was under way.[47] The anti-JCP factions and the Zenkyōtō councils were riven with internal battles over future agenda, now that October-November protests against Okinawa, Vietnam, and the treaty had failed. Their quondam allies among the New Left civic movements had lost all sympathy for the ceaseless violence that marred radical demonstrations, and the Narita airport problem as well as environmental and consumer issues

were sapping the resistance to Satō's foreign policy by mid-1970.

Even the Old Left approached the extension of the treaty far less vigorously than might have been expected a few years earlier. The communists made big gains in the December 1969 election by turning themselves into a fully indigenous party, putting the Sino-Soviet quarrel aside but also admitting that the security pact was a long-term issue that could not be solved in June 1970. The JSP had blundered in the election campaign by overemphasizing foreign policy to the point where inner divisions within the party came to light. When the returns were in the party knew at once that it could not hope to topple the military alliance the following summer. Sōhyō's membership had leveled off in the mid-sixties and fallen steadily thereafter, challenged by Dōmei and smaller labor federations that were concerned mainly with economic issues. The union movement as a whole began to lose ground after 1968, as workers sought out alternative associations and adopted middle-class habits that vitiated their solidarity with organized labor. Before the treaty question resurfaced, the writer Minaguchi Kōzō asked rather plaintively: "in the so-called Shōwa Genroku [flush times] of Japan today, with its my-homeism and leisure boom, is there enough energy to sustain the struggle in 1970?"[48] Evidently the chairman of Sōhyō, Horii Toshikatsu, knew there was not: a week before the climactic demonstrations set for June 23, he flew off to an antipollution conference in the United States.[49]

Most huge rallies earlier in the Vietnam War had drawn their numerical strength mainly from labor and the opposition parties, but this time the Old Left botched its feeble efforts at joining forces and ended up staging an uncoordinated series of events. In contrast with the 2 million workers who struck on October 21, 1966 against the Vietnam War as well as for economic reasons, Sōhyō managed to get just 350,000 of is members to walk out for an hour or two on June 23, 1970. The police estimated that another 202,000 persons attended joint meetings held around the country by Sōhyō and the JSP.[50] The

CHAPTER 7

transport workers in Dōrō and Kokurō, normally among the
most active unions, confined their protests to refusing to touch
American military cargoes. Because the JSP no longer offered
"expense" money to laborers to attend political demonstrations, many of them did not bother to come. Those who did
saw a rallier who bowed to changing times by carrying a placard that read, "the security treaty brings pollution with it."[51]
The general impression left by the Old Left meetings on June
23 was that there was far less frustration and disillusionment
than in 1960 because the protesters' expectations of success on
the treaty question were lower and because there were still
many other pressing issues, including the environment, to be
faced in the future.[52]

Yet paradoxically June 23 produced the most massive outpouring of demonstrators of the entire era. The bulk of the rallies throughout the country were organized by Beheiren via
the June Action committee, including the largest meeting ever
held at Shimizudani Park. *Yomiuri* reported that the 6 P.M.
gathering "greatly exceeded police forecasts,"[53] with 5,000
people packed into the small park and another 15,000 spilling
into the streets nearby. Oda and the other organizers cut the
meeting off early so that the throng could begin its long
march, spearheaded by a women's federation, to Yaesu and
Ōtemachi by nightfall. What made the day different from all
other protests in the antiwar and antitreaty movements was
that hundreds of thousands of ordinary people unaffiliated
with any party, union, or civic group showed up at one or another of the 150 events sponsored by the Old and New Left.
This surprising turnout seemed to bear out Oda's predictions
a year earlier about a whirlpool of humanity to protest Satō's
diplomacy. Even some of the demonstrators from the 1960
imbroglio were drawn into the swirl, taking to the streets to
oppose the treaty again even though they were much less
drawn to Marxism or to the existing opposition parties than a
decade earlier.[54]

Most of those who appeared on June 23, *Yomiuri* concluded,
"were 'citizens against the security treaty' who did not show

210

the sense of pathos or frustration evident in the 1960 treaty demonstrations."[55] Many were there out of simple conviction that the treaty was ill-advised, that the conditions for regaining Okinawa were unfavorable, or that the recent reescalations in Vietnam were wrong. At the same time, the protests were less focused on overt policy matters that in 1960, since the nation had lived with the issues themselves for a long time, and they were correspondingly more affected by a new mood of generalized resistance to the establishment found most notably in the citizens' and consumers' movements of the late sixties. In this sense Beheiren was a transitional phenomenon between the established opposition parties, ban-the-bomb groups, and labor organizations of the Old Left and the citizens' movements of the late sixties and early seventies. Its loose leadership style and lack of structural frippery foreshadowed the civic organizations arising shortly after the antiwar movement began, yet in focusing on international political questions Beheiren still resembled the opposition parties and unions. June 23 suggested the conversion in both the style and the substance of Japanese protests that was confirmed in the early seventies when civic issues and local movements displaced overtly political demonstrations as the dominant agenda.

The giant deluge of ralliers on June 23 was overwhelmingly peaceful, but the riot police still arrested 501 persons in Tokyo alone. Hansen and the Zenkyōtō councils drew more than 30,000 young people at Meiji Park, including many wearing helmets. Afterward some of them joined radicals from the anti-JCP sects armed with timbers and metal pipes to battle the police. The Kakumaru faction held a separate demonstration attended by nearly 3,000 protesters. Violent students threw Molotov cocktails and rocks at police booths around town, and a crowd of about 5,000 took over venerable Shinbashi station after the last train of the evening had departed and spent the night roaming the streets of Ginza. Yet despite their attacks on the police, there was little indiscriminate property damage or even simple vandalism (at the height of the 1968–1969 violence there was surprisingly little random destruction of prop-

211

erty). June 23 was a last spree for the violent radicals in the capital; their battles after that date were usually more localized and aimed at more specific targets.[56]

The events of June 1970 showed that most citizens had learned to accept, if not positively support, the security treaty which bound their country to an American foreign policy that was only beginning to shed its Cold War outlook, thanks in part to the lessons of Vietnam. The lack of a crisis mentality, Satō's adept leadership, the public's greater realism about the value of the relationship with the United States, and the disarray of the opposition forces all helped Japan avert an upheaval when the treaty came up for renewal. But the mammoth demonstrations clearly indicated that a large number of people were still very concerned about war. They were anxious about whether Okinawa after reversion would still be used as a nuclear arsenal and launch pad for bombing Vietnam and whether the treaty would continue to keep them out of war.

An *Asahi* survey published the morning of the biggest demonstrations revealed that only 13 percent of the public favored allowing the Americans to use bases in Japan for combat in South Korea if war should break out there, whereas 54 percent opposed the idea.[57] This report spotlighted the contradictions in public attitudes on defense, inasmuch as the only purpose of the treaty after the Satō–Nixon summit in November 1969 was to permit precisely this sort of military operation. Yet the diplomatic menu after June 1970 quickly shifted away from security matters to troublesome questions of trade with the United States, recognition of the People's Republic of China, and development assistance to Southeast Asia. Moreover, now that the tide of public protests had peaked, the latter part of the Vietnam era produced an even greater diversity of activity by the Japanese antiwar movement.

CHAPTER 8

Preparing for the
Post-Vietnam Era

"THE antiwar movement tapered off just about the same time in Japan as in the United States, give or take a few months,"[1] according to Oda Makoto, but not entirely for the same reasons. The acme of the American campaign against the war came in May 1970 after the invasion of Cambodia; Japan reached the pinnacle of dissent a month later in the mammoth nationwide demonstrations of June 23. Then war weariness and public ennui began to spread in each country, dissipating the vitality of the broad antiwar movement and clearing the track for a handful of radicals to commit even greater violence than before. Once the furor over Cambodia receded, the Japanese and American people both seemed satisfied that United States ground forces were steadily withdrawing and that diplomats would somehow devise what President Nixon called "peace with honor."

The antiwar effort in Japan went limp after 1970 for reasons that "were not Japanese but global," according to Ishida Takeshi. "The movement depended on the mass media to make people aware of the war. When the media stopped reporting the war and turned to other issues, the protests grew smaller."[2] Several domestic factors were also at work: 1) the Left felt let down after the security treaty was automatically renewed in June 1970; 2) activists began to fragment their energies into antipollution, antibureaucratic, proconsumer, and anarchist campaigns; 3) trade relations with the United States soured and ties with China became a source of agonizing debate, especially after the Nixon shocks of mid-1971; 4) the nation was both proud and relieved when Okinawa reverted on May 15,

213

1972; and 5) Prime Minister Satō left office in July 1972, removing the most visible target for anyone who opposed the government's Vietnam policies. Even though the antiwar and citizens' movements came together at Sagamihara for one last outcry against the Vietnam conflict in late 1972, it was clear by then that the endless war had outlasted almost all active opposition to it by a public that had become perplexed, exhausted, and numbed into near silence. By the time a complete American withdrawal was negotiated at Paris in January 1973, the blaze of dissent in Japan had subsided to little more than scattered sparks.

A PATCHWORK OF PROTESTS

The day after the security treaty was extended on June 23, 1970, Japan broke off textile negotiations with the United States, a fitting sign that economic issues had replaced war and defense as the main irritations between the two allies in the 1970s. The Japanese refused to bow to requests for self-regulation in exporting their fabrics and garments to the United States, a cause for pride among the press and public because their country had at last told the Americans no. Within fifteen months the outlook changed to humiliation and bitterness when Washington forced Japan to accept a distasteful settlement, driving America still lower in the opinion polls taken in Japan.[3]

While the cabinet and foreign ministry were immersed in economic diplomacy, the antiwar movement continued to find new channels for agitating against American policy in Indochina and the Japanese government's support for it. Shimada Seisaku, a young progressive without party affiliation, was elected on an antibase, anti-Vietnam War platform to the Tachikawa municipal council on June 28, the second antiwar candidate to be seated in the city where the Sunagawa struggle had raged for fifteen years. Even in local races in areas near American military installations, such instances were rare during the war, which is why Shimada's victory was heartening

to protesters who felt crestfallen after the fight against the treaty ended in failure.[4] The Old and New Left rebounded by October 21, 1970, to stage a very large and uncommonly peaceful international antiwar day, with meetings at 530 places throughout the country attended by more than a million people. The goals of antiwar day were to aid the peoples of Indochina, resist the security treaty system, and upset the terms of Okinawan reversion—familiar aims expressed with much greater calm than previously. Both the JCP and the JSP called for repealing the treaty and establishing democratic government, whereas Beheiren and other groups without party ties hammered away at the Okinawa agreement and its links to the Vietnam War.[5]

Protests on university campuses all but evaporated by the end of the year, leaving a stagnant pool of radicals who soon adopted causes that were only remotely connected with the controversial foreign policy questions of a year or two before. By 1971 the campus chapters of Beheiren had shrunk to "a youth movement on a limited scale," according to Muro Kenji, a former member, who called them "a cell of radical students who don't know where to go."[6] The young activists who had formed Zenkyōtō councils to evade the factionalism of the anti-JCP Zengakuren found themselves without venue or support when the campus disputes virtually came to a halt in 1970. The national federation of Zenkyōtō organizations limped along until June 1971, when it was destroyed by internal bickering. This left the field of radical activism to Hansen and the anti-JCP sects, who moved off campus and abandoned all pretense of antiwar idealism in favor of violence against the police. In 1971 nearly 1,500 officers were hurt in battles with extremists, almost double the number in 1970. Much of the carnage took place at Narita airport, where three police officers were ambushed and murdered in September 1971. Two others were killed in separate clashes with radicals that year and forty-nine were seriously injured—a toll even more severe than during the antiwar protests of 1967–1969 at their bloodiest.[7]

The Narita demonstrations began with protests by local farmers against land condemnation in 1967 and have continued sporadically ever since. The anti-JCP factions joined the farmers in early 1968, equating their struggle against bureaucratism and official indifference with the efforts of the Viet Cong to achieve liberation. The main issues propelling the Narita conflict were domestic, but starting in February 1968 Hansen and the Chūkaku faction of Zengakuren shrilly insisted that the new airport would be an instrument of the war in Vietnam. Iwadare Hiroshi summarized their outlook: "even though they say Narita airport will be a civilian airport, we can't trust them. It certainly will become a military airport. . . . The reason Haneda has become full is that planes used for aggression in Vietnam have muscled their way in. Narita airport will increase this still more."[8] With air bases closing in Fuchū and Tachikawa midway through the war, the radicals' assumption that Narita might become a military transshipment center was not farfetched, even though the Japanese government probably considered such a "use for the airport as a remote contingency at best."[9] The battle over the new airport dragged on for twelve years; even though the facility was largely ready by 1972, it finally opened on May 20, 1978, after eleven previous attempts to put it into service had failed because of strife between protesters and the riot police.[10]

Another splinter from the radical student movement was a terrorist band known as the United Red Army (Rengō Sekigunha), which was formed on July 15, 1971 through a merger of the Red Army faction and an anarchist group called Keihin Anpo Kyōtō. The Red Army, which was evidently unconnected with any overseas organization, first attracted wide attention in March 1970 when it hijacked a Japan Air Lines plane to Seoul and Pyongyang, while the Keihin Anpo Kyōtō was noted for breaking into gun shops, raiding police boxes, and tossing Molotov cocktails onto United States bases. Up to February 1972, according to the Tokyo metropolitan police, the newly combined group was responsible for 132 shootings and explosions. Then, in a televised standoff that gripped the

nation's attention for ten days starting on February 19, the United Red Army held police at bay from a fortress on the slopes of Mt. Asama near the posh summer resort of Karui-zawa. Officers finally shot their way into the enclave, ending the holdout and driving the tatters of the faction underground in Japan or into exile abroad. Three terrorists affiliated with the United Red Army later took part in the Lod airport massacre in Israel on May 30, 1972, in which twenty-six persons—many of them pilgrims from Puerto Rico—were killed and seventy-two others injured.[11] Except for firebombing American bases in Japan, there was nothing to tie the United Red Army to the movement against the Vietnam War.

The radicals at Narita and Asama were aberrations of the political ferment that boiled over in the late sixties, but the citizens' movements that grew up off campus at the same time came into fullest flower in the early 1970s. Whereas the antiwar effort coordinated by Beheiren was national in scope and international in aims, the citizens' campaigns were usually local in membership, and they increasingly focused on precise issues affecting specific groups of people. Specialists disagree about whether neighborhood lobbying by residents of apartment projects or other defined city districts about sewers, playgrounds, and day care qualifies as a citizens' movement, and some of them also distinguish consumer campaigns by organizations of housewives against high prices, hoarding, and false advertising from the broader citizens' efforts against pollution, urban nuisances, nuclear power plants, immigration restrictions, and abuses of civil rights. Certain citizens' activities were overtly antiwar in the 1960s, but their chief point of contact with Beheiren was style rather than ideology.

The civic groups were grass-roots in their makeup, consciously rejecting the top-heavy structure and discipline of the Old Left. They were unaffiliated with any existing party and prided themselves on the spirit of voluntarism, something that was rarely found in Japanese social movements before the sixties. Most citizens' organizations were led by adults who had regular occupations and family responsibilities, in sharp con-

217

trast to the youth protests based at the universities. Beheiren often cooperated with the civic movements but stressed that the antiwar campaign had "no official ideology" and that its membership included workers, students, and others who did not usually join in citizens' rallies on other issues.[12] Although Beheiren provided a decentralized model of organizational spontaneity and democratic participation, the true parallel for the civic units was the citizens' movements of the sixties in Western Europe. Ishida Takeshi, a leading expert on Beheiren and the civic groups, says, "I am rather pessimistic about citizens' movements since the late seventies compared with Germany where the energy of the late sixties continues even today. The antinuclear movement too is stronger in Germany and in Europe than it is in Japan today. One reason is that the antinuclear issue is not new in Japan"—where the factional rivalry among ban-the-bomb groups has long been a scourge.[13]

Oda Makoto and the other antiwar leaders continued their crusade against the war after the catharsis of June 1970, drawing more than 30,000 persons to their rallies around the country on international antiwar day the next October and continuing their monthly meetings outside commuter stations in the biggest cities. At the same time, Tsurumi Yoshiyuki called for diversifying the movement still further, refining its efforts into a multiplicity of actions—a process he called *saibunka* (breaking into small parts).[14] Beheiren members began setting up antiwar coffeehouses outside United States military bases at Misawa, Yokosuka, Iwakuni, and Itazuke. They also sponsored rock concerts, kite-flying festivals, and other entertainments nearby to denounce the war, but apparently the Japanese antiwar leaders had only indirect contact with the peace movement among troops on the bases. By late 1970 Beheiren also lent its support to farmers who protested outside the Self-Defense Force firing range at Kitafuji, chanting, "don't connect Mt. Fuji with Vietnam!"[15]

A number of antiwar protesters the following spring began to adopt the American tactic of purchasing single shares of stock in companies that manufactured arms so they could hec-

kle management at annual meetings and place questions on stockholder ballots. The favorite target was Tōjō Teruo, son of the wartime prime minister and head of the Mitsubishi aircraft plant at Nagoya. About 250 single-shareholders from Beheiren attended the annual meeting of Mitsubishi Heavy Industries on May 28, 1971, at Hibiya public hall, wearing death masks emblazoned with the warning symbol for radioactivity—three diamonds in a pattern like the Mitsubishi corporate symbol. When they started shouting "death to the merchants of death," thugs hired by management roughed up the demonstrators and squelched their protest. Big business paid out $27 million to 3,000 of these enforcers (*sōkaiya*) in 1971 alone to preserve order at meetings held by some of the biggest polluters as well as profiteers from the Vietnam War.[16]

The main object of antiwar resistance that spring was the reversion agreement under which Okinawa would be returned to Japan in May 1972. Local resentment spilled over after a United States military court found an allegedly intoxicated American soldier not guilty of negligent driving when his car struck and killed an Okinawan woman in Naha on September 18, 1970. When the verdict was announced on December 20, about 5,000 residents burned cars and an American elementary school at Koza, Okinawa.[17] April 28, 1971 was Okinawa Day in Tokyo and became the last raucous demonstration by the Zenkyōtō radicals before their national federation collapsed the following June. A week later Beheiren gathered roughly 2,000 demonstrators for an antiwar rally that also opposed the terms of reversion, held on May 5 near Yokota air base. The crowd set off fireworks and also flew aluminum-foil kites to interfere with the American planes. Zengunrō led a twenty-four-hour strike involving 75,000 Okinawan teachers and base workers on May 19 to demand the withdrawal of United States troops and nuclear weapons before reversion was completed a year hence.[18]

Hirose Michisada, head of the *Asahi* bureau in Naha, observed that in mid-1971 Okinawans almost uniformly welcomed reunification with Japan but were anxious because 1)

"MERCHANTS OF DEATH"
Beheiren demonstrators wearing death masks outside
the annual stockholders' meeting of Mitsubishi
Heavy Industries, Japan's largest defense
contractor, at Hibiya public hall, Tokyo, on
May 28, 1971. (Photo: Mainichi Shinbunsha)

the military character of their islands would not change, perpetuating their dependence on the United States forces as well as prolonging the possibility that Vietnam would be attacked from Kadena once again; 2) no one could be sure that nuclear arms would be removed; 3) Okinawan claims against the United States for losses of life and property before reversion were explicitly waived; and 4) Tokyo might not assist the Ryūkyūan economy sufficiently once wartime procurement from the Indochina conflict ended.[19] Most of these concerns were shared by the protesters on the mainland who carried out a spate of demonstrations on June 17, 1971, the day the agreement was signed by the two governments. About 90,000 persons rallied against the reversion treaty throughout Japan and Okinawa, including terrorists in Meiji Park who threw a bomb directly at riot police, injuring thirty-seven. Under the agreement, the United States returned thirty-four military installations but retained eighty-eight others, including all the important ones except Naha airport. Ten days later the LDP scraped through the national election for the House of Councillors with a loss of just five seats, no threat to its majority. The reversion treaty was forcibly ratified by the House of Representatives on November 24, 1971, but leftist opposition to the agreement continued right up to the final restoration of Okinawa to Japanese authority the following spring.[20]

THE NIXON SHOCKS AND THE FALL OF SATŌ

Prime Minister Satō met with President Nixon at the end of October 1970 to iron out details of Okinawa's reversion and to discuss Japanese aid to the Saigon regime. At the same moment a top Japanese diplomat was making a series of secret trips to Hanoi to hold conversations that eventually led to recognition of the DRV after the Paris agreements of January 1973. But the top agenda between Japan and the United States involved trade restrictions, not Vietnam or the status of Okinawa under the security treaty, and by the time of the Nixon-Satō summit each country was determined not to be outwres-

tled by the other in the acrimonious textile dispute that had begun to overshadow all other issues between the allies. Then a series of jolts delivered by the president during the second half of 1971 concerning policies toward China, the international monetary system, and bilateral trade protectionism stunned the Japanese government and embarrassed Satō so greatly that he eventually lost control over his party and decided to resign as prime minister in July 1972.

Satō promised a "forward-looking posture" toward aid to the Government of Vietnam at the October 1970 summit, and shortly after he returned to Japan he proposed an assistance package of $140 million to the noncommunist regimes in South Vietnam, Cambodia, and Laos. Yet Tokyo had no intention of abandoning its small but important trading connections with Hanoi. During his unpublicized talks with leaders of the DRV, Miyake Wasuke of the foreign ministry recalls, "I repeatedly impressed on Hanoi the Japanese government's view that the war should end through negotiations, which were then taking place in Paris. I told the leaders in Hanoi that Japan would extend its economic cooperation after the war. After the unification of Vietnam in 1975, Japan had a great deal of contact with Hanoi concerning economic cooperation, but the peace talks themselves were concluded in Paris, and it's difficult to say that Japan had a direct role in achieving peace."[21]

While the textile negotiations remained stymied, Nixon suddenly shocked Japan and the world by announcing on July 15, 1971 that he would shortly visit China. Once again Satō was caught by complete surprise, and he was also acutely chagrined after years of tenaciously supporting Taiwan and refusing to recognize the PRC. The president's trip undermined one of the main premises of American intervention in Vietnam (that Hanoi was a proxy for Chinese expansion) and severely damaged the basic principles on which Japanese foreign policy, at John Foster Dulles's insistence, had been grounded since 1952. Nixon's new opening to China also appeared to remove Taiwan from the scope of the Japan–United States se-

curity treaty, effectively reducing the pact to an elaborate set of bases for the defense of South Korea. The Park government in Seoul was even more shocked than the Japanese by Nixon's announcement, especially because the United States had decided unilaterally in March 1970 to withdraw a division of American troops from South Korea despite Park's faithful support of the war in Vietnam. Conservatives in Japan were especially taken aback by détente with China and began to consider Washington an unreliable ally; from this point on some of them took perverse satisfaction in the success of Hanoi and the Viet Cong, believing that the communists were teaching the United States some humility after it had treated Japan and other allies in a very cavalier fashion.[22]

The astounding disclosure of Nixon's trip to China irritated the Japanese mainly because of the abrupt way it was revealed, not because they opposed rapprochement with China. The second Nixon shock, by contrast, was dismaying to many of them in both form and substance. On August 15, 1971, the president imposed a 10 percent surcharge on imports, abandoned the Bretton Woods monetary system that had been in effect since 1944, and forced an upward revaluation of the yen that eventually stabilized at ¥308 to the dollar, a 16.88 percent increase. The United States took these steps to defend the dollar against inflation and to make American products more competitive abroad. It was probably unavoidable that such stiff medicine was administered suddenly, but once again the Japanese were miffed at not being consulted in advance. Even more importantly, they were dissatisfied with the effects these measures seemed likely to have on Japanese exports. In the short run the American tactics helped to shore up the dollar; in the long run they helped erode the assumptions of trust and reliability that Japanese, perhaps naively, had long embraced in their relations with the United States.[23]

Another facet of what the economist Gary R. Saxonhouse has called "the Great American Economic Offensive against Japan" was the forced settlement of the synthetic textile dispute on October 15, 1971. As with the dollar-defense strategy,

Japan was clearly the main target of the import restraints imposed by the United States on that date. Many people in Japan reacted bitterly to Washington's strong-arm methods, which may have resulted from President Nixon's and Secretary of State Henry Kissinger's scorn for *seikei bunri*.[24] The lesson of 1971 was that the United States would act out of political as well as economic self-interest, whereas the Japanese were nearly blind to the political dynamics of the textile issue. Nixon faced protectionist pressures at home and much sentiment in the Congress that Japan should play a greater political and defense role to accompany its new economic importance. Because the textile row involved such modest stakes for its economy, the United States was obviously unwise to choose so petty an issue to make an important point about Japan's place in the world of economic superpowers. Incensed at America's patronizing stubbornness, most Japanese took the China shock, the dollar-defense package, and the textile settlement as national affronts to Japan rather than as an overdue rearrangement of economic and diplomatic relations in the Asian and Pacific region.[25]

Prime Minister Satō reacted with characteristic placidness to the textile wrangle, partly because he knew the public anger at America's bullying would soon subside and partly because the final timetable for regaining Okinawa was still under discussion. But he was reportedly furious because of the shame he suffered over the question of seating Beijing rather than Taipei at the United Nations. Fujiyama Aiichirō, a leader of the Asian-African group within the Liberal Democratic Party and a former foreign minister, had taunted Satō for more than a year on the China issue: "our foreign ministry," he said, "is just following the Washington line."[26] Japan continued to support the American position that the Chinese seat was an important question when the new United Nations session took up the matter in September 1971; late the next month, while China's representation was under debate and Japan was laboring to retain membership for Taipei, Satō was angered to learn

that Kissinger was in Beijing preparing for President Nixon's visit the following February.[27]

Four days after the textile settlement brought a shuddering finale to the shocks administered by the United States in 1971, the Chūkaku faction of Zengakuren mobilized 6,000 demonstrators in Hibiya Park on October 19 against the impending ratification of the Okinawa reversion agreement. Fights broke out among subfactions at the meeting, and someone set fire to the famous Matsumoto-rō restaurant in the park. The fifth international antiwar day on October 21 was similarly ripped by violence, partly because most of the ordinary citizens who had made the previous year's event so tranquil stayed away. Various extreme groups from the New Left cited Okinawa as the pretext for their demonstrations but used the occasion for an orgy of bombings, car burnings, and battles with the riot police, who arrested 453 of the activists. The terrorism recurred on Christmas Eve 1971 when a pipe bomb exploded at a police box in Shinjuku, injuring twelve police officers and passersby.[28] By then any connection between radical violence and genuine dissent over foreign policy seemed to be irreversibly severed.

Beheiren continued its peaceful protests during 1971–1972, working closely with artists once again to publicize the unfinished war in Vietnam. Jane Fonda brought the antiwar touring show "FTA" from the United States in December 1971, playing to American troops near Yokota with active cooperation from the Tokyo Beheiren. Fonda, who had earlier visited Hanoi, criticized the Japanese antiwar movement for being "too male chauvinist." Yoshikawa Yūichi recalls that "if such criticism had come early in the war, we would have accepted it. But now we rejected it, accusing Fonda of practicing 'American antiwar imperialism' in criticizing Beheiren. When we told her this, she quickly agreed with us." Yoshikawa calls the tendency toward greater autonomy and diminished influence from the American peace campaign "a kind of conversion within ourselves during the war, produced not by theory but by practice."[29] Even if he overstates the separation between the

Japanese and American movements, Yoshikawa is doubtless correct that Beheiren felt much more self-confidence in its choice of tactics and targets than was true when the war first escalated.

The formal reversion of Okinawa on May 15, 1972 was both the climactic moment of Satō's prime ministership and the last chapter of his political career. It was also one of the final milestones for the Japanese antiwar movement because it coincided with Operation Linebacker I, the torrent of aerial firepower unleashed by the United States in response to the Easter offensive by the communists that spring in Vietnam. Once again the newspapers lashed out at President Nixon for prolonging the war and attacked the Saigon government for not agreeing to a reasonable settlement at Paris. By now the Thieu government considered *Asahi*'s editorials "unfriendly" and routinely delayed visa applications, making it hard for the paper to rotate its staff. Maruyama Shizuo, the chief editorialist, privately called the bombing and mining of the north "almost identical to the Nazis' atrocities at Auschwitz."[30] The same group of writers, scholars, and critics who had denounced the war in petitions to Satō in April 1965, led by Ōuchi Hyōe, Ōkōchi Kazuo, Kozai Yoshishige, and Matsumoto Seichō, renewed their appeal on May 10, 1972, in a statement also signed by 130 other cultural leaders. They were heartened by a Tokyo high court ruling that afternoon permitting public employees to wear antiwar badges without violating rules banning political activity on the job. Yet the judges did not defend the practice on constitutional grounds of free expression; instead their extraordinary argument was that wishing for peace in Vietnam was "not a political act" but instead "shows the general opinion of the people and thus does not violate the political neutrality" of the government agency concerned.[31]

The semiannual surveys taken by the Institute of Statistical Research seemed to bear out the court's view, and they also showed that America's popular image had plunged even further from the previous low point in 1968. Largely because of

the Linebacker bombings but also because of war weariness, the proportion of those polled who thought the United States was principally at fault in the war rose to 43 percent in 1972, compared with 36 percent after Tet, Johnson's withdrawal, and the heavy bombardments in 1968.[32] Public events on the day of Okinawa's return seemed to mirror the ambivalence many Japanese felt toward the United States by May 1972: radicals threw incendiary bombs at train cars and Sōhyō encouraged the national railway workers to stage a work-to-rule slowdown on May 15. That evening the Chūkaku faction rallied at Sukiyabashi against the treaty handing back the Ryūkyūs, while thousands of shoppers and officer workers felt proud as they glanced up at the lights on the wall of the Sony building across the street spelling out "Okinawa reverts."[33]

Prime Minister Satō presided over a splashy ceremony the next day at the Budōkan to celebrate the recovery of Okinawa, but the press, the opposition, and some of the factions within the LDP treated the occasion not as a triumph but as the start of a fresh round of problems: Okinawa was poor, the bases there might be needed to defend South Korea as America otherwise pulled back from Asia, and the militarized Ryūkyūs might become a sticking point in normalizing relations with the PRC. Ever since the Nixon announcement of July 15, 1971 that he would visit China, Satō had felt enormous pressure to recognize Beijing. Now that reversion was completed, there was every reason for Japan to modify its relations with Taiwan and the mainland, but Satō's political strength in the Diet and the LDP was too vitiated for him to take on this challenge even if he had been disposed to overhaul his foreign policy. The Nixon shocks, the textile agreement, and the embarrassing debacle over Taiwanese representation at the United Nations all cost the prime minister heavily, both among party leaders and the general public. So did his stubborn refusal to shift course from the policy of high economic growth inherited from Ikeda, in spite of a growing clamor for antipollution measures and social welfare programs at home. By the time of the Budōkan rites the popularity of the Satō cabinet had shrunk to

just 16 percent, the lowest figure for any government since World War II. (When he took office in November 1964 he had the support of 46 percent of the public.)[34] When Satō resigned from the prime ministership on July 6, 1972, he strode into the press room for a farewell interview and made the most Nixonesque statement of his career. Bluntly ordering the print journalists to leave, he shouted, "you only write lies! Get out! I shall speak to the people directly through television."[35] He addressed an almost deserted room.

Tanaka Kakuei, the new prime minister, quickly restored ties with the PRC, softened Japan's attitude toward North Korea, and tried to stabilize relations with the Soviet Union, moves that received the support of big business and enthusiastic approval from the public at large. When Tanaka met President Nixon at Honolulu on August 31, their communiqué did not even mention Taiwan, paving the way for Sino-Japanese normalization on Beijing's terms in an agreement signed by Tanaka and Zhou Enlai on September 29, 1972. Tanaka's diplomacy was a partial repudiation of the Satō-Nixon position in November 1969, which had stressed the defense of Taiwan and South Korea, but the new prime minister's policies paralleled Nixon's own by mid-1972 in many respects. The Japan Socialist Party and Kōmeitō silently cooperated with Tanaka on the China question, while Beijing ceased its shrill talk of revived Japanese militarism the instant Satō left office.[36] Even though Tanaka managed to downplay the security treaty by building a more flexible relationship with the communist states in Asia, the opposition parties were still flabbergasted in the summer of 1972 when the PRC suddenly announced its support for the Japan–United States military alliance and the Self-Defense Forces. Equally importantly, the new cabinet set about healing the rift with Washington over trade by revaluing the yen upward and opening Japan to more foreign capital and manufactures.[37] This whirlwind of changes soon overcame the impasse into which Satō's diplomacy had fallen by mid-1972, but it was also a reminder that the former prime minister's policies had protected Japan's interests remarkably well, given the

assumptions of American diplomacy in the Kennedy-Johnson years.

The last big antiwar campaign of the Vietnam era in Japan began while Tanaka was negotiating with the Chinese in August 1972 and continued until his government bulldozed the protesters into submission through administrative intervention two months later. The issue was the transport of American tanks and armored personnel carriers between the port of Yokohama and an army repair facility at Sagamihara, a distance of thirty-four kilometers. By one estimate as many as 40 percent of M-113 armored personnel carriers damaged in battle were junked early in the Vietnam War, but by 1972 virtually all of them were being shipped to Sagamihara or a facility in Taiwan for repair, as were a number of M-48 tanks.[38] On August 5 some local units of the JSP and JCP blocked the passage of five tanks at Murasame bridge in Yokohama for nearly two days to protest the war. Supported by the leftist mayor of the city and several thousand local residents, the antiwar leaders later tried to stall several convoys of tanks and APC's under the slogan "don't connect route 16 with Vietnam!"[39] Soon a tent city sprang up outside the gates of the repair depot, filled with representatives of Old and New Left groups who watched for repaired vehicles on their way back to the war zone.

Declaring that local traffic laws and the national vehicle control ordinance were being systematically violated by oversize and overweight flatbed trucks hauling tanks and APC's, five progressive mayors in Kanagawa prefecture denounced the shipments in a statement on August 15, 1972 and said they "unanimously demand once again that the United States forces obey the domestic laws."[40] The confrontation turned hostile when the national government ordered the riot police to arrest local officials if they halted the convoys to inspect them for possible violations of municipal traffic regulations. This action drew local residents into nightly sit-downs in the streets; dozens were seized by the police and treated as though they were radical students. The national headquarters of the

JSP and JCP were lukewarm about being associated with Hansen and the remnants of the anti-JCP student factions at Sagamihara, so that leadership of the movement passed by the end of August to a local committee of citizens to stop the tanks (Tada no Shimin ga Sensha o Tomeru Kai).[41] At this point the protests became a joint venture of the antiwar and citizens' campaigns, probably the purest example of cooperation between the two at any point during the Vietnam conflict.

Both the Tanaka cabinet and the opposition parties saw national elections on the horizon and tried to resolve the impasse, finally prevailing on the local authorities to issue the necessary permits so the tanks could get through freely. In response about 10,000 persons from Beheiren, other New Left organizations, and the surrounding neighborhood showed up on September 19 outside the gates of the depot to block a shipment of ten M-113 APC's. About half the crowd sat down in the roadway, causing the riot police to move in. The unarmed protesters were doused with water cannon and prodded with sticks and shields, leading to twenty-five arrests. The police also tore down fifty-two "vigilance" tents nearby. This fracas won the demonstrators a good deal of public sympathy throughout Japan, especially when it became apparent that the repaired vehicles were intended for the ARVN, not the United States. Finally the mayor of Yokohama agreed to reinforce Murasame bridge, and on October 17 the government abruptly and unilaterally revised the vehicle control ordinance so that municipal road use permits would no longer be needed—an embarrassment to Foreign Minister Ōhira Masayoshi, who had promised the foreign affairs committee of the House of Councillors on August 22 that "we have no intention of permitting exceptions to the domestic law."[42] The government's sudden action squashed the resistance of local authorities, and soon the protests faded away.

Sagamihara was the last important instance of direct action in Japan to oppose the Vietnam War. Soon both the citizens' movement and the campaigns against the American military bases turned from civil disobedience and large-scale rallies to

the courts for relief, a long-term approach that recognized the inadequacy and ineffectiveness of the earlier street protests. With Okinawa reclaimed and American troops withdrawing from Vietnam, it is not surprising that on October 21, 1972, only 100,000 persons attended rallies on international antiwar day, just half the number who took part a year earlier when the protests had been marred by bombs and fights.[43]

JAPAN AND THE AMERICAN WITHDRAWAL FROM VIETNAM

Looking back at the futile struggle against the tanks at Saga-mihara and the modest demonstrations on October 21, Tsu-rumi Yoshiyuki defined the future tasks of Beheiren as "stopping the aid" from Japan to capitalist economies in Southeast Asia and "stopping the trade" with the region—even though he admitted that these slogans had far less appeal than "stopping the war." Tsurumi also criticized the government for taking very little interest in refugees from the conflict—a charge often lodged against Beheiren itself, with only minor justification.[44] Instead the government responded to the final spasm of American bombings in Vietnam exactly as it had to the first attacks back in February 1965: whereas Swedish Prime Minister Olof Palme and many other world leaders bitterly denounced the Christmas 1972 saturation raids in Hanoi, Foreign Minister Ōhira dutifully defended them as "one process toward a peaceful solution."[45]

Japan, like the rest of the world, welcomed the news of the cease-fire in Vietnam on January 9, 1973 with more relief than jubilation. Beheiren went ahead with an antiwar rally at Shimizudani Park scheduled for January 20, timed to coincide with similar demonstrations in the United States on the day of President Nixon's inauguration to a second term. About 2,000 persons, including delegates from many civic organizations, heard Oda Makoto and other speakers call for the immediate withdrawal of American forces from Indochina. Afterward the crowd marched along the main street of Akasaka, bearing placards with slogans such as "now of all times oppose the

Vietnam War" and "sign the peace agreement at once." A number of the protesters sat down in the street for twenty minutes in front of the United States embassy. The JCP was equally determined to maintain its resistance to the war until the very end, convening a meeting of several thousand followers that same day in Hibiya Park. Other demonstrations were held throughout the country by partisans of both the Old and New Left.[46]

The combatants in Vietnam signed the Paris agreement on January 27, 1973, providing for the withdrawal of foreign military forces from Indochina. The document allowed the North Vietnamese and Viet Cong armies to remain in place, recognized the sovereignty, independence, and territorial integrity of Vietnam, and called for a Council of National Reconciliation and Concord consisting of communist, anticommunist, and neutral elements to determine the political future of the south. Japan was excluded from the Paris conference, unlike China, the Soviet Union, France, or Great Britain, even though Tokyo was expected to play a major part in reviving the economies of the region after the war. Prime Minister Tanaka treated the Paris accord as an economic event. Two nights before Nixon announced the suspension of hostilities, Tanaka told a national television audience that "the greatest, perhaps only merit of a cease-fire in Vietnam will be the strengthening of the dollar."[47] On the day the agreement was signed, he addressed a plenary session of the House of Representatives: "peace has come to Vietnam," he stated optimistically, and "the urgent agenda facing Japan is to contribute to solidifying the peace that is being realized in Vietnam." He pledged "every effort possible to restore and rebuild war-torn Indochina."[48] Ōhira Masayoshi led a chorus of approval from the foreign ministry, which took an exceedingly rosy view of South Vietnam after the Paris negotiations were concluded.[49] The government's upbeat prognosis almost surely reflected the outlook of Japanese companies doing business in the region.

Ishibashi Masashi, secretary-general of the Japan Socialist

Party, called the cease-fire "a victory of the heroic Vietnamese people" in "America's war of aggression in Vietnam" and also "a victory for the forces of peace throughout the world who assisted" the Vietnamese. The JCP leader Murakami Hiroshi agreed, noting that "the indomitable will of the Vietnamese people cannot be crushed."[50] The press treated the Paris settlement calmly, generally pointing out that the arrangements confirmed what the newspapers had long predicted: America could not gain its objectives militarily and would sooner or later have to withdraw.[51] The unspoken echoes of "I told you so" reverberated throughout the dailies. But the press was also pessimistic that the cease-fire would stick. A day after the Paris agreement was signed Beheiren and sixty other antiwar groups declared that they would continue to help the people of Vietnam until true peace came, no matter what putative termination of the conflict the diplomats had decided. Oda Makoto tried to put a bright face on the accord, calling it "a victory for the people over those in power," not the triumph of the DRV or NLF. He said that the agreement was at least a first step toward national self-determination, because the Americans promised to go home, even if no one could be sure that a workable political solution could be reached by the reconciliation council.[52] Kamiya Fuji and Rōyama Michio, the tough-minded scholars of international relations, noted in the April 1973 *Jiyū* that a number of Japanese had hoped the United States would lose in Vietnam, especially after the Nixon shocks. Rōyama pointed out that European criticism of American actions during the war might have been more outspoken than was the case in Japan but that few persons in Europe wanted the United States to suffer defeat.[53] "Once the clouds of the Cold War had dispersed," Rōyama recalled a decade later, "the Vietnam War was revealed for what it was: a struggle between indigenous people for power."[54]

Whatever the public made of the American agreement to withdraw from Vietnam, most Japanese were surprised to learn on March 9, 1973 that their country was still being used as an arsenal for South Vietnam two months after the cease-

fire. On that date officials of the United States military sea transport service in Kure admitted that they were still sending ammunition, especially 105 millimeter shells, to stock the ARVN under a program known as Operation Enhance Plus. The agency Japan Press reported that the Americans had moved several thousand tons of munitions to South Vietnam from Hiroshima prefecture and Okinawa since mid-February, apparently in violation of the Paris arrangements. Foreign Minister Ōhira confirmed on March 12 that 15,000 tons had been shipped from Kure alone but said that the United States did not consider the resupply activity improper.[55]

The Americans continued to fund the Thieu regime until its collapse on April 21, 1975, and the Japanese government kept on supporting the American position right to the very end. Japan also backed the nationalist Lon Nol government as the legitimate representative of Cambodia at the United Nations in December 1973 and November 1974, only to see the regime crushed when the Khmer Rouge marched triumphantly into Phnom Penh on April 17, 1975. Early in April 30, 1975 Vietnamese communist forces overran Saigon, seizing the sumptuous presidential palace where French governors-general had once resided and accepting the surrender of the Government of Vietnam from its interim leaders. By then American policy in Indochina was in tatters, but not so the wartime diplomacy of Washington's most important Pacific ally. Japan had experienced a sustained public outcry against the war, but otherwise the costs it incurred from supporting the United States were minimal in relation to the considerable benefits that accrued—and by January 1973 Tokyo had long since prepared for the post-Vietnam era by revamping its policies toward communist states in Asia and gearing up for a big economic offensive in Southeast Asia as soon as the fighting ended.

The cease-fire and subsequent military withdrawal from Vietnam did nothing to improve the public image of the United States among the Japanese, according to opinion polls taken in 1973. Only 18 percent of those surveyed listed America as their favorite foreign country, and 13 percent said they

disliked the United States—a postwar low and high, respectively.[56] The Arab oil embargo of 1973–1974 further undermined their confidence in America's ability to cope with its own economic problems, let alone defend its allies in case of need. Vietnam, the Guam doctrine of July 1969, and the oil shock all propelled Japan into greater independence of Washington, particularly in its Middle East policy and its efforts to secure raw materials around the globe.[57]

The Paris agreement also brought an end to the antiwar movement in most parts of Japan. *Asahi* reported on April 22, 1973 that the Kyoto Beheiren would officially disband at a meeting on April 30 at Kyoto University. The group declared: "it is important to wrap up neatly the movement we've carried out over the past eight years. This isn't an ending; it's the first step toward linking up with the new citizens' movement."[58] The Tokyo Beheiren decided to carry on its efforts, opening a two-week campaign on April 21 to protest the resumption of bombings in Cambodia, the fortification of United States bases in Thailand, and the imminent likelihood that Vietnam would lapse into war once again. A delegation of antiwar activists visited the South Vietnamese embassy in Moto Yoyogi that day to hand over a petition with 3,306 signatures demanding the release of all political prisoners held by the Thieu regime. An embassy employee refused to accept the document, telling the crowd, "you are acting on the basis of false information from the communist side."[59]

Later in the year Beheiren demonstrated on behalf of a ban on poison gas, held a symposium on defense industries in Japan and another on the Self-Defense Forces, and planned a conference of Asian peoples for the summer of 1974 to discuss combatting the penetration of Japanese capitalism in Southeast Asia. Still, it is true that the vitality of the antiwar movement dwindled rapidly after the Americans withdrew from Vietnam in the spring of 1973. Less than a year later the Tokyo Beheiren decided to close up shop for good. Speaking at a parting ceremony held on January 26, 1974, at Kyōritsu Kōdō in the

235

Hitotsubashi section of Kanda, Tsurumi Shunsuke told an audience of 1,000 that the antiwar movement was now ending, "but another day I think Beheiren—although not as Beheiren—will want to make an appearance once again. Beheiren is dissolved. Long live Beheiren!"[60]

CHAPTER 9

Adjusting to Peacetime

WHEN Saigon fell to the North Vietnamese armies on April 30, 1975, the reaction in Japan showed how polarized attitudes still were after ten years of bickering over the Vietnam War. Miyazawa Kiichi, the new foreign minister, told a press conference that day that the government "didn't believe America's motives were wicked" in Vietnam, so "from this standpoint Japan cooperated with America's war goals."[1] The next morning *Asahi*, the most trenchant critic of Japan's official stance toward the war, expressed its "heartfelt rejoicing" that the fighting was over. "From first to last," the newspaper said editorially, "it was a war of national liberation. That it ended in victory for the liberation effort shows that the age when great powers can restrain nationalism by force has ended."[2] The titanic gulf between how the public in general and the government-business elite viewed the conflict had scarcely shrunk at all during ten years of warfare, nor have opinions softened very much since. This raw divergence of outlooks was politically tolerable only because the Satō and Tanaka governments managed to avoid overcommitting Japan to the war while scoring highly popular successes on other foreign policy issues and boosting national prosperity at home.

The end of the fighting in Vietnam dispersed the energies of the antiwar movement, but a small band of Beheiren leaders converted their efforts from resisting the war to publicizing the malign side effects of Japanese business expansion in Southeast Asia after 1975. The collapse of the Saigon government had "very little" impact on Japan's military planning, according to Sakata Michita, head of the self-defense agency, who told a reporter in November 1975 that its influence was

237

"purely psychological."[3] In fact the psychology of Japanese security became critical not when South Vietnam fell but when President Jimmy Carter suddenly proposed to withdraw more American troops from South Korea in February 1977.

The latter part of the Vietnam War also coincided with a switch in goals for Japanese economic aid in Southeast Asia from pump-priming credits that spurred the import of Japanese goods to greater technological assistance and capital investment. The changes were capped by an ambitious development program unveiled in Manila by Prime Minister Fukuda Takeo in August 1977. The final and perhaps most disturbing aftereffect of the war for Japan was the arrival of boatload after boatload of Indochinese refugees at the end of the decade. After stormy debates and much soul-searching by the government and the public at large, the Japanese revised their immigration laws and ended up offering permanent residence to nearly 4,000 of the newcomers by 1985.

THE ANTIWAR LEADERS AFTER 1975

While Sōhyō and the ban-the-bomb organizations were making a vigorous effort to compose their differences and pursue a common strategy against nuclear war in the late seventies, many people accused Oda Makoto and the antiwar movement of washing their hands of Vietnam after the country was unified in April 1975. In retrospect, the political scientist Rōyama Michio believes Oda was "irresponsible" for giving the impression in his writings that the Indochina problem was solved once the United States withdrew its forces and support. Rōyama credits the antiwar movement with showing concern for refugees while the fighting was in progress, but he and many other critics have faulted Beheiren for seemingly ignoring the unfinished agenda from three decades of conflict once Saigon fell to the communists.[4] Yet, ironically, the harshest denunciations of Oda's alleged lack of interest in the Vietnamese after 1975 have come from conservatives who them-

selves had usually shown indifference toward the plight of civilians in the war zone while the shooting was still going on.

Oda agrees that the refugee crisis of 1978–1979 forced him to pay more attention to the ravages of war. He visited a number of refugee camps along the Thai border and "clarified my position" on the issue after returning to Japan.[5] After Vietnam invaded Cambodia with 100,000 troops on Christmas Day 1978 and China retaliated by attacking the northern border of Vietnam, Oda and fifty-eight other intellectuals from the antiwar movement issued a statement charging Hanoi with flouting the Khmer people's right of self-determination, however dreadful the atrocities of the Pol Pot regime had been. They also blasted China for intervening and called for the removal of all foreign forces.[6] Yoshikawa Yūichi, the former secretary-general of Beheiren, concedes that "the right-wing criticism of the antiwar leaders' attitudes after April 1975 is. partly valid, but from the opposite standpoint." Yoshikawa thinks that Beheiren should have pressed the Japanese government much harder "to give aid to Hanoi after 1975. The Vietnamese were forced to turn to Moscow because no one else would give them assistance to rebuild the country."[7] Perhaps even more isolated was the viewpoint of Mutō Ichiyō, the philosopher and Beheiren activist, who regretted that the antiwar movement had not supported revolutionary elements in Southeast Asia after 1975, although he attributed the hands-off attitude to Beheiren's firm commitment to Vietnam for the Vietnamese.[8]

Despite such second-guessing by people inside and outside the campaign against the war, several long-range effects of the antiwar movement on its adherents are clear. First, many of the best younger social scientists in Japan today were immersed in the Vietnam protests, and a number of them have continued to pay attention to Southeast Asia in their scholarly research. Second, the war stimulated a great deal of peace research by leading Japanese humanists and social scientists, beginning with the Japan Peace Research Group formed by Kawata Tadashi and others in 1966. Another society, the Peace

239

Studies Association of Japan, took a somewhat more scientific and less purely pacifistic approach to the subject when it was established in September 1973 under the leadership of Seki Hiroharu.[9] A third and "almost unknown effect of the war" on those who denounced it, according to Tsurumi Yoshiyuki, was the increase in the number of Japanese volunteers who spent time working with international relief organizations in Southeast Asia after 1975. Most were men and women in their late twenties or thirties who took as much as a year off from their occupations in Japan to work with refugees in Thailand and Malaysia or to help with public health and agricultural development projects throughout the region.[10]

Probably the most visible avatar of the antiwar movement was the Pacific Asian Research Center (PARC, or Ajia Taiheiyō Shiryō Sentā), founded in 1973 by Tsurumi Yoshiyuki and a handful of other Beheiren veterans. PARC continued to publish *Ampo* after Beheiren was dissolved in 1974, giving international publicity to the center's muckraking studies of Japanese corporate activities in Southeast Asia.[11] PARC looked into pollution and other effects of multinational corporations from Japan on local societies in the region, especially in the capitalist developing countries. Its efforts were concentrated for a time on the banana industry in the Philippines; more recently the group has collected information on the Japanese maritime interests that have been "cleaning the seabed of shrimp in India and Southeast Asia."[12] Like Beheiren, PARC's income came from small contributions, subscriptions to its publications, and royalties donated by its best-known partisans when they sold manuscripts to major publishers. Its leaders claim that these sources were sufficient to finance the overseas research carried out by its investigators,[13] although this cannot be independently verified.

Public attention in Japan was directed mainly toward China, not Southeast Asia, for the balance of the decade. Then in the early eighties, as the PRC turned to capitalist models of enterprise, there were signs of revived interest in Southeast Asia among scholars, writers, and journalists as well as LDP poli-

ticians and business leaders.[14] Tsurumi Yoshiyuki's books began to attract a certain following, after years of obscurity, and
publishers reported a boomlet in sales of works on Southeast
Asia. Oda compares the renewed popularity of the region to
the fascination with Southeast Asia on the eve of World War
II. "At Rotary Club meetings, gatherings of youth groups,
and the like there are speech contests and many discussions
about Southeast Asia. Business people always refer to 'developing countries' (hatten tōjōkoku), never to the 'third world.'
They think the latter sounds revolutionary, the former safe."[15]
Oda himself continued to campaign for peace and democrati-
zation despite a hectic schedule of deadlines for his fiction and
criticism with some of Japan's leading journals.

Uncorking the Defense Debate

When the Americans pulled out of Vietnam and then Saigon
fell to the communists, people in Japan grew just uneasy
enough about whether the United States would really protect
them in the event of trouble that it became politically possible
to begin talking again about defense without lapsing into an-
tipodal controversies like those stirred by the security treaty in
1960. At the same time the extinction of the Saigon regime
helped reinforce the conviction among Japan's military plan-
ners that they should once again draw close to the United
States, after a period of uncertainty in the early seventies about
America's commitment in light of the Guam Doctrine. During the weeks before the Thieu government collapsed, both
President Gerald R. Ford and Prime Minister Miki Takeo
stressed that the security treaty was the cornerstone of Pacific
stability. Under pressure from conservative factions in the
LDP, Foreign Minister Miyazawa Kiichi visited Washington
in mid-April 1975 and reportedly extracted a United States
"reconfirmation of its pledge concerning Japan's defense."[16]
Miki and Ford issued a joint statement in Washington on August 6, the thirtieth anniversary of the Hiroshima bombing,
reemphasizing that the security of South Korea was essential

to the peace and stability of Japan and the rest of Asia. Japan soon pledged $78 million in development loans to Seoul for agriculture and fisheries and offered another $500–600 million in 1977.[17] After discussions between defense chief Sakata Michita and Secretary of Defense James Schlesinger, Japan and the United States also agreed to set up a consultative mechanism for the "operational coordination" of American forces and the Self-Defense Forces in August 1975.[18]

These steps reflected a fear harbored by certain people in Japan that as the Americans pulled back from Indochina, Korea might be the next trouble spot in Asia. No specific event provoked this worry, although President Kim Il-sung of North Korea visited Beijing in April 1975 and President Ford went out of his way the next autumn to warn Pyongyang in the midst of the *Mayaguez* episode not to mistake America's commitment to defend South Korea. Secretary of State Henry Kissinger told the Japan Society of New York in June 1975 that the United States would not "turn away" from Asia and said that Washington had "learned from experience" during the tense moments in the Japan–United States relationship in the early seventies.[19] The apparent threat from North Korea soon eased; the real friction between Pyongyang and Tokyo later in the decade was caused by disputes over fishing rights.

The fall of South Vietnam and the seemingly reduced role of the United States in Asia made defense a legitimate topic of discussion in Japan, but the public remained rock-hard in its support for the three nonnuclear principles first adopted by Satō in January 1968. An *Asahi* poll taken in June 1975 showed that people favored the principles by almost eight to one.[20] The following year Prime Minister Miki made two moves that won him much popularity: he widened the ban on exporting weapons that Ikeda had first imposed, and he officially established a ceiling of 1 percent of GNP for military expenditures—a limit that remained in effect for the next decade.[21] At the same time the press, the opposition parties, and the intellectual establishment all grew more "mature and realistic" about international military affairs, as Rōyama Michio has

pointed out.[22] In the five months after the unification of Vietnam, the major Japanese dailies carried 318 articles on defense issues, compared with just 78 during the same period a year earlier.[23] American bases in Japan were used during the *Mayaguez* incident with little protest from the Left or the press. The Japan Socialist Party, the Democratic Socialist Party, and Kōmeitō all redefined their positions on defense and the security treaty during the winter of 1975–1976, partly because China had declared its support for both the treaty and the Self-Defense Forces in 1972 and partly because of the outcome in Vietnam. Nearly all specialists agree that the fall of Saigon resolved the tension in Japanese-American military relations and opened up discussion of defense questions in far more practical terms than had been possible previously.[24]

Prime Minister Miki and self-defense chief Sakata tried to upgrade Japan's armed forces by preparing an outline for a national defense program and publishing a second defense white paper in 1976 (the first had caused such an outcry in 1970 that none had appeared since). By this point nearly 80 percent of the public accepted the necessity of the Self-Defense Forces, but various surveys showed that only 40–45 percent thought that they were constitutional, even though the courts had never found them incompatible with the no-war clause (Article IX). At the end of the decade about one-fourth of Japan's high schools still refused to allow military recruiters to visit their students, and most universities did not admit Self-Defense Force officers for graduate study.[25]

The biggest jolt to Japanese strategic planning in the mid-seventies came when Vice President Walter F. Mondale suddenly told Japanese leaders during a visit to Tokyo in Feburary 1977 that the United States would revive former President Nixon's policy of reducing American commitments to South Korea by withdrawing additional troops beyond the division that Nixon had removed in 1970. This decision was made after only cursory consultations with Japan and South Korea, and it ignited anxieties in both countries because it appeared that the new American president, Jimmy Carter, was reneging on

Ford's and Kissinger's assurances of continuing support after the downfall of Saigon in 1975. Although Carter eventually shelved the plan in 1979 and the troops were not phased out, the defense expert Momoi Makoto believes that this "unfortunate" episode so close on the heels of the Vietnam debacle "reawakened the Japanese people to the potential of war in this area."[26]

The self-defense agency launched a campaign in early 1978 for $4.5 billion in improvements for its air and antisubmarine forces, and at budget time that year the new head of the agency, Kanemaru Shin, warned legislators that so many Soviet ships were appearing "in the Sea of Japan these days that we may as well refer to those waters as the Sea of Russia."[27] In November 1978 Japan and the United States agreed on guidelines for defense cooperation that provided for joint operations in East Asia. After a number of combined field and sea exercises and many additional strategic studies, the two governments signed binding documents of cooperation on December 26, 1984 and conducted their first joint command post exercise in 1985.[28]

The proposed reduction of American troops in South Korea, followed by a greater awareness of Soviet military activity at the end of the decade, helped to dampen public and parliamentary resistance to joint military maneuvers, even though the Miki, Fukuda, and Ōhira cabinets were careful to keep defense budgets under the 1 percent ceiling despite pressure from Washington to bear far more of the security costs in the region. The opposition parties were stunned by Vietnam's invasion of Cambodia in December 1978, China's counterattack early the following year, and then the Soviet Union's intervention in Afghanistan later in 1979. It was particularly shocking to the Japanese Left, the scholar Tanigawa Yoshihiko has written, that after "the NLF managed to win following many years of sacrifices, Vietnam—which should have known better than anyone else the importance of national independence—underwent a complete change and turned into an aggressor, attacking the small country of Cambodia and in effect taking over

244

control of Laos too."[29] The events of 1977–1979 completed the process of expanding the public's realism and sophistication about international affairs that began in February 1965 when the first American bombers over Vietnam shattered Japan's post-Hiroshima idyll of peace and harmony in Asia. At the same time, as Shibusawa Masahide has pointed out, the Japanese in the mid-eighties remain pervasively committed to pacifism: their national goal is to be "a major power without major military power."[30]

JAPAN AND POSTWAR VIETNAM

The morning after the Paris agreement of January 27, 1973, the Liberal Democratic Party unfurled a giant banner from the rooftop of its national headquarters in Tokyo: "Congratulations, Vietnam cease-fire. Next let's cooperate in reconstruction and development."[31] Soon the government set aside $10.8 million for postwar rehabilitation in all parts of Vietnam, and on September 21 it opened diplomatic relations with the Democratic Republic of Vietnam, twenty-eight years after the Hanoi regime was first established. Yet because the Tanaka and Miki cabinets kept on giving Saigon financial aid until the bitter end, the North Vietnamese refused to receive Japanese diplomats or allow embassies to open in the two capitals until mid-1975. Tokyo recognized the new Khmer Rouge government under Pol Pot two days after it captured Phnom Penh on April 17, 1975 and wasted little time before recognizing the provisional revolutionary government in Saigon on May 7. Despite the fact that their country had just given South Vietnam $10 million in additional humanitarian aid a month earlier, anticommunist business and political leaders in Japan understood that the future of Vietnam belonged to Hanoi and that they did not want to be left behind.[32]

As of the end of 1970 Japan had done little to implement Prime Minister Satō's vision of a "new Pacific age" mentioned at Washington the year before. Apart from medical and other humanitarian assistance the amount of Japanese economic aid

actually paid to South Vietnam during 1965–1970 was just $1.8 million. Then as Vietnamization took hold and the end of the war seemed in sight, Japan's aid policies began to encourage greater technical transfers and capital investments rather than credits for purchasing Japanese goods. A diplomatic white paper published on July 7, 1971 made it clear that Japan planned "to continue to extend aid after peace is achieved under a broad program of international cooperation for the rehabilitation and recovery of Vietnam and neighboring countries."[33] In fact Satō did not wait for the fighting to end; he committed $30 million in grants and credits during 1971 and proposed a $150 million Vietnam reconstruction program to be financed by various nations.[34] Shortly after taking office in July 1972, Prime Minister Tanaka announced plans for a $50 million loan for agricultural development in Phan Rang, the hometown of President Thieu. Further promises of technical and commercial aid were made during the final years of the Saigon regime, but because of wartime instability the amount actually paid to South Vietnam by the Japanese government during 1971–1975, including humanitarian assistance, apparently did not exceed $61 million[35]—a huge leap, nonetheless, from the period 1965–1970. Even so, South Vietnam ranked just eighteenth among all countries receiving Japanese economic assistance at the end of 1973 because of the great increases in overall foreign aid commitments during the early seventies.[36] Still, it is not surprising that North Vietnam was slow to exchange embassies with Japan when Tokyo was supporting the South Vietnamese so substantially while the war was in progress.

Japanese private investment in the south also grew toward the end of the conflict. According to official Japanese sources, private investors in Japan had put $2.5 million of their capital in South Vietnam as of March 1972, mainly into machinery, television, and vehicle assembly plants. After Saigon liberalized the terms of foreign investments in April of that year, Japanese firms committed an additional $2 million during 1973–1975 to enterprises specializing in fishing, textiles, and the pro-

duction of household appliances. Although the dollar value of the capital participation was small, a 10 percent investment in a joint venture was sufficient to give the Japanese partner a monopoly within South Vietnam on sales of products assembled locally.[37]

Perhaps more important than the amount of private funds was the attitude with which they were invested. A semiofficial report issued in early 1973 by a committee of business and bureaucratic leaders in Japan encouraged investors in terms that reeked of a leftover colonialist mentality: "the Vietnamese are an extremely outstanding people. They are clever, industrious, and quick because they remember things well. Perhaps in this respect they are next only to the Chinese as a superior nation."[38] If such an outlook prevailed as Japanese companies entered Southeast Asia in the early seventies it is small wonder that Hanoi was so cautious about a Japanese role in postwar Vietnam or that Prime Minister Tanaka encountered such hostility during his ill-starred tour of Thailand and Indonesia in January 1974. Yet there was an air of inevitability even more than resentment about the soaring economic strength of Japan in the region. By the end of 1974 the anti-Japanese protests had died down and Japan had become the leading commercial power in Southeast Asia. Moreover except for Laos, South Vietnam, and Burma, every country in the area received more aid and private investment from Japan by 1975 than from the United States.[39]

After Vietnam was unified the goal of Japanese policy was to cultivate harmonious relations with both the Association of Southeast Asian Nations and the communist states of Indochina, in order to promote regional stability and maximize trade. After months of careful diplomacy, Prime Minister Fukuda Takeo visited the ASEAN summit meetings in August 1977 at Kuala Lumpur, after which he toured Burma and the five ASEAN states. He announced the three-point Fukuda doctrine in a speech on "The Age of Southeast Asia" at Manila on August 18: 1) Japan would not become a military power or produce nuclear weapons; 2) it would foster "heart-to-heart

contacts" with the nations of Southeast Asia on an equal basis; and 3) it would try to improve relations with Vietnam and contribute to peace in the region.[40] He also offered a total of $1.55 billion in aid to the area. Fukuda's program greatly improved Japan's image in Southeast Asia, and it encountered very little resistance from any quarter in Japan.

As soon as the war ended Japan made progress with adjusting its economic relations with the Socialist Republic of Vietnam, as the unified country was known after 1976. The two-way volume of trade between Japan and all of Vietnam rose from $123 million in 1975 to $216 million the following year, mainly because of a big jump in Japanese exports. Japan also offered a $16.6 million loan for economic rehabilitation in September 1976 and the following month became the first country to sign a nongovernmental commercial pact with Vietnam.[41] A few months after Fukuda announced his doctrine for Southeast Asia, Prime Minister Pham Van Dong of Vietnam expressed the hope that his country and Japan "can develop economic, scientific, and technical cooperation on the basis of mutual respect, equality, and mutual benefit." He also said, "we attach importance to relations with Japan both at the State and at the people's level. There are many similarities between the Vietnamese and the Japanese people."[42] These words were a prelude to the big trade agreement reached by the two countries on April 28, 1978. Vietnam pledged to repay $75.7 million owed to Japan by the former Thieu regime, in return for which Tokyo quietly dropped its claims to about $4 million in Japanese assets taken over by the communists when they seized Saigon. Japan also agreed to provide a series of loans, credits, and other forms of economic assistance totalling $100 million during the next four years.[43] Attractive as the arrangements may have been to both parties, the scale of Japanese aid was still very small—less than 2 percent of the total extended by Tokyo that year to its trading partners worldwide.[44]

Vietnam soon scuttled the hopes for rapprochement between Indochina and ASEAN when Hanoi dispatched its armies in December 1978 to oust the Pol Pot regime in Cam-

bodia and install a more compliant government headed by Heng Samrin and Ieng Sary. Shortly after the Chinese leader Deng Xiaoping visited Tokyo in January-February 1979, the Japanese suspended all economic assistance to Vietnam, including supplemental grants from the fiscal 1979 budget announced just a few weeks earlier. Japan sided with ASEAN, China, and the United States in opposing the Vietnamese takeover of Cambodia. Not until October 1984 did Tokyo and Hanoi officially discuss lifting the ban on aid to Vietnam, at which point Foreign Minister Abe Shintarō reaffirmed Japan's intention to offer about $170–250 million per year to the states of Indochina when Vietnam withdrew from Cambodia. The Vietnamese foreign minister, Nguyen Co Thach, responded that his country would pull out in five to ten years.[45] Although there were hints in mid-1984 that Japan might partly lift its freeze if Vietnam began removing some of its troops, Japanese aid policies took a more political turn in early January 1985 when Abe and George Shultz, the American secretary of state, agreed in Los Angeles that Japanese economic assistance would be given to "unstable" countries to keep them from becoming communist.[46] In short, Japanese trade with Southeast Asia as a whole soared 700 percent in nominal terms during the Vietnam War and kept on rising so fast that by 1979 it was double the value of American trade with the region,[47] but Vietnam short-circuited its own modest but promising share of the postwar boom through expansionist military policies and cruel treatment of the refugees who tried to flee its harsh rule.

Frosty Reception

No aspect of the Vietnam War pierced the mystique about the homogeneity of Japanese society more deeply than the international refugee crisis at the end of the 1970s. Few if any peoples have surpassed the Japanese in spinning out legends of racial and cultural distinctiveness to bind its population together. As recently as August 1983, the prime minister made a widely

criticized remark in this vein: Nakasone Yasuhiro told patients in a home for atomic bomb survivors in Hiroshima that "the Japanese have been doing well for as long as 2,000 years because there are no foreign races" in the country.[48] Such views conveniently overlook the sizable numbers of Korean-Japanese and Chinese-Japanese scattered throughout the nation and minimize the foreign origins of much in culture that the Japanese consider uniquely their own.

When more than 3,000 refugees from Indochina appeared in Japanese ports the latter half of the 1970s, exclusionist sentiments clashed so fiercely with humanitarian impulses among the Japanese leadership and general public that only an unremitting campaign of criticism from abroad caused the government to start admitting refugees as permanent residents of the world's second richest country. The question of how Japan dealt with people fleeing Indochina is only a footnote to the Vietnam War and a relatively minor scene in the drama of recent Japanese history, but it brought to the surface the racial and cultural exclusionism of what the photojournalist Maekawa Makoto calls "the frosty Japanese" (*tsumetai Nihonjin*).[49] It was also one of the purest examples of how the Japanese government used foreign pressures as a means of modifying a basic national policy to Japan's advantage. As Katō Mikio points out, "Japan acted out of self-interest, not out of real concern for the refugees. Japan wanted to avoid further international criticism for failing to take more refugees, and it also wanted to retain its trade relations with all its partners."[50]

Well over 2 million persons are believed to have fled Laos, Cambodia, and Vietnam during the period 1975–1981, far more of them by foot into Thailand and Malaysia than by sea. The great wave of boat people escaping from Vietnam caught the world's attention in the second half of 1978 and continued throughout 1979. The majority were ethnic Chinese, known generally as Hoa, even though they represented only 3 percent of the Vietnamese population. In 1979 alone, perhaps 250,000 boat people drowned in the South China Sea before reaching safety.[51] Of this enormous hegira, slightly more than 8,000

refugees arrived in Japan between May 1975 and the beginning of 1985, less than four-tenths of 1 percent of the total who fled Indochina. The greatest upsurge took place between May 1979 and early 1981, but new arrivals continued to appear into the mid-eighties. As of 1985 roughly 3,800 of the refugees still remaining in Japan had received the status of permanent residents and another 1,400 were classified as temporary residents, either because they were awaiting resettlement in another country or because they had not yet been approved for permanency in Japan. At that point the Japanese government's immigration quota of 5,000 Indochinese refugees seemed unlikely to be filled.[52]

These figures mask far more than they reveal about the tortuous route nearly all the immigrants traveled to win even qualified acceptance in Japan. The Japanese government donated hundreds of millions of dollars to the international effort to rescue homeless Laos, Cambodians, and Vietnamese but for years took an exceedingly chilly view of admitting them to Japan for anything more than a temporary stay. When the exodus from Indochina first started, both Japanese and foreign ships bound for Japan began picking up boat people at sea and depositing them when they reached port. But by 1979 only 4 percent of the refugees were arriving in Japanese vessels, leading the government to warn its maritime industry not to invite further bad publicity by sailing past boats in distress without stopping.[53] At first the newcomers were given special landing permission for fifteen days under Article XII of the immigration control law; this was extended to thirty days in the case of Japanese carriers in July 1976 and foreign ships in November 1978. The following May the period of stay was lengthened to a half year, although in practice it sometimes had to be extended as much as four years because a permanent country of resettlement could not be found.[54]

Only in September 1977, after more than 1,000 refugees had taken temporary shelter in Japan, did the government begin to coordinate the work of bureaucratic agencies, the Japan Red Cross, religious groups, and the office of the United Nations

High Commissioner for Refugees (UNHCR) in coping with the stream of homeless Indochinese. Soon after President Carter pressed Prime Minister Fukuda to give humanitarian aid as well as financial assistance, the government announced on April 30, 1978 that it would begin accepting certain refugees as permanent residents. A year later Japan finally set the quota for permanent status at 500, but the prerequisites were so stiff that initially just three persons were approved. *Asahi* reported in June 1979 that the public was more sympathetic to the newcomers than was the justice ministry, which controlled immigration: 50 percent of those polled said that more refugees should be allowed to settle in Japan, even though nearly everyone agreed that most Indochinese would probably not find Japan an especially hospitable place to live.[55]

More foreign pressure at the Tokyo summit in June 1979 led to a new cabinet policy, announced on July 13, that eased the requirements for permanent residence and broadened the rights of refugees. Prime Minister Ōhira Masayoshi ran into furious bureaucratic infighting when he attempted to liberalize Japan's approach still further in early 1980, mainly because the justice ministry feared that other nationals, such as Filipinos, Taiwanese, and Koreans, would cry for more generous immigration status if Japan were flexible with the war refugees. The health and welfare ministry worried because the UNHCR was urging Japan to grant permanent residents from Indochina such benefits as public housing, pensions, and loans, even though other resident aliens did not enjoy these rights. The foreign ministry, sensitive to international criticisms and aware of the adverse effect that exclusion might have on Japan's exports, lobbied successfully to revise the quota for permanent residents to 1,000 when the initial 500 had been reached. The change, announced on June 17, 1980, was followed by a leap to 3,000 on April 28, 1981 and to 5,000 by 1984.[56]

Although Japan was very reluctant before the 1980s to take in large numbers of refugees, it was so cooperative about contributing money for relief work abroad that many critics ac-

cused the government of trying to buy its way out. Even while the war was still in progress, Japan had given at least $3 million to help people fleeing the fighting, including $1.6 million to the International Red Cross.[57] After the exodus reached the crisis level in 1978, the UNHCR convened a conference at Geneva in December of that year, during which Japan pledged $10 million in aid. Foreign Minister Sonoda Sunao stunned a meeting of ASEAN diplomats at Bali the following July by announcing that henceforth Japan would pay half the costs incurred by the UNHCR for resettling Indochinese refugees, a sum that eventually came to $31.5 million for 1979 and nearly $60 million the next year.[58] About $2.8 million of the 1979 contribution and $1.9 million of the 1980 figure were recycled back to Japan by the UNHCR to assist refugees under its care in Japanese shelters, because the Ōhira cabinet could not legally authorize direct payments to the religious organizations with which the UNHCR had contracted to operate them.[59] The government also provided funds to UNICEF, the World Food Program, the International Red Cross, and the Thai refugee camps, so that its total outlay for Indochinese relief work in 1979 was $91.9 million.[60] Altogether Japan gave $270 million in public monies to the UNHCR alone during 1979–1984, and when the funds provided to other agencies and governments are included, Japan has surpassed the United States as the single largest source of financial aid for resettlement work abroad.[61]

Most of the early duties of caring for refugees while they were waiting in Japan for reassignment elsewhere fell to nongovernmental organizations like the Japan Red Cross, the Salvation Army, Risshō Kōseikai, Tenrikyō, and especially the Roman Catholic agency Caritas Japan. The plight of the Indochinese visitors tapped the nascent spirit of voluntarism in Japan that had first appeared in the citizens' movements a decade earlier. Private groups operated about thirty shelters, mainly in the Tokyo region, and in February 1980 roughly twenty civic organizations active in raising private funds to help the newcomers formed a coordinating committee to as-

sist Indochinese refugees (Indoshina Nanmin Kyūen Renra-kukai). That same month the Japan Volunteer Center (Nihon Hōshi Sentā) was established to coordinate Japanese work in Southeast Asian refugee camps and solicit contributions of money, medical supplies, clothing, and vehicles from Japanese individuals and corporations. Altogether private sources raised several million dollars during 1980–1984 to help home-less Indochinese both in Japan and Southeast Asia, and several thousand Japanese volunteers donated their services to work-ing with refugees.[62] Even the restaurant Shiko, a lunch counter in the most hedonistic entertainment district of Shinjuku, was swept by the spirit of sharing. Starting in 1981 the owner, Takagi Masayuki, sold Chinese noodles for ¥100, not the usual ¥320, on the third Tuesday of each month under a ban-ner reading "let's try to rid mankind of starvation and war." Takagi attracted 200–300 customers each time and through mid-1984 had donated more than $2,000 in proceeds to help the refugees.[63]

The Japanese government belatedly opened two training centers to prepare Indochinese for permanent residence during the winter of 1979–1980 at Himeji in Hyōgo prefecture and Yamato in Kanagawa prefecture. Later another center at Shin-agawa was added. All three offered classes in Japanese lan-guage, job training and counseling, help with finding foster families, and socialization in Japanese ways of life. Refugees spent up to six months in the centers at government cost, and most who eventually found jobs ended up in small manufac-turing firms or service industries ranging from beauty shops to hospitals, usually in low-paying positions. Of the 3,800 In-dochinese with permanent resident status as of 1985, only a minority were graduates of the training centers and only 1,500 of the total were employed.[64]

Why were the Japanese government and people so slow to welcome refugees in the late seventies? A cabinet report issued in October 1980 summarized the official view: Japan is a nar-row country with a large population; half or more of its land area is mountainous or otherwise not inhabitable. "What is

more, heretofore we have not taken in immigrants or foreign workers, nor have we actively taken in refugees." The program to train permanent residents "can be called our country's first experience" with absorbing refugees.[65] Again in June 1984, when the foreign ministry established a human rights and refugees division, its director Masui Tadashi pleaded that "we had no experience. Japan has no history of small communities of refugees."[66] Although the diplomat Watanabe Koji argued that Japan had "no practice of bringing in foreign immigrants into its labor markets,"[67] actually hundreds of thousands of Korean and Chinese workers were forcibly imported to toil in mines, ports, and factories during World War II, and many stayed on as resident aliens after the surrender. Japan also took in about 500 White Russian refugees in the late 1950s, more than 100 of whom were eventually allowed to settle there permanently.

Even the United States was sympathetic at first to Tokyo's reluctance about accepting foreigners. On May 6, 1980, the state department's coordinator for refugee affairs, Victor H. Palmieri, said of the Japanese: "the difficulty is that they can't find 500 refugees who want to live there because it is a very tradition-bound society."[68] Not a single opposition party protested the government's restrictive immigration policies, nor did intellectuals or the newspapers make much effort to help the newcomers before the mid-1980s. Instead the excuses heard from left and right were "Japan is a single race," "the language is difficult," "even if they settle here it will be hard for them to melt into society," "there is no need to take in people who have abandoned their native countries," and especially "there is the fear that next time refugees will flow in from Taiwan and Korea."[69] As Maekawa Makoto lamented in 1980, Japan gave the appearance of still being "a closed country," and "there are many Japanese who continued to scorn Asians."[70] The ASEAN countries blasted the barriers to immigration in 1980, declaring that "Japan is an Asian country and should attach more importance to Asia."[71] Others argued that Japan had a moral obligation to accept refugees because of

its strong political support for United States policy during the war and its large profits from special procurement.[72]

Like many people who opposed the war in the United States, Beheiren members at first took relatively less interest than other citizens' groups in the plight of the Indochinese reaching their country because the newcomers were often seen as collaborators with the Americans during the war who helped to perpetrate aggression against their fellow nationals.[73] Later when it became apparent that most of the Vietnamese refugees were ethnic Chinese from the cities who had been evicted by a new rural elite, some of the Beheiren leaders became more involved in relief work. Muchaku Seikyō traveled to Thailand with a group of Sōtō Buddhists in August 1980 and stayed on to teach reading and writing to children in refugee camps. Yoshikawa Yūichi maintains that Beheiren clamored for more aid to homeless Indochinese, "but Japan is very exclusive. We demanded that the government admit people not only from Indochina but also from elsewhere in Asia, including China and Korea."[74] At length the Japanese government changed its outlook toward Southeast Asians: shortly before his sudden death in mid-1980, Prime Minister Ōhira said, "with the refugee problem, the doors of our country's true internationalization have been opened."[75] The United States, on the other hand, grew more critical as Japan expanded its immigration quotas and aid payments. In November 1984 Eugene Douglas, ambassador at large and coordinator of refugee affairs, said, "I cannot imagine that a society that has built itself to the pinnacle of international success and respect cannot manage to take 1,000 or 2,000 people who need help every year."[76]

Japan took a big step in this direction by finally agreeing in June 1981 to sign the thirty-year-old international Convention Relating to the Status of Refugees and its ancillary protocol developed in 1967. Japan was the eighty-fourth country to endorse the convention but only the third in Asia, nor had any communist government yet signed. Most refugees in the 1950s were located in Europe, and only after the Vietnam War

did the issue have a big impact in East Asia. Even though the convention applied only to refugees once they had been admitted to a given country, before signing it the Japanese felt obliged to standardize their own procedures for four categories of Indochinese immigrants: 1) boat people picked up at sea by vessels bound for Japan; 2) land people who arrived in Japan after fleeing their home countries on foot and spending time in camps elsewhere in Southeast Asia; 3) Laos, Cambodians, and Vietnamese stranded in Japan while studying or working during the war who feared returning home because their governments had changed; and 4) persons who entered Japan on Thai or Taiwanese passports and then overstayed their temporary visas. The justice ministry considered the first three groups bona fide refugees (*nanmin*) but looked on the fourth as displaced persons (*ryūmin*). Japan's membership in the international convention took effect on January 1, 1982, but only in January 1983 did Minister of Justice Hatano declare that the eighty or so displaced persons would have the same right to seek permanent residence as the refugees.[77]

Yamagami Susumu, a top immigration official in the justice ministry who helped to draft legislation to bring Japanese practices into line with the refugee convention and protocol, has pointed out how the issue made many Japanese fear that a flood of immigrants from Korea might deluge the island of Kyushu if massive internal disturbances should break out in the Korean peninsula. The government's response was that large numbers of Koreans would likely flee to Japan whether or not it was a signatory of the international convention.[78] Perhaps the Vietnam War's most important social residue for Japan was an improvement in the rights of all resident aliens because of the refugee crisis, and especially so for the 700,000 of Korean descent. In order to qualify for membership in the international convention on refugees, Japan finally gave resident aliens the same benefits of children's medical care, national health insurance, family dependents' payments, housing, loans, and pensions that had been previously reserved for Japanese citizens alone.[79] The changes, which took effect with Ja-

pan's participation in the convention on January 1, 1982, were an important step toward lifting the inferior status of Korean-Japanese and ungluing the clubby social cohesion that has perpetuated for so long the myth of homogeneity among the Japanese people.

CHAPTER 10

Fire Across the Sea

JAPAN emerged from the stormy Vietnam era more prosperous than ever, but the country was also very much sobered by the war. From start to finish the public opinion polls reflected a belief that the United States was bullying the Vietnamese, and nearly everyone in Japan was appalled by the American bombing campaigns that went on for almost eight years and dropped many more explosives on Indochina than had fallen everywhere in World War II. But the war was far away, almost no Japanese blood was being shed, and times were good for nearly all workers in the late sixties and early seventies. Most people in Japan felt too removed from the fighting to convert their misgivings about American policy into concrete actions against the war or their government's support for it.

Prime Minister Satō Eisaku was astonishingly successful at keeping the gap between popular and elite views of the Vietnam conflict from turning into a political liability. Satō correctly calculated that the LDP's conservative electorate would pay Vietnam little heed unless Japan became embroiled in combat. "Satō did almost everything his government could do" to help the Americans "short of sending troops," according to the critic Katō Shūichi, "but he did it secretly, with a low posture, to avoid antagonizing more people than necessary."[1] Rather than stirring up a constitutional crisis by trying to undo the ban on foreign wars in Article IX, Satō used the security treaty to justify Japan's aid and comfort to the Americans. This tactic cleverly appealed to the public's consciousness of being victimized (*higaisha ishiki*) by a security system foisted on an isolated and helpless Japan by John Foster Dulles at the San Francisco Peace Conference in 1951. Because Japan

259

was stuck with the treaty, many people assumed the government had no choice but to cooperate in the war.

The prime minister was also remarkably skillful at using the threat of massive left-wing opposition as a tool to pry loose Okinawa and the Ogasawaras from the United States, maintain free trade and close defense ties with the Americans, and minimize Japan's direct role in Vietnam. On the one hand he moved closer to the United States in November 1967 in order to regain autonomy over the Ryūkyūs; on the other he renounced nuclear weapons in January 1968 in order to maintain Japan's key role as a rear echelon for the war. Despite Vietnam, no crisis flared up in 1970 over the automatic renewal of the security treaty because of Satō's low-keyed but effective leadership, the promised return of Okinawa, greater economic prosperity, and the weakness of the antitreaty forces. Throughout the endless war, Japanese businesses earned at least $1 billion a year from direct and indirect procurement, but these added exports were incidental windfalls, not major reasons why the government supported the American position. In the end it was not his Vietnam policy but economic and diplomatic developments that finally did Satō in. The dollar-defense measures of August 1971, the textile settlement in October 1971, and President Nixon's new opening to China in February 1972 left Satō far behind, still clinging to a menu of anticommunism and free trade that had worked well for Japan in the 1960s but now seemed stale in the 1970s.

It was easy for Japan during the war to satisfy both its conscience and its purse because Vietnam was a fire across the sea. For exporters and conservative politicians alike the risks of cooperating in the war were slight and the benefits considerable. For opponents of the war, there was no military draft or serious police repression to raise the stakes of dissent, nor was there any real danger that Japan would be drawn into the fighting. Both supporters and critics of the war were protected by constitutional freedoms and the no-war clause, by Satō's cautious diplomacy of avoiding overcommitment, and by 2,500 kilometers of open sea. Perhaps because they viewed Indo-

china through the lenses of distance and insularity, both leftists and rightists in Japan had difficulty seeing the war as a series of revolutionary power struggles between indigenous groups for control. Instead, many opponents of the conflict believed the Vietnamese were engaged in a romantic and heroic effort at liberation from American imperialism. Japanese conservatives, like those in the United States, thought the war was a doctrinal contest between freedom and communism. Only gradually have people come to realize the actualities of power politics in Vietnam that were masked for so long by ideological deflection.

The fighting in Southeast Asia gave birth to the largest antiwar movement in Japanese history and helped clear the path for a new form of citizen involvement in public issues in a country where individuals have traditionally preferred to leave everything to the authorities. Beheiren and the other civic groups opposing the war operated outside the established parliamentary system, so they had almost no effect on electoral politics. Beheiren, Hansen, the anti-JCP student factions, and other antiwar civic groups carved out a new style of protest based on greater personal participation, spontaneous action, and a rejection of the doctrinaire authoritarianism of the opposition parties, big labor, and the ban-the-bomb organizations. The lack of compatibility between the Old and New Left made it harder for either to succeed in stopping the war. Beheiren turned out to be a transitional phenomenon between the tightly structured Marxist parties that flourished right after World War II and the citizens' movements which sprang up beyond the formal political framework in the late 1960s and early 1970s. It is clear that Beheiren had no measurable impact on shortening the war, but it seems equally certain that the antiwar campaign as a whole placed certain limits on how positively the Japanese government could support the American policy in Vietnam. Most importantly, Beheiren was an expression of conscience by a large number of citizens who were upset about the war and their government's role in it.

Beheiren was antiwar but not fundamentally anti-Ameri-

261

can, whereas the Old Left usually attacked the United States and yet treated the Vietnam War as an issue secondary to the security treaty. Beheiren had no ties to any political party and no ambition for power; its only reason for existing was to work for change in foreign affairs. The Old Left, by contrast, used the war, the treaty, and anti–Americanism as instruments to achieve its ultimate goal of gaining political power. Beheiren insisted on showing solidarity with American peace marchers who felt loyal to their country but alienated from its current policy in Southeast Asia. It also insisted on confining its protests to criticizing specific United States policies and actions, because Oda Makoto and the other leaders knew that slogans such as "Yankee go home" were counterproductive.

An important result of the antiwar movement in Japan was that ordinary people felt free to criticize the United States once again, after twenty years of unrealistic admiration. It was entirely predictable that the euphoric view of America shared by most Japanese in early 1965 would gradually be replaced by a more hardheaded attitude as citizens became more knowledgeable about international affairs. Their regard for the United States plunged from a peak at the beginning of 1965 to a postwar low in 1973 in direct response to the Indochina conflict, but it seems likely that with growing prosperity and national confidence the Japanese would sooner or later have taken a more measured view of America anyway. In the decade after the fighting ended, Japan became the economic giant of Asia, drew closer to the United States militarily, and experienced rifts with various trading partners as it piled up huge surpluses year after year. With the war safely in the past and Japan and America increasingly interdependent, it was not surprising that 75 percent of the people surveyed by the prime minister's office in 1984 said they felt friendly toward the United States or that 43 percent thought it was more important to maintain friendly relations with America than with any other country.[2] But underlying this benign outlook was a new realism about the weaknesses as well as the strengths of the United States. A TBS poll disclosed in August 1985 that the

Japanese regarded their own industries and products as more technologically advanced, their business and industrial managers more capable, and their blue-collar employees much harder working than those in the United States.[3]

At the level of popular culture Japan seemed more pro-American in the mid-eighties than ever before, even though a large number of affluent Japanese had traveled to the United States only to discover that subways were cleaner, cities more livable, workers more industrious, and clerks more attentive back home. Many Japanese seemed to regard their country and the United States as extensions of each other's material cultures, with the same Disneyland, pop music, consumer products, and fast-food chains. Such an outlook reinforced the satisfying feeling that Japan had learned the lesson of Ichikawa's *Tokyo Olympiad* and become comparable to America as number one. Actually what had happened was not equivalence but selectivity. Like the Meiji reformers who borrowed only the best from Europe in the late nineteenth century, Japanese consumers in the mid-1980s understandably chose those features of middle-class American culture that fitted their own increasingly comfortable life-styles without importing the social and economic problems confronting American society. Such a discriminating approach made the pro-Americanism of Japanese popular culture very partial and incomplete, and it also probably helped to inflate the friendly image many Japanese seemed to hold of the United States because they knew America mainly through certain cheerful symbols of mass culture at their most marketable.

Japanese intellectuals in the mid-eighties did not often share this enthusiasm for material artifacts, but many of them seemed to find American society relatively open and tolerant compared with other foreign countries. At the same time they were usually resentful of the United States for supporting repressive regimes abroad, especially in the developing world. Still, as Katō points out, most Japanese were even more critical of the Soviet Union: "this is an age of bitter disillusionment. American democracy is tarnished, but the socialist countries

263

are even worse."[4] The traumas of Vietnam, Czechoslovakia, the Chinese cultural revolution, Cambodia, and Afghanistan caused the Japanese to turn inward for direction—but not to nationalism. Instead there seemed to be renewed tentativeness, a lack of commitment, a fragmentation of ambitions, and a distinct privatization of personal goals. The war in Indochina set in motion the process that gradually diminished America as a model for national emulation in Japan, but as of the mid-eighties the Japanese seemed uncertain about where their vast prosperity and international respect would lead them now that they depended less on foreign examples to set their agenda for the future.

NOTES

PREFACE

1. NSC 61, January 27, 1950, in *America in Vietnam*, ed. Williams et al., p. 83.
2. Tanigawa, ed., *Betonamu*, p. 1; Maruyama, *Betonamu—sono tatakai*, p. 13; Iwasaki, *Japan and Southeast Asia*, pp. vii–xi.

INTRODUCTION: JAPAN, THE UNITED STATES, AND VIETNAM

1. *Bunka hyōron*, no. 94 (July 1969), 73.
2. Miyamoto, *Keizai*, p. 254. Polls are summarized in NHK, *Zusetsu*, pp. 179, 185. See Destler, "U.S.–Japanese Relations," pp. 194–195.
3. NHK, *Zusetsu*, pp. 179, 185; Shibusawa, *Japan*, p. 162.
4. *Asahi shinbun* (evening edition), May 31, 1966, in *Nichibei*, ed. Saitō et al., p. 399. See *Asahi jānaru*, November 10, 1972, p. 20.
5. C. A. Johnson, "Japanese Relations," p. 35. I have benefited from conversations on this point with Jackson N. Huddleston, Jr., December 13, 1984.
6. Haryū interview, November 22, 1984.
7. Mainichi, *Ichiokunin*, 8:148.
8. Inoue, "Betonamu sensō," p. 33. On these points I am indebted to T. J. Pempel (correspondence, August 16, 1983) and Daniel I. Okimoto (correspondence, August 24, 1983).
9. Sodei, "What Vietnam War Means," p. 317.
10. Maruyama, *Ronsetsu*, p. 167.
11. *Pentagon Papers*, 1:450. See Shibusawa, *Japan*, pp. 16–19.
12. U.S. Department of State, *Foreign Relations, 1952–54* 14, excerpted in *New York Times*, June 7, 1985.
13. Allison, "American Foreign Policy," p. 7.
14. See Inoue, "Betonamu sensō," pp. 33–34; Shibusawa, *Japan*, pp. 18–19; Iwadare, "Heiwa," pp. 50–53; *Japan Quarterly* 22:4 (October 1975), 309–310.

NOTES TO PP. 10–18

15. Packard, *Protest in Tokyo*, p. 261; Ishida Takeshi, "Emerging," p. 416.
16. See Shibusawa, *Japan*, pp. 20, 93–94.
17. Katō et al., *Nihon rekishi*, 3:253; Halliday, *Political History*, p. 223.
18. Iwadare, "Heiwa," pp. 53–56; Katō et al., *Nihon rekishi*, 3:253–254; *Japan Quarterly* 22:4 (October 1975), 310–311; *Kodansha Encyclopedia of Japan*, 6:166.
19. Asahi, *Pacific Rivals*, pp. 221–222; Honda interview, November 28, 1984.
20. The text of the treaty is given in Borton, *Japan's Modern Century*, pp. 589–590. See Mendel, "Japanese-American Relations," p. 322; Shibusawa, *Japan*, pp. 94–95.
21. Young C. Kim, "Japan's Security," p. 64; *Kodansha Encyclopedia of Japan*, 8:165.
22. Matsuda, *Nihon no shinsei*, p. 32.
23. See *Kodansha Encyclopedia of Japan*, 8:191; Buttinger, *Vietnam*, pp. 121–131, 156–157.
24. Buttinger, *Vietnam*, p. 188.
25. Ibid., pp. 189–190. See Harrison, *Endless War*, pp. 92–97.
26. Ho Chi Minh, "Letter From Abroad" (1941), in *Ho Chi Minh on Revolution*, ed. Fall, pp. 133–134; Ho Chi Minh, "Declaration of Independence of the Democratic Republic of Viet-Nam" (September 2, 1945), in *Ho Chi Minh on Revolution*, ed. Fall, pp. 141–143.
27. Buttinger, *Vietnam*, p. 288.
28. See *Kodansha Encyclopedia of Japan*, 8:192; Ebashi and Yamada, *Shinsei*, p. 399.
29. Japan External Trade, *Economic Cooperation 1980*, pp. 24, 46, 174; Maruyama, *Betonamu kaihō*, p. 250; Yanaga, *Big Business*, p. 227; Mainichi, *Fifty Years*, p. 269.
30. Kameyama, *Betonamu*, p. 194; Matsuda, *Nihon no shinsei*, pp. 207–208; Yanaga, *Big Business*, pp. 226–227; Ebashi and Yamada, *Shinsei*, p. 399; Hasegawa, *Japanese Foreign Aid*, p. v.
31. Ebashi and Yamada, *Shinsei*, p. 411. See Fukuda Kan'ichi, "Japan's Reaction," p. 24; *Japan Quarterly* 22:3 (July 1975), 277.
32. Nihon Keizai Chōsa, *Betonamu jōsei*, p. 125; Ebashi and Yamada, *Shinsei*, p. 411; Olson, *Japan*, pp. 218–222; Hasegawa, *Japanese Foreign Aid*, pp. 103–105; *Far Eastern Economic Review*, March 20, 1969, p. 567.

33. Ebashi and Yamada, *Shinsei*, p. 384; Iwai, "Nihon," pp. 256, 261–264; Shibusawa, *Japan*, p. 22.
34. Ebashi and Yamada, *Shinsei*, pp. 385–389, 411.
35. Seki Hiroharu, *Kiki*, p. 212.
36. Shibusawa, *Japan*, p. 25. See also pp. 22–24; Fukuda Kan'ichi, "Japan's Reaction," p. 25; Hiroharu Seki, "International Environment," p. 441.
37. *Kodansha Encyclopedia of Japan*, 1:290. See Shibusawa, *Japan*, p. 23.
38. *Far Eastern Economic Review*, January 28, 1965, p. 177. See Shibusawa, *Japan*, p. 24; Katō et al., *Nihon rekishi*, 3:249–250.
39. Kajitani, "Hannin," p. 35.
40. Betonamu ni okeru, *Jenosaido*, p. 129.
41. "Sono toki," p. 16.
42. J. Clark, *Japanese Foreign Policy*, p. 80.
43. *Shōwashi jiten*, p. 590; Young C. Kim, "Japan's Security," p. 65.
44. *Shōwashi jiten*, p. 590; Matsuda, *Nihon no shinsei*, p. 267; *Far Eastern Economic Review*, February 23, 1967, p. 314; J. Clark, *Japanese Foreign Policy*, pp. 78–79.
45. *Far Eastern Economic Review*, April 1, 1965, p. 18. See *Pentagon Papers*, 3:723; Matsuda, *Nihon no shinsei*, p. 268.
46. *New York Times*, September 30, 1964.
47. "Sono toki," p. 16; Fukuda Kan'ichi, "Japan's Reaction," pp. 25–26.

CHAPTER 1: THE WAR COMES TO JAPAN

1. Biographical details are taken from *Nihon kingendaishi jiten*, p. 252; *Nihon gaikōshi jiten*, pp. 326–327; Barnet, *Alliance*, pp. 184–185, 268–269; Mainichi, *Ichiokunin*, 8:244–246; Takagi et al., "Secrets," pp. 309–312.
2. *Far Eastern Economic Review*, April 1, 1965, p. 18. I am indebted to Rōyama Michio for helpful comments on this point. Rōyama interview, November 26, 1984.
3. "Satō-Jonson kyōdō kōmei" (January 14, 1965, Japan Standard Time), *Nichibei*, ed. Saitō et al., pp. 365–366; Togawa, *Satō*, pp. 142–143; Matsuda, *Nihon no shinsei*, p. 272; Yara, "Report," p. 290; Lu, "Sato," p. 38.
4. See Nihon Heiwa, *Heiwa undō*, p. 243.
5. U.S. Department of State, *Bulletin* 237:1336, February 1, 1965, p.

135. See Fukuda Kan'ichi, "Japan's Reaction," pp. 25–26; Matsuda, *Nihon no shinsei*, pp. 271–272; Kajima, *Modern Japan's Foreign Policy*, p. 107; Takagi et al., "Secrets," p. 309.

6. *Far Eastern Economic Review*, February 14, 1965, p. 40.

7. Heiwa, *Sensō*, p. 241; Betonamu ni okeru, *Jenosaido*, p. 117.

8. *Asahi jānaru*, December 5, 1965, p. 13.

9. *Asahi jānaru*, November 10, 1972, p. 21.

10. Harrison, *Endless War*, p. 241.

11. Oda interview, December 9, 1984.

12. *Asahi jānaru*, November 10, 1972, p. 21.

13. *Pentagon Papers* (1971), excerpted in "Sono toki," p. 19.

14. Iida, "Shimin," p. 26; Inaba, "Nikkan," p. 257; Iwadare, "Hansen," p. 231.

15. Inaba, "Nikkan," p. 257.

16. *Far Eastern Economic Review*, March 4, 1965, p. 369.

17. *Far Eastern Economic Review*, February 25, 1965. See Heiwa, *Sensō*, pp. 245–246; Ōmura, *Shōwashi*, p. 90; Matsueda and Moore, "Japan's Shifting Attitudes," pp. 614–616.

18. Shiina statement, February 14, 1965, excerpted in *Asahi jānaru*, November 10, 1972, p. 20.

19. Fukuda Kan'ichi, "Japan's Reaction," p. 27.

20. Betonamu ni okeru, *Jenosaido*, p. 129; Young C. Kim, "Japan's Security," p. 65.

21. *Public Papers of the Presidents of the United States: Lyndon B. Johnson, 1965* (Washington, D.C., 1967), in *America in Vietnam*, ed. Williams et al., pp. 242–244; Olson, *Japan*, p. 145.

22. See Fukuda Kan'ichi, "Japan's Reaction," p. 25; Emmerson, *Arms*, p. 84.

23. Kumakura, *Nihon*, p. 123; Heiwa, *Sensō*, pp. 249–250; Iida, "Shimin," p. 25; Arasaki, "Okinawa's Reversion," pp. 287–288; Iwadare, "Hansen," p. 231; *No More Hiroshimas!* 12:3 (April 1965), 1.

24. *Mainichi nenkan 1966*, p. 310; Maruyama, "Japanese Opinion," p. 305; Maruyama, *Ronsetsu*, p. 225; Kyōdō, *Kono*, p. 190.

25. Inoki's criticism appears in *Chūō kōron* (April 1965) and Hayashi's in *Jiyū* (April 1965).

26. Ōuchi et al., "Petition," pp. 73–75. The full text appears in *Nichibei*, ed. Saitō et al., pp. 395–396.

27. Maruyama, "Japanese Opinion," p. 306. See "Japan and the Vietnam War," p. 245.

28. *Asahi shinbun*, April 21, 1965, in *Nichibei*, ed. Saitō et al., p. 396. See Maruyama, "Japanese Opinion," p. 310.

29. Fukuda Tsuneari, "Let's," p. 82.

30. Fukuda Tsuneari, "Amerika," p. 92.

31. Kaikō, "Fukuda," pp. 18–29; Tonooka, *Genronjin*, pp. 45–46; Maruyama, "Japanese Opinion," pp. 309–310; Saeki Kiichi, "Betonamu sensō," pp. 7-9; *Journal of Social and Political Ideas in Japan* 4:2 (August 1966), 21–22; Ishida Takeshi, *Seiji to bunka*, p. 274.

32. "Yobikake," in Betonamu ni Heiwa, *Shiryō*, 1:5. See also 1:10; Eguchi, *Gendai*, pp. 231–232.

33. "Betonamu ni heiwa o!" April 24, 1965, in Betonamu ni Heiwa, *Shiryō*, 1:7.

34. *Asahi shinbun*, April 24, 1965, and *Mainichi shinbun*, April 24, 1965, in Betonamu ni Heiwa, *Shiryō*, 1:10. See Eguchi, *Gendai*, p. 233.

35. Michio Umegaki (correspondence, July 25, 1983).

36. Inoue, "Betonamu sensō," p. 35; Maruyama, "Japanese Opinion," pp. 306–307; Lockheimer, "Vietnam," pp. 6–8; Miwa interview, November 22, 1984; Iwadare interview, November 28, 1984.

37. Jansen, "China War," pp. 20–28. See Mori Kyōzō, "Judgments," p. 298.

38. Maruyama, *Betonamu—sono tatakai*, pp. 285–286.

39. See *Journal of Social and Political Ideas in Japan* 4:2 (August 1966), 20, for a letter from Katō Shūichi and five other scholars, dated April 4, 1965.

40. Matsumoto Shigeharu, "Future," p. 20. See Inoue, "Betonamu sensō," p. 35; Sannosuke Matsumoto, "Introduction," p. 3; Mori, "Two Ends," p. 17.

41. Dore, *Energy*, p. 3.

42. Momoi interview, January 9, 1985.

43. Katō Shūichi, "Ushinawareta," p. 19.

44. Kataoka, *Waiting*, p. 24. For comments on this point I am grateful to Kent C. Smith.

45. Honda interview, November 28, 1984.

46. Irie, *Sengo*, p. 143.

47. Tai Sung Kim, "Japan's Security," pp. 143–144. The figures are for 1968.

48. Sneider, *U.S.–Japan*, p. 58.

49. Maruyama, *Betonamu—sono tatakai*, p. 72; Morinaga, "Shinbun," pp. 10–11; Irie, *Sengo*, p. 138; Murakami interview, December 20, 1984; Inoue, "Betonamu sensō," p. 34.
50. Morinaga, "Shinbun," p. 13; Murakami interview, December 20, 1984; Oda interview, December 9, 1984; Tokuoka interview, December 3, 1984.
51. Lee, "Professional and Political Attitudes," pp. 97–124; "Nihon no Betonamu hōdō," p. 42.
52. Matsumoto Shigeharu, "Future," p. 19.
53. Maruyama, *Ronsetsu*, pp. 171–172, 241. See Tsurumi Shunsuke, *Sengo*, pp. 109–110.
54. Maruyama, *Ronsetsu*, pp. 168–177; Kugai, ed., *Shiryō*, 2:311–374. See Young C. Kim, *Japanese Journalists*, pp. 189–192.
55. Maruyama, "Japanese Opinion," pp. 303–304. See Ishida Takeshi, *Japanese Society*, p. 86; Iwadare, "Hansen," p. 230.
56. Iwadare, "Hansen," p. 231.
57. Maruyama, *Ronsetsu*, p. 160. Criticisms of the major dailies are found in Urushiyama, *Shinbun, passim*; Irie, *Sengo, passim*; Morinaga, "Shinbun," pp. 10–19; Tonooka, *Genronjin, passim*.
58. Tonooka, *Genronjin*, p. 331.
59. Honda interview, November 28, 1984. On television, see Maruyama, "Japanese Opinion," p. 304; "Japan and the Vietnam War," p. 239.
60. Nichols interview, November 28, 1984.
61. Inaba, "Nikkan," p. 259; *Asahi jānaru*, November 10, 1972, pp. 139–140; Betonamu ni okeru, *Jenosaido*, p. 118.
62. Maruyama, *Ronsetsu*, p. 157. See Inaba, "Nikkan," p. 258.
63. *Asahi shinbun*, April 16, 1965.
64. "Japan and the Vietnam War," p. 246.
65. Matsumoto Shun'ichi, "Seifu," p. 21.
66. Ibid., p. 23.
67. "Gokai teisei ni kansuru Beikokumushō kōmei" (May 1, 1965), in *Nichibei*, ed. Saitō et al., p. 384. See Barnet, *Alliance*, p. 270; Katō Shūichi, "Ushinawareta," p. 18.
68. Betonamu ni okeru, *Jenosaido*, p. 118; *Mainichi nenkan 1966*, p. 189; Kesavan, "Vietnam," pp. 509–510; *Far Eastern Economic Review*, May 27, 1965, p. 387.
69. Reischauer statement, quoted in *Asahi Evening News*, April 30, 1965. See Hayakawa, "Raishawā," pp. 134–137; Maruyama,

Ronsetsu, pp. 157–160; Inaba, "Nikkan," p. 258; Kesavan, "Vietnam," pp. 507–508.

70. *Asahi shinbun*, May 1, 1965. See "Japan and the Vietnam War," p. 247.

71. Narita, *1970*, p. 86.

72. *Asahi jānaru*, November 10, 1972, p. 21; Betonamu ni okeru, *Jenosaido*, p. 130.

73. Mainichi, *Anpo to seiji*, p. 18.

74. *Far Eastern Economic Review*, July 7, 1966, pp. 12–13. On the LDP Right, see Dower, *Empire*, p. 445; Kurzman, *Kishi*, pp. 316–317.

75. J. Clark, *Japanese Foreign Policy*, p. 121. On these points I am indebted to Rōyama Michio. Rōyama interview, November 26, 1984.

76. "Tōitsu kenkai," May 18, 1965, in *Asahi jānaru*, June 6, 1965, p. 15.

77. *Seisaku geppō*, May 1965, pp. 59–60.

78. *Far Eastern Economic Review*, May 27, 1965, p. 387. See Young C. Kim, "Japan and the Vietnam War," p. 154.

79. "Undō hōshin," 1966, in Irie, *Sengo*, p. 138. See *Mainichi nenkan 1966*, p. 189; Stockwin, *Japan*, pp. 154–155.

80. Storry, "Repercussions," p. 74.

81. Sōhyō resolution, March 4, 1965, quoted in Scalapino, *Japanese Communist Movement*, p. 244.

82. Haryū interview, November 22, 1984. On Sōhyō, see Iwadare, "Hansen," pp. 231-232; Hatada, "Betonamu," p. 70; Ishida Takeshi, *Japanese Political Culture*, p. 154; *Mainichi nenkan 1966*, p. 189.

83. Japan Communist Party declaration, November 15, 1964, quoted in Scalapino, *Japanese Communist Movement*, p. 215. See Young C. Kim, "Japan and the Vietnam War," p. 154; Nihon Heiwa, *Nihon no kokusho*, introduction, p. 20; J. Clark, *Japanese Foreign Policy*, p. 117; Nihon Kyōsantō, *Betonamu, passim*.

84. Young C. Kim, "Japan and the Vietnam War," p. 153; Eguchi, *Gendai*, p. 230; J. Clark, *Japanese Foreign Policy*, p. 127.

85. *Asahi Evening News*, June 9, 1965. See Mainichi, *Anpo to seiji*, pp. 18–19; Katō Shūichi, "Ushinawareta," p. 16; *Far Eastern Economic Review*, June 17, 1965, p. 536.

86. Miyake interview, December 28, 1984. See Katō Bunzō et al., *Nihon rekishi*, 3:252; Mainichi, *Ichiokunin*, 8:129; Iwadare, "Hansen," p. 231.

87. *Asahi jānaru*, July 18, 1965, p. 15; *Far Eastern Economic Review*, August 12, 1965, p. 282.
88. Rōyama, "Domestic Factors," p. 6.
89. Kamiya interview, November 30, 1984.
90. Katō Shūichi interview, December 10, 1984. I am grateful for comments on this point to Rōyama Michio. Rōyama interview, November 26, 1984.
91. "*Asahi* Poll," pp. 463–465. See Hayashi Chikio, "Chōsa," p. 36; J. Clark, *Japanese Foreign Policy*, p. 130.
92. "*Asahi* Poll," pp. 463–465.
93. NHK, *Zusetsu*, p. 164.
94. Ibid., p. 181; Hayashi Chikio, "Chōsa," p. 38.
95. Mendel, "Japan, Okinawa," p. 1.
96. I have benefited from conversations with Akimoto Ritsuo, December 2, 1984, and Kusumoto Satoshi, January 6, 1985, on these points.
97. Katō Shūichi interview, December 10, 1984; Katō, quoted in *Asahi jānaru*, November 10, 1972, p. 34.
98. Rōyama interview, November 26, 1984.
99. Kaiko, *Darkness*, p. 184.

CHAPTER 2: THE PROTESTS THICKEN

1. Harrison, *Endless War*, p. 255.
2. Tsurumi Shunsuke, "Beheiren," p. 1.
3. The group's representative work is *Tenkō* (3 vols., 1959–1962). See Asahi, *Pacific Rivals*, pp. 353–354; Packard, *Protest in Tokyo*, pp. 274–275.
4. Kishi Nobusuke, press conference, May 28, 1960, quoted in *Ampo*, no. 1 (November 1969), 8. See *Koe naki koe no tayori*, no. 34 (June 10, 1965), 2–5; Kobayashi, "Koe," pp. 44–46.
5. Takabatake, "Citizens' Movements," pp. 195–196. See Kobayashi, "Koe," p. 46.
6. Tsurumi Yoshiyuki, "Beheiren," p. 445; Tsurumi Yoshiyuki, quoted in *Asahi Jānaru*, November 10, 1972, p. 101.
7. Asahi, *Pacific Rivals*, p. 354.
8. Etō interview, December 20, 1984. On Beheiren members, see Tsurumi Shunsuke, "Beheiren," pp. 3–4; Shisō, *Bōhatsu*, pp. 131–135; Takahashi, "Beheiren wa," p. 110; Ishida Takeshi, *Japanese Political Culture*, p. xi.

9. Oda interview, December 9, 1984. See Sodei, "What Vietnam War Means," p. 315.

10. Tsurumi Yoshiyuki, "Beheiren," p. 447; Tsurumi interview, December 24, 1984.

11. Tsurumi Shunsuke, "Beheiren," p. 2; Lummis interview, December 27, 1984.

12. Tsurumi Yoshiyuki, "Beheiren," p. 448.

13. See Oda, *Nan de mo.*

14. Katō Shūichi interview, December 10, 1984. See Takahashi, " 'Beheiren' o," p. 27; Fukashiro, "New Left," p. 30.

15. Oda, *Gimu*, p. iii; Takahashi, " 'Beheiren' o," p. 27.

16. Fukashiro, "New Left," p. 31; Oda, *"Betonamu" no kage*, pp. 45–46; Takabatake, "Citizens' Movements," p. 196.

17. Takahashi, "Beheiren wa," p. 110.

18. Oda interview, December 9, 1984. See Oda, *Mao*; Oda, "Making," p. 130.

19. Postscript in Oda, *Heiwa.*

20. See Takahashi, " 'Beheiren' o," p. 29; Takahashi, "Beheiren wa," p. 117.

21. *Asahi jānaru*, February 9, 1973, quoted in Tonooka, *Genronjin*, p. 77.

22. Oda, ed., *Shimin, passim*; Takahashi, "Beheiren wa," p. 119; Fukashiro, "New Left," p. 31; Wheeler, "Japan's Postmodern Student Movement," p. 205.

23. Oda, "Demo," p. 54.

24. Ibid., pp. 54–55.

25. Ibid., p. 53; Oda interview, December 9, 1984.

26. Oda, "Demo," pp. 49–53; Oda, "Making," p. 136.

27. Tsurumi Yoshiyuki, "Beheiren," p. 448.

28. Ibid., pp. 447–448.

29. Oda, " 'Ikitsuzukeru,' " p. 444.

30. Oda and Tsurumi, eds., *Hansen*, pp. 6–7.

31. Eguchi, *Gendai*, pp. 233–234; *Nihon kingendaishi jiten*, p. 601; Iwadare interview, November 28, 1984; *Mainichi nenkan 1974*, p. 350.

32. Oda interview, December 9, 1984; Ishida interview, December 5, 1984; Katō Mikio interview, November 28, 1984; Béraud, *La gauche*, p. 104.

33. Tsurumi Yoshiyuki, "Beheiren," p. 446; Eguchi, *Gendai*, p. 233; Shisō, *Bōhatsu*, p. 90; Inaba, "Nikkan," p. 259.

34. Tonooka, *Genronjin*, p. 121.
35. *Asahi shinbun* (evening edition), August 15, 1965, in Betonamu ni Heiwa, *Shiryō*, 1:36. See Eguchi, *Gendai*, p. 233; "Japan and the Vietnam War," p. 251; Inaba, "Nikkan," p. 259.
36. Betonamu ni Heiwa, *Shiryō*, 1:37.
37. *New York Times*, November 16, 1965, in Betonamu ni Heiwa, *Shiryō*, 1:58; *Washington Post*, April 3, 1967, ibid., 1:209. See *Mainichi nenkan 1967*, p. 458; Tsurumi Yoshiyuki, "Beheiren," p. 446; Takahashi, " 'Beheiren' o," pp. 23, 28.
38. Ishida interview, December 5, 1984. See Tsurumi Shunsuke et al., eds., *Heiwa*, p. 13.
39. Oda, "Demo," p. 53. I am grateful to Ishida Takeshi for comments on this point. Ishida interview, December 5, 1984. See Iida, "Shimin," p. 27.
40. Lummis interview, December 27, 1984; Lummis correspondence, February 8, 1985.
41. Oda interview, December 9, 1984. I am grateful for comments from Yoshikawa Yūichi on this point. Yoshikawa interview, January 7, 1985.
42. Tonooka, *Genronjin*, p. 74. See also pp. 64, 72–73; Saeki Shōichi, *Kyōki, passim*.
43. Etō interview, December 20, 1984; Kamiya interview, November 30, 1984.
44. Miyake interview, December 28, 1984.
45. Mishima conversation with Tokuoka Takao, cited in Tokuoka interview, December 3, 1984. On October 15, 1969, Mishima discussed the war protests and Japan's defense policies in a speech marking the hundredth anniversary of the finance ministry. This speech was first published as "Nihon to wa nani ka" in *Bungei shunjū*, December 1985, pp. 192–209.
46. Oda interview, December 9, 1984.
47. Oda notes that "the right-wingers said they were going to kill us." Oda interview, December 9, 1984.
48. *Mainichi* polls, November 1964–October 1966, cited in J. Clark, *Japanese Foreign Policy*, p. 146.
49. Yoshikawa, "Beheiren wa," p. 21.
50. Nikkan, *Kensetsu*, pp. 105–106. See Takahashi, "Beheiren wa," pp. 113–116.
51. Shisō, *Bōhatsu*, p. 86.
52. Lummis correspondence, February 8, 1985.

53. *Japan Quarterly* 23:2 (April 1976), 132.
54. Ishida interview, December 5, 1984.
55. Rōyama interview, November 26, 1984. See Oketani, "Chishik-ijin," pp. 33–34.
56. Tsurumi interview, December 24, 1984.
57. Tsurumi Shunsuke, "Beheiren," p. 4.
58. Asahi, *Pacific Rivals*, p. 67.
59. Tsurumi interview, December 24, 1984; Yoshikawa interview, January 7, 1985.
60. Katō Shūichi interview, December 10, 1984.
61. Lummis interview, December 27, 1984; Lummis correspondence, February 8, 1985.
62. Oda interview, December 9, 1984. For comments on this point I am grateful to Donald Keene (correspondence, July 17, 1983).
63. *No More Hiroshimas!* 12:6 (August 1965), 4.
64. See Harada, *Shōwa*, p. 261; Maruyama, *Betonamu—sono tatakai*, pp. 73–74.
65. Nichols interview, November 28, 1984. See *No More Hiroshimas!* 12:6 (August 1965), 5; Takahashi, "Betonamu," pp. 108–109.
66. Takahashi, "Betonamu," pp. 111–112.
67. Oda interview, December 9, 1984. See Shinobu, ed., *Nihon gaikōshi 2*,581; Takahashi, "Betonamu," pp. 110–111.
68. Takahashi, "Betonamu," p. 114; Yoshikawa interview, January 7, 1985; Mellen, *Waves*, p. 396.
69. Bock, *Japanese Film*, pp. 319–320; Mellen, *Waves*, pp. 413–416, 419; Takahashi, "Betonamu," p. 113.
70. Oda interview, December 9, 1984.
71. *Asahi shinbun* (evening edition), July 31, 1965, in *Nichibei*, ed. Saitō et al., p. 397.
72. *Mainichi nenkan 1966*, p. 189.
73. *Asahi shinbun* (evening edition), July 31, 1965, *Nichibei*, ed. Saitō et al., p. 397.
74. *Mainichi nenkan 1966*, p. 189.
75. *Asahi jānaru*, November 10, 1972, p. 22.
76. Ibid., p. 21; *Far Eastern Economic Review*, August 12, 1965, p. 280; Langdon, *Japan's Foreign Policy*, p. 112.
77. *Asahi shinbun* (evening edition), July 31, 1965, in *Nichibei*, ed. Saitō et al., p. 398. See *Mainichi nenkan 1966*, p. 188.
78. *Asahi jānaru*, December 5, 1965, p. 12.

79. *Boston Globe*, August 7, 1965. See *Asahi jānaru*, December 5, 1965, p. 13.
80. Reischauer, "Watakushi," p. 28.
81. Reischauer, "Role," p. 327.
82. Matsuda, *Nihon no shinsei*, pp. 272–273; Nihon Heiwa, *Heiwa undō*, p. 284; Arasaki, "Okinawa's Reversion," p. 289; Miyamoto, *Keizai*, p. 254.
83. Edwin O. Reischauer press conference, September 1, 1965, quoted in *Asahi shinbun* (evening edition), September 1, 1965, in *Nichibei*, ed. Saitō et al., p. 398 (retranslated from Japanese). See Maruyama, *Ronsetsu*, p. 165.
84. Edwin O. Reischauer press conference, October 5, 1965, in Betonamu ni okeru, *Jenosaido*, p. 119 (retranslated from Japanese).
85. *Far Eastern Economic Review*, August 14, 1971, p. 17.
86. Edwin O. Reischauer press conference, October 5, 1965, in Betonamu ni okeru, *Jenosaido*, p. 120 (retranslated from Japanese).
87. Axelbank, *Black Star*, pp. 187–188.
88. Hayakawa, "Raishawā," p. 136.
89. Betonamu ni okeru, *Jenosaido*, p. 120; Inaba, "Nikkan," p. 260.
90. Ōmori Minoru, *Kita*, pp. 168–178.
91. Ōmori Minoru, *Ishi ni kaku*. See Storry, "Repercussions," p. 80.
92. See *Far Eastern Economic Review*, August 14, 1971, p. 17.
93. *Asahi shinbun*, October 7, 1965, in *Nichibei*, ed. Saitō et al., p. 392.
94. Betonamu ni okeru, *Jenosaido*, p. 120; *Mainichi nenkan 1967*, p. 452; *Far Eastern Economic Review*, January 6, 1966, p. 7.
95. Reischauer, "Role," p. 326.
96. Togawa, *Satō*, p. 162; Shibusawa, *Japan*, p. 41.
97. *No More Hiroshimas!* 12:10 (December 1965), 11. See Katō Bunzō et al., *Nihon rekishi*, 3:251; Matsuda, *Nihon no shinsei*, p. 274; Bix, "Report—Part II," p. 20.
98. Heiwa, *Sensō*, p. 247. See Mainichi, *Ichiokunin*, 8:21; Ishida Ikuo, *Anpo*, p. 33; Togawa, *Satō*, pp. 162–166.
99. See *Asahi jānaru*, December 5, 1965, pp. 13–14; *Mainichi nenkan 1966*, p. 189.
100. *New York Times*, December 23 and 29, 1965. See *Far Eastern Economic Review*, January 6, 1966, p. 10.
101. *Asahi jānaru*, December 5, 1965, pp. 12–14. See *Far Eastern Economic Review*, August 14, 1971, p. 17.

CHAPTER 3: THE SILENT PARTNER

1. Young C. Kim, "Japan and the Vietnam War," p. 156.
2. U. A. Johnson, *Right Hand*, p. 453.
3. Betonamu ni okeru, *Jenosaido*, p. 104.
4. Aoshima and Shinta, *Kichi*, p. 15; Buck, ed., *Modern Military*, p. 242; *Kodansha Encyclopedia of Japan*, 8:160.
5. *Kodansha Encyclopedia of Japan*, 8:161.
6. Aoshima and Shinta, *Kichi*, pp. 17–18; Buck, ed., *Modern Military*, p. 242.
7. Betonamu ni okeru, *Jenosaido*, p. 115; Nihon Heiwa, *Nihon no kokusho*, p. 3. For details on American bases, see Nihon Keizai Shinbun, *Kore*, p. 11; Aoshima and Shinta, *Kichi*, pp. 15–18; Betonamu ni okeru, *Jenosaido*, pp. 81–82; Dower, "Superdomino," p. 118; Kōmeitō report on bases, December 5, 1968, in *Nichibei*, ed. Saitō et al., pp. 450–453.
8. A. Watanabe, *Okinawa*, p. 64.
9. Ibid., pp. 64–65, 68; Selden, "Okinawa," pp. 284–285; Dower, "Superdomino," p. 118.
10. Betonamu ni okeru, *Jenosaido*, p. 104; *Far Eastern Economic Review*, April 10, 1971, p. 14.
11. *Far Eastern Economic Review*, October 10, 1968, p. 111.
12. Hirose, "Okinawan Disappointment," p. 408.
13. Young C. Kim, "Japan and the Vietnam War," p. 158.
14. Reischauer, *Japan the Story*, p. 357. On prior consultation, see Tai Sung Kim, "Japan's Security," pp. 73–74; Young C. Kim, "Japan's Security," pp. 66–75.
15. Young C. Kim, "Japan's Security," pp. 78–79; Tai Sung Kim, "Japan's Security," p. 75.
16. Honda Katsuichi, *Betonamu*, p. 331. See Betonamu ni okeru, *Jenosaido*, pp. 109–111; Kyōdō, *Kono*, p. 201; Nihon Heiwa, *Nihon no kokusho*, p. 57; *No More Hiroshimas!* 16:2 (June 1969), 13; Mainichi, *Ichiokunin*, 8:147.
17. *Sekai*, no. 259 (June 1967), 192; Nihon Heiwa, *Nihon no kokusho*, p. 56; Honda Katsuichi, *Betonamu*, p. 329.
18. Betonamu ni okeru, *Jenosaido*, p. 131.
19. *Sekai*, no. 259 (June 1967), 193.
20. U. A. Johnson, *Right Hand*, p. 452; Murakami interview, December 20, 1984; Momoi interview, January 9, 1985.
21. Congressional Quarterly Service, *Global Defense* (Washington,

D.C.: U.S. Government Printing Office, 1969), quoted in Dower, "Asia," p. 142. Figures are for fiscal years.

22. Asahi, *Pacific Rivals*, p. 231.

23. Mainichi, *Ichiokunin*, 8:243.

24. U. A. Johnson, *Right Hand*, p. 451; J. Clark, *Japanese Foreign Policy*, p. 155.

25. Harada, *Shōwa*, p. 289; *Far Eastern Economic Review*, October 24, 1970, p. 4; January 2, 1971, pp. 18–19.

26. *Sekai*, no. 253 (December 1966), 136–137. See Halliday, *Political History*, pp. 293, 430.

27. Asahi, *Pacific Rivals*, p. 304.

28. Naikaku Kanbō Naikaku, *Betonamu*, p. 147; Nihon Keizai, *Betonamu*, pp. 118, 121; Shepler and Campbell, "United States Defense," pp. 42–46; *Far Eastern Economic Review*, August 25, 1966, p. 351; "Vietnam Special Procurement," p. 13; Bix, "Security," p. 34.

29. Nihon Keizai, *Betonamu*, pp. 118, 121. Figures for yen sales and United States deposits are from the ministry of international trade and industry; those for contracts are from United States embassy records. On special procurement, see "Vietnam Special Procurement," p. 16; Economist, *Economic Effects*, pp. 1–2. For calculation variables, see Nihon Keizai, *Betonamu*, p. 132; Keizai, *Betonamu*, p. 116; Economist, *Economic Effects*, p. 9. On Okinawa, see Dower, "Superdomino," p. 120; J. Clark, *Japanese Foreign Policy*, p. 34.

30. Keizai, *Betonamu*, p. 116.

31. *Far Eastern Economic Review*, April 4, 1968, p. 13; J. Clark, *Japanese Foreign Policy*, pp. 10, 44.

32. Nihon Keizai, *Betonamu*, p. 131; "Vietnam Special Procurement," pp. 13–14; *Far Eastern Economic Review*, July 14, 1967, p. 53. Growth rates are calculated from *The Oriental Economist's Japan Economic Yearbook* 1967, p. 68; 1969, p. 68; 1970, p. 62; 1971, p. 69; 1972, p. 78; 1973, p. 76.

33. Economist, *Economic Effects*, p. 3; J. Clark, *Japanese Foreign Policy*, p. 21; *Far Eastern Economic Review*, April 4, 1968, p. 13.

34. "Vietnam Special Procurement," p. 15; Betonamu ni okeru, *Jenosaido*, p. 113.

35. Nihon Keizai, *Betonamu*, p. 133.

36. Ibid., pp. 133–134.

37. Keizai, *Betonamu*, p. 116.

38. Naikaku Kanbō Naikaku, *Betonamu*, p. 147; "Vietnam Special Procurement," p. 15.
39. See "Vietnam Special Procurement," p. 15; Naikaku Kanbō Naikaku, *Betonamu*, pp. 147, 151–152.
40. *Sekai*, no. 245 (April 1966), 159–164; Betonamu ni okeru, *Jenosaido*, p. 112.
41. Murakami interview, December 20, 1984.
42. Nihon Heiwa, *Nihon no kokusho*, p. 92; Betonamu ni okeru, *Jenosaido*, p. 114; *Far Eastern Economic Review*, April 14, 1966, p. 50; January 19, 1967, p. 97.
43. Betonamu ni okeru, *Jenosaido*, p. 114; Nihon Heiwa, *Nihon no kokusho*, pp. 88–92, 110–120; "Vietnam Special Procurement," p. 14; Honda Katsuichi, *Betonamu*, p. 331; Saitō et al., eds., *Nichibei*, p. 452. For comments on this point I am grateful to Donald M. Peppard, Jr.
44. Nihon Heiwa, *Nihon no kokusho*, p. 87; Betonamu Hansen, *Shi*, pp. 6–11; Betonamu ni okeru, *Jenosaido*, p. 115; " 'Nihonsei,' " p. 151. For technical advice I am grateful to Gary G. Giachino.
45. " 'Nihonsei,' " pp. 150–151.
46. Ibid., p. 151.
47. *Far Eastern Economic Review*, April 14, 1966, p. 50. See Murakami, *Nihon bōei*, p. 200; Okakura, *Betonamu*, pp. 43–45; Nihon Heiwa, *Nihon no kokusho*, p. 91.
48. Murakami, *Nihon bōei*, p. 199; Kyōdō, *Kono*, p. 219. See Langdon, *Japan's Foreign Policy*, p. 107.
49. Mainichi, *Anpo to bōei seisan*, p. 13.
50. *Ampo*, no. 15 (December 1972), 29. See p. 28; Sodei, "What Vietnam War Means," p. 315.
51. Okakura, *Betonamu*, p. 45; *No More Hiroshimas!* 13:4 (May–June 1966), 7; Betonamu Hansen, *Shi*, pp. 21, 28, 60–62.
52. Betonamu ni okeru, *Jenosaido*, pp. 114–115; Kyōdō, *Kono*, pp. 213–216; *No More Hiroshimas!* 16:2 (June 1969), 13; Nihon Keizai Chōsa, *Betonamu*, pp. 121–123.
53. *Mainichi nenkan 1968*, p. 330; Economist, *Economic Effects*, pp. 13–15; Andō Shinzō, *Betonamu*, pp. 15–17.
54. Aoshima and Shinta, *Kichi*, pp. 69–70; *Sekai*, no. 253 (December 1966), p. 137; *Zusetsu*, 13:72; Nihon Heiwa, *Nihon no kokusho*, pp. 59–60.
55. *Asahi jānaru*, June 4, 1967, pp. 22–23; Mainichi, *Ichiokunin*, 8:12; Bix, "Security," p. 40.

56. Ebashi and Yamada, *Shinsei*, p. 411; *Far Eastern Economic Review*, February 23, 1967, p. 314; March 20, 1969, p. 567.
57. Economist, *Economic Effects*, pp. 21–22; Ebashi and Yamada, *Shinsei*, pp. 403–407.
58. Ebashi and Yamada, *Shinsei*, p. 411; *Far Eastern Economic Review*, March 26, 1971, p. 64; Halliday and McCormack, *Japanese Imperialism*, p. 56.
59. Emmerson, *Arms*, p. 287; Nihon Keizai Chōsa, *Betonamu*, p. 128; Krause and Sekiguchi, "Japan," p. 418; Hellmann, *Japan*, p. 129.
60. *Far Eastern Economic Review*, October 13, 1966, p. 47; Naikaku Kanbō Naikaku, *Betonamu*, p. 125; Krause and Sekiguchi, "Japan," pp. 418–419.
61. Ebashi and Yamada, *Shinsei*, pp. 403, 411; Tsūshō, *Tsūshō hakusho* (1973), 367, 370.
62. See *Mainichi nenkan 1969*, p. 333.
63. J. Clark, *Japanese Foreign Policy*, p. 39. See Shibusawa, *Japan*, p. 152; Hayashi Risuke, "Where," p. 260; Emmerson, *Arms*, pp. 288–293.
64. Emmerson, *Arms*, p. 288.
65. Ebashi and Yamada, *Shinsei*, pp. 401–402; Hasegawa, *Japanese Foreign Aid*, p. 16; Shibusawa, *Japan*, p. 43; Kajima, *Modern*, p. 221.
66. Ebashi and Yamada, *Shinsei*, 402; Japan External Trade, *Economic Cooperation 1980*, pp. 25, 48.
67. *Far Eastern Economic Review Yearbook 1969*, p. 200; Maruyama, *Tōnan*, pp. 68–69; Kosaka, *100 Million*, p. 238.
68. Ebashi and Yamada, *Shinsei*, pp. 389–391, 397–398, 411; *Far Eastern Economic Review*, April 8, 1965, p. 68; September 8, 1966, p. 437; February 3, 1967, p. 320; *No More Hiroshimas!* 14:7 (December 1967), 36; Hellmann, *Japan*, p. 170; Halliday and McCormack, *Japanese Imperialism*, p. 235.

CHAPTER 4: STEADY STATE

1. *Far Eastern Economic Review*, February 10, 1966, p. 224.
2. "Betonamu mondai ni kansuru Hariman taishi hatsugen" (January 7, 1966), in *Nichibei*, ed. Saitō et al., p. 399. See Shinobu, ed., *Nihon gaikōshi 2*, p. 579.
3. Ibid. (retranslated from Japanese) See *Mainichi nenkan 1967*, p. 189.

4. Morse testimony, quoted in *Japan Times*, February 12, 1966.
5. Kennan, "American Involvement," p. 324.
6. *Asahi jānaru*, November 10, 1972, p. 22. See Kajima, *Modern*, p. 111; *Mainichi nenkan 1967*, p. 189; J. Clark, *Japanese Foreign Policy*, p. 123.
7. See J. Clark, *Japanese Foreign Policy*, pp. 83–85.
8. Betonamu ni okeru, *Jenosaido*, p. 121. On the polls, see p. 120; J. Clark, *Japanese Foreign Policy*, pp. 141–142.
9. Betonamu ni okeru, *Jenosaido*, p. 120.
10. *Far Eastern Economic Review*, April 14, 1966, p. 50.
11. *Far Eastern Economic Review*, March 10, 1966, p. 432; *Mainichi nenkan 1967*, p. 188.
12. *Mainichi nenkan 1967*, p. 188; Betonamu ni okeru, *Jenosaido*, p. 115; *Far Eastern Economic Review*, February 24, 1966, p. 344.
13. *Asahi shinbun* (evening edition), May 31, 1966, in *Nichibei*, ed. Saito et al., p. 399.
14. Eguchi, *Gendai*, p. 187.
15. Betonamu ni okeru, *Jenosaido*, pp. 130–131.
16. Takahashi, "Betonamu," p. 108; *Far Eastern Economic Review*, July 7, 1966, p. 4.
17. Takahashi, "Betonamu," p. 108.
18. *Far Eastern Economic Review*, July 7, 1966, p. 4. See J. Clark, *Japanese Foreign Policy*, p. 104; Mendel, "Japan, Okinawa," p. 3.
19. Okakura, *Betonamu*, p. 42. See Betonamu ni okeru, *Jenosaido*, p. 130.
20. Kawashima Shōjirō interview with Douglas H. Mendel, Jr., July 22, 1966, in Mendel, "Japan, Okinawa," p. 3.
21. Griffin, "Politics," p. 148.
22. Ibid.
23. Zinn, *Vietnam*, p. 15.
24. Asahi, *Pacific Rivals*, p. 223.
25. Ibid., p. 224.
26. Rōyama, "Japan," p. 5. See Colbert, "National Security," pp. 210–211; *Far Eastern Economic Review Yearbook 1967*, pp. 232–233; *Far Eastern Economic Review*, April 7, 1966, p. 11; Shibusawa, *Japan*, p. 42; E. Satō, "Pacific," pp. 1–2.
27. Langdon, *Japan's Foreign Policy*, p. 188; Colbert, "National Security," pp. 210–211; Rōyama, "Japan," pp. 5–6; Mainichi, *Ichiokunin*, 8:129.
28. Packard, "Living," p. 41.

29. "Japan and the Manila Conference," p. 4.
30. Shibusawa, *Japan*, pp. 34, 37–39, 45; *Far Eastern Economic Review Yearbook 1968*, p. 208.
31. Young, "Involvement," p. 174; Rōyama, "Japan," p. 5; Shibusawa, *Japan*, p. 42; Yasutomo, *Japan*, p. 69.
32. *Mainichi nenkan 1967*, p. 393; *Japan Quarterly* 13:2 (April 1966), 247; Inaba, "Nikkan," p. 261.
33. *No More Hiroshimas!* 13:5 (July-August 1966), 16. On Baez, Nichols interview, November 28, 1984; Inaba, "Nikkan," pp. 262–263; Betonamu ni okeru, *Jenosaido*, p. 121.
34. Takahashi, "Betonamu," pp. 113–116; Mainichi, *Ichiokunin*, 8:129; Betonamu ni okeru, *Jenosaido*, p. 132.
35. *Asahi jānaru*, November 17, 1972, p. 26; *Bunka hyōron*, no. 66 (April 1967), 146; Betonamu ni Heiwa, *Shiryō*, 1:147.
36. Tsurumi interview, December 24, 1984. See Kameyama, *Betonamu*, pp. 175–176; Shinobu, ed., *Nihon gaikōshi 2*, p. 582; Ishida Takeshi, *Japanese Political Culture*, pp. 156–157.
37. Yoshikawa interview, January 7, 1985; Tsurumi interview, December 24, 1984. See Eguchi, *Gendai*, p. 228.
38. *Bunka hyōron*, no. 63 (January 1967), 1–2, 44; no. 66 (April 1967), 146; Itō Yoshiaki, "Shinryaku," pp. 24–34.
39. Hatada, "Betonamu," p. 71. See *No More Hiroshimas!* 13:4 (May-June 1966), 9; *Bunka hyōron*, no. 81 (June 1968), 26.
40. Mutō, " 'Beheiren,' " p. 84.
41. *Asahi jānaru*, August 14, 1966, p. 21. See Tsurumi Yoshiyuki, "Beheiren," p. 446; Shisō, *Bōhatsu*, pp. 93–94; Takahashi, " 'Beheiren' o," p. 27; Zinn, *Vietnam*, p. 9.
42. Takabatake, "Citizens' Movements," p. 197. Yoshikawa interview, January 7, 1985; *Asahi jānaru*, August 14, 1966, p. 21.
43. *Zusetsu*, 13:22, 206; Betonamu ni Heiwa, *Shiryō*, 1:124, 138–139; Takahashi, " 'Beheiren' o," p. 27; Takahashi, "Beheiren wa," p. 113; Yoshioka, "Tenki," p. 67.
44. Postscript, in Oda, *Heiwa*. See Shisō, *Bōhatsu*, pp. 95–98.
45. Betonamu ni okeru, *Jenosaido*, p. 121; *Sekai*, no. 253 (December 1966), 82–121.
46. *Mainichi nenkan 1967*, p. 296; Heiwa, *Sensō*, p. 253.
47. Okakura, *Betonamu*, p. 2.
48. *Sekai*, no. 253 (December 1966), 157.
49. *Asahi jānaru*, November 6, 1966, p. 95; Shibata, "Gendai," pp. 49–50; Duke, *Japan's Militant Teachers*, pp. 182–184.

50. Sodei, "What Vietnam War Means," p. 314. See *Far Eastern Economic Review*, February 3, 1966, p. 145; Miyamoto, *Keizai*, p. 207; Iwadare interview, November 28, 1984; *Asahi jānaru*, November 6, 1966, pp. 90, 95.

51. *Asahi jānaru*, November 6, 1966, p. 95. See *Far Eastern Economic Review*, January 12, 1967, p. 36; Katō Shūichi, "Ushinawareta," p. 18.

52. *Asahi jānaru*, November 6, 1966, p. 95. For survey data, see Mendel, "Japan, Okinawa," p. 8.

53. Betonamu ni Heiwa, *Shiryō*, 1:180–181; Arasaki, "Okinawa's Reversion," p. 288.

54. Betonamu ni Heiwa, *Shiryō*, 1:160; Takahashi, " 'Beheiren' o," p. 27; Konaka, *Tezukuri*, p. 92.

55. *Nihon kingendaishi jiten*, p. 931; *Far Eastern Economic Review Yearbook 1968*, p. 207.

56. Shinobu, ed., *Nihon gaikōshi 2*, p. 583. See also p. 580.

57. Ibid., p. 583; Young C. Kim, "Japan's Security," pp. 65–66.

58. Irie, *Sengo*, p. 140. See J. Clark, *Japanese Foreign Policy*, p. 105; *Asahi jānaru*, June 5, 1967, p. 12.

59. Inaba, "Nikkan," pp. 263–264.

60. Ibid., p. 272; Togawa, *Satō*, p. 184.

61. Mita, "Political Attitudes," p. 548.

62. Aoshima and Shinta, *Kichi*, pp. 49–51; Okakura, *Betonamu*, p. 45; Harada, *Shōwa*, p. 270.

63. Miyamoto, *Keizai*, p. 207; Kugai, ed., *Shiryō*, 2:534–538.

64. *Asahi jānaru*, September 10, 1967, pp. 10–11; McNelly, *Politics*, pp. 65–66; *Mainichi nenkan 1968*, p. 330.

65. "Betonamu ni okeru Amerika no sensō hanzai," p. 813. See p. 809; Betonamu ni okeru, *Jenosaido*, p. 78; Shinobu, ed., *Nihon gaikōshi 2*, p. 583.

66. The evidence on Japan is given in Betonamu ni okeru, *Jenosaido*, and Betonamu ni okeru, *Rasseru*. It is summarized in "Betonamu ni okeru Amerika no sensō hanzai," pp. 809–813.

67. "Betonamu ni okeru Amerika no sensō hanzai," pp. 811–812.

CHAPTER 5: CHOPPY WATERS

1. Poll data taken from J. Clark, *Japanese Foreign Policy*, p. 140. See Shinobu, ed., *Nihon gaikōshi 2*, p. 582; Stockwin, *Japan*, p. 208.

2. See Kameyama, *Betonamu*, pp. 174–176. Kameyama observed some people voting five times in this election.

3. Rōyama, "Japan," p. 7; "Mr. Satō's Visits," p. 3; Langdon, *Japan's Foreign Policy*, pp. 113–114.

4. *Far Eastern Economic Review Yearbook 1968*, p. 208. See Togawa, *Satō*, p. 182.

5. See Togawa, *Satō*, p. 183.

6. "Mr. Satō's Visits," p. 5; Kameyama, *Betonamu*, p. 174.

7. *Shōwashi jiten*, p. 629; *Kodansha Encyclopedia of Japan*, 6:167.

8. Morris-Suzuki, *Showa*, p. 307. See Kazuko Tsurumi, "Student Movements," p. 209; *Kodansha Encyclopedia of Japan*, 6:167.

9. Iwadare, "Hansen," p. 232. See Dowsey, ed., *Zengakuren*, pp. 125–126.

10. Iwadare, "Hansen," p. 233.

11. Dowsey, ed., *Zengakuren*, pp. 125–128; *Shōwashi jiten*, p. 629; Mainichi, *Fifty Years*, p. 388; *Mainichi nenkan 1972*, p. 427; Packard, *Protest in Tokyo*, p. 296.

12. Béraud, "La gauche," pp. 119–121; Hashii, "Shichijūnen," pp. 228–229; Takami, ed., *Hansen*, pp. 107–108; Dowsey, ed., *Zengakuren*, p. 265.

13. "Mr. Satō's Visits," p. 6.

14. *Pentagon Papers*, 4:156.

15. *Asahi jānaru*, November 10, 1972, p. 21; "Mr. Satō's Visits," pp. 5–6; Kameyama, *Betonamu*, p. 174.

16. *Mainichi nenkan 1968*, pp. 324–330.

17. *Asahi jānaru*, November 5, 1967, pp. 8–9; *Mainichi nenkan 1968*, p. 324.

18. Maruyama, *Ronsetsu*, p. 228. See *Asahi jānaru*, November 26, 1967, pp. 15–16; *No More Hiroshimas!* 14:6 (October–November 1967), 6.

19. *Asahi jānaru*, November 26, 1967, pp. 10–15; Dowsey, ed., *Zengakuren*, pp. 128–129.

20. Shinobu, ed., *Nihon gaikōshi 2*, p. 579. I am grateful for advice from Rōyama Michio on this point. Rōyama interview, November 26, 1984.

21. *No More Hiroshimas!* 16:2 (June 1969), 11.

22. *Far Eastern Economic Review*, November 30, 1967, p. 395.

23. *No More Hiroshimas!* 16:2 (June 1969), 11.

24. Asahi, *Pacific Rivals* p. 224.

25. *Joint Communiqué Between Prime Minister Eisaku Satō and President*

Lyndon B. Johnson, November 15, 1967, quoted in Rōyama, "Japan," p. 7. For full text, see *Nichibei,* ed. Saitō et al., pp. 428–430.

26. Asahi, *Pacific Rivals,* p. 224. See Togawa, *Satō,* p. 186; Langdon, *Japan's Foreign Policy,* p. 127.

27. Betonamu ni okeru, *Jenosaido,* p. 117. See U. A. Johnson, *Right Hand,* p. 482; Langdon, *Japan's Foreign Policy,* p. 127.

28. *Yoron nenkan 1967,* pp. 429–431.

29. Togawa, *Satō,* p. 186; *Far Eastern Economic Review,* December 7, 1967, pp. 443–444.

30. Rōyama, "Japan," p. 7.

31. Katō Shūichi, "Ushinawareta," p. 18; Shibusawa, *Japan,* p. 96; Murakami interview, December 20, 1984.

32. Parker, *In One Day,* pp. 20–21. It is generally estimated that several hundred thousand American troops overstayed their status as absent without official leave and were classified as deserters during the Vietnam War. Many rejoined their units. Few desertions took place in the war zone.

33. Takahashi, "Beheiren wa," p. 113. The phrase is *ningen no shutaisei jiyū.* See Iwadare, "Hansen," pp. 234–235.

34. Lummis correspondence, February 8, 1985.

35. Betonamu ni Heiwa, *Shiryō,* 1:274.

36. Ibid., 1:267–268; Tsurumi interview, December 24, 1984; Yoshikawa interview, January 7, 1985; Konaka, *Tezukuri,* p. 93.

37. Betonamu ni Heiwa, *Shiryō,* 1:262–275; *Far Eastern Economic Review,* October 10, 1970, p. 18; *No More Hiroshimas!* 14:7 (December 1967), 4; Saitō et al., eds., *Nichibei,* pp. 427–428; *New York Times,* June 17, 1985.

38. Tsurumi interview, December 24, 1984.

39. Tsurumi Yoshiyuki, "Beheiren," p. 447; *No More Hiroshimas!* 14:7 (December 1967), 4.

40. Betonamu ni Heiwa, *Shiryō,* 1:275.

41. Yoshikawa interview, January 7, 1985. See Whitmore, *Memphis,* pp. 130–149.

42. The Soviet position is discussed in Zagoria, *Vietnam,* pp. 31–62; McGovern, "Moscow and Hanoi," pp. 64–71.

43. Oda et al., eds., *Kokka,* pp. 198–244; Betonamu ni Heiwa, *Shiryō,* 1:350, 2:37; Konaka, *Tezukuri,* p. 100; Shisō, *Bōhatsu,* pp. 109–111; Oda interview, December 9, 1984; Yoshikawa interview, January 7, 1985; *Ampo,* no. 2 (1970), 4. See *Far Eastern Economic Review,* October 23, 1969, p. 222.

44. Oda interview, December 9, 1984. See *Shōwashi jiten*, p. 630.
45. Oda interview, December 9, 1984.
46. Tsurumi interview, December 24, 1984.
47. Yoshikawa interview, January 7, 1985.
48. *Asahi shinbun*, January 1, 1968. Translation taken from *Japan Quarterly* 15:2 (April 1968), 246.
49. Togawa, *Satō*, pp. 190–191.
50. Irie, *Sengo*, p. 143; Miyamoto, *Keizai*, p. 204; *Asahi shinbun* (evening edition), in *Nichibei*, ed. Saitō et al., p. 363; Mainichi, *Ichiokunin*, 8:129; *Asahi jānaru*, July 4, 1965, p. 15; *Japan Times*, December 3, 1984; *Asahi Evening News*, December 4, 1984.
51. Sneider, *U.S.–Japan*, pp. 23–24. See *Far Eastern Economic Review*, February 24, 1966, p. 344; Young C. Kim, "Japan's Security," pp. 75–76.
52. *Seisaku geppō*, April 1968, p. 55. See Emmerson, *Arms*, p. 87.
53. U. A. Johnson, *Right Hand*, p. 490. See *Seisaku geppō*, April 1968, p. 55.
54. U. A. Johnson, *Right Hand*, p. 490. Momoi Makoto confirmed this point in Momoi interview, January 9, 1985.
55. U. A. Johnson, *Right Hand*, p. 493.
56. For details on Sasebo, see Ishida Ikuo, "Sasebo," pp. 58–68; Ishida Ikuo, *Anpo*, pp. 129, 132; Usami, "Zengakuren," p. 233; Dowsey, ed., *Zengakuren*, p. 131; Young C. Kim, "Japan's Security," p. 78.
57. Togawa, *Satō*, p. 191; Ishida Ikuo, "Sasebo," p. 58.
58. U. A. Johnson, *Right Hand*, p. 490. See Usami, "Zengakuren," p. 233; Ishida Ikuo, "Sasebo," pp. 59–60.
59. *No More Hiroshimas!* 15:2 (March–April 1968), 14–15; Togawa, *Satō*, p. 191.
60. Ishida Takeshi, *Japanese Political Culture*, p. 156.
61. Usami, "Zengakuren," p. 236; Dowsey, ed., *Zengakuren*, p. 131; Ishida Ikuo, "Sasebo," p. 58.
62. Mainichi, *Ichiokunin* 8:134–135; Togawa, *Satō*, p. 191; Mainichi, *Fifty Years*, p. 386; Ishida Takeshi, "Emerging," p. 421.
63. Ishida Ikuo, *Anpo*, p. 102; Takahashi, "Beheiren wa," p. 110.
64. Inaba, "Nikkan," p. 266; *Japan Times*, December 11, 1984. As of 1985 there had been only four calls in total.
65. U. A. Johnson, *Right Hand*, p. 493; Sneider, *U.S.–Japan*, p. 24; Suzuki, "Declining," p. 125; Lu, "Sato," p. 39; Mainichi, *Ichiokunin*, 8:246. The *New York Times* reported on August 11, 1985,

that United States bases in Japan stored nuclear weapons from 1955 to 1957.

66. The best account of Tet is Oberdorfer, *Tet!*
67. Tokuoka interview, December 3, 1984. See Aoshima and Shinta, *Kichi*, p. 12; *Asahi jānaru*, November 10, 1972, p. 140; Tonooka, *Genronjin*, pp. 191–192; Iwadare interview, November 28, 1984.
68. Etō, *Mukoku*, p. 237.
69. Lockheimer, "Further Reflections," pp. 8–9; Lockheimer, "Vietnam," p. 2; Kameyama, *Betonamu*, pp. 181–186; Tokuoka interview, December 3, 1984; *Asahi jānaru*, April 21, 1968, p. 90.
70. A. Watanabe, *Okinawa*, p. 64; J. Clark, *Japanese Foreign Policy*, p. 69; *Far Eastern Economic Review*, October 10, 1968, p. 111; Marcot, "Japanese Foreign Policymaking," p. 258.
71. *Japan Quarterly* 16:2 (April 1969), 142.
72. U. A. Johnson, *Right Hand*, p. 502; Selden, "Okinawa," p. 298.
73. Marcot, "Japanese Foreign Policymaking," p. 259. See *Far Eastern Economic Review*, March 7, 1968, p. 400; Mainichi, *Ichiokunin*, 8:138; U. A. Johnson, *Right Hand*, p. 502.
74. Harada, *Shōwa*, p. 275; Marcot, "Japanese Foreign Policymaking," pp. 260–261; A. Watanabe, *Okinawa*, p. 67; *Far Eastern Economic Review*, January 2, 1969, p. 4; February 13, 1969, p. 270.
75. *Shōwashi jiten*, p. 637; Aoshima and Shinta, *Kichi*, p. 65.
76. J. Clark, *Japanese Foreign Policy*, pp. 164–165, 174–175; Dowsey, ed., *Zengakuren*, p. 133; Mainichi, *Ichiokunin*, 8:136–137; *Shōwashi jiten*, p. 637.
77. Betonamu ni Heiwa, *Shiryō*, 1:346.
78. Aoshima and Shinta, *Kichi*, p. 63; Ishida Takeshi, *Japanese Political Culture*, p. 155; Ishida interview, December 5, 1984; Harada, *Shōwa*, p. 274; J. Clark, *Japanese Foreign Policy*, pp. 157–158.
79. Aoshima and Shinta, *Kichi*, pp. 63–65; Nihon Heiwa, *Nihon no kokusho*, p. 59; Iwadare interview, November 28, 1984; J. Clark, *Japanese Foreign Policy*, pp. 161–162, 167–172, 180–181.
80. J. Clark, *Japanese Foreign Policy*, p. 196; U. A. Johnson, *Right Hand*, pp. 499–500.
81. U. A. Johnson, *Right Hand*, p. 500.
82. Ibid.; J. Clark, *Japanese Foreign Policy*, pp. 104, 145, 196.
83. Yoshikawa, "Beheiren to," p. 10.
84. Ishida Takeshi, *Japanese Society*, pp. 104–105. See Nagai, *Takyoku*, p. 83; Ishida Takeshi, *Japanese Political Culture*, p. 128. I am

grateful to Katō Mikio for comments on this point. Katō Mikio interview, November 28, 1984.

85. *Asahi shinbun* (evening edition), April 3, 1967, quoted in *Sekai*, no. 259 (June 1967), 193; Nihon Heiwa, *Nihon no kokusho*, p. 51; Okakura, *Betonamu*, p. 43.

86. Aoshima and Shinta, *Kichi*, pp. 71–72; Kyōdō, *Kono*, pp. 195–196.

87. Aoshima and Shinta, *Kichi*, p. 71; *Sekai*, no. 259 (June 1967), 193; Young C. Kim, "Japan's Security," p. 70.

88. Young C. Kim, "Japan's Security," pp. 70–71; Apter and Sawa, *Against*, p. 124.

89. Sasebo, *Shimin*, p. 54. See Heiwa, *Sensō*, pp. 242–244.

90. Aoshima and Shinta, *Kichi*, p. 90; *Far Eastern Economic Review*, October 10, 1968, p. 109.

91. Horie, "Sasebo," pp. 78–79; Gotō, "Crisis," p. 425; Aoshima and Shinta, *Kichi*, pp. 67–68; U. A. Johnson, *Right Hand*, pp. 496–498.

92. *Shōwashi jiten*, p. 639; Emmerson, *Arms*, p. 94; *No More Hiroshimas!* 15:3 (May–June 1968), 7; Gotō, "Crisis," p. 421.

93. *Mainichi nenkan 1968*, p. 330; *Far Eastern Economic Review*, July 20, 1967, p. 136; Miyaoka, *Sunagawa*, p. 226; *Asahi jānaru*, June 29, 1969, p. 17.

94. *Asahi jānaru*, October 19, 1969, p. 7. See Nihon Heiwa, *Nihon no kokusho*, p. 44; Miyaoka, *Sunagawa*, pp. 9–11, 209–229.

95. See Mellen, *Voices*, p. 16; Mellen, *Waves*, pp. 436–438.

96. Mendel, "Japanese-American Relations," p. 325.

97. U. A. Johnson, *Right Hand*, pp. 506–507.

98. *Mainichi shinbun* (evening edition), December 23, 1968, in *Nichibei*, ed. Saitō et al., pp. 453–454. See J. Clark, *Japanese Foreign Policy*, p. 172; U. A. Johnson, *Right Hand*, pp. 506–507.

CHAPTER 6: WAVES OF DISSENT

1. Oda Makoto et al., "Yobikake," April 26, 1968, quoted in *Asahi jānaru*, June 23, 1968, p. 41.

2. Ishida Ikuo, *Anpo*, pp. 41, 57; Ishida Takeshi, *Japanese Political Culture*, p. 132.

3. Gomi, "Behan," p. 50; *Asahi jānaru*, June 23, 1968, p. 44; Betonamu ni Heiwa, *Shiryō*, 1:364, 370–372.

4. Hidaka, "Chokusetsu," p. 374.

5. *Nihon kingendaishi jiten*, pp. 933–934.
6. Takahashi, "Beheiren wa," p. 110; Shisō, *Bōhatsu*, pp. 100–104.
7. Yoshioka, "Tenki," p. 68.
8. Shisō, *Bōhatsu*, p. 104; Yoshioka, "Tenki," pp. 69–70; Tonooka, *Genronjin*, p. 84.
9. *Asahi jānaru*, November 3, 1968, p. 11.
10. Ibid., p. 12; *Far Eastern Economic Review*, December 12, 1968, p. 629.
11. Ishida Ikuo, *Anpo*, pp. 177–185; Shinobu, ed., *Nihon gaikōshi 2*, p. 585; *Asahi jānaru*, November 3, 1968, p. 12.
12. *Asahi shinbun* (evening edition) December 29, 1984. See Kikuchi, *Sugao*, pp. 245–247; Mainichi, *Fifty Years*, p. 387.
13. Ishida Ikuo, *Anpo*, p. 177; *Asahi jānaru*, November 3, 1968, p. 13.
14. Kikuichi, *Sugao*, p. 246.
15. Morris-Suzuki, *Showa*, p. 307.
16. Saitō et al., eds., *Nichibei*, p. 406.
17. Mendel, "Security," pp. 102–103; Mendel, "Japanese Opinion," p. 637; NHK, *Zusetsu*, p. 164.
18. Asahi, *Pacific Rivals*, p. 225.
19. *Asahi jānaru*, February 16, 1969, p. 113.
20. Konaka, *Watakushi*, p. 153. See Shisō, *Bōhatsu*, p. 107; Fukashiro, "New Left," p. 30.
21. Mainichi, *Ichiokunin*, 8:138, 144; Apter and Sawa, *Against*, p. 124; Beer, *Freedom*, p. 365; *Japan Quarterly* 22:3 (July 1975), 279–280.
22. Haryū interview, November 22, 1984. See *Asahi jānaru*, August 4, 1968, p. 48; Moriyama, "Minshuteki," p. 55.
23. *Asahi jānaru*, December 22, 1968, p. 26; Higuchi, "Betonamu," pp. 116, 120; Tonooka, *Genronjin*, pp. 167–168; Satō, "Ongaku," p. 48.
24. T. Sato, *Currents*, pp. 204–205; Mellen, *Waves*, p. 444; Ishiko, "Senkyūhyakushichijūnen," p. 45; *Bunka hyōron*, no. 98 (November 1969), 138.
25. Harada, *Shōwa*, p. 281.
26. Mainichi, *Ichiokunin*, 8:115; Dowsey, ed., *Zengakuren*, pp. 181–183.
27. Dowsey, ed., *Zengakuren*, p. 183; Lockheimer, "Vietnam," pp. 1–2; *Asahi jānaru*, November 2, 1969, p. 4.
28. Kikuchi, *Sugao*, p. 24. See pp. 18–23; *Mainichi nenkan 1970*, p. 80; Hashii, "Shichijūnen," p. 233; Takami, ed., *Hansen*, p. 118.
29. *Ampo*, no. 1 (November 1969), 8.

30. Shisō, *Bōhatsu*, p. 80. See Yoshikawa, "Beheiren to," pp. 7–8; Eguchi, *Gendai*, p. 234; *Asahi jānaru*, June 29, 1969, p. 102.

31. Shisō, *Bōhatsu*, pp. 78–81; *Asahi jānaru*, June 29, 1969, p. 102; Tsurumi Yoshiyuki, "Beheiren," p. 444; Yoshikawa, "Beheiren to," pp. 7–8, 14–16; *Far Eastern Economic Review*, June 26, 1969, p. 688.

32. Takahashi, "Beheiren wa," p. 111. See Dowsey, ed., *Zengakuren*, p. 266.

33. Shisō, *Bōhatsu*, p. 115.

34. Tsurumi Yoshiyuki, "Senkyūhyakushichijūnen," p. 54. See Takahashi, "Beheiren wa," pp. 110–111, 120; Itō Shin, "Hansen," pp. 109–117; Iwadare, "Heiwa," pp. 49–50.

35. Mainichi, *Ichiokunin*, 8:139; Miyazaki, "Political Rights," pp. 82–94.

36. *Ampo*, no. 2 (1970), 10–11; *Far Eastern Economic Review*, October 30, 1969, p. 264; Halliday, *Political History*, p. 234.

37. Kyōdō, *Kono*, p. 192; Maruyama, *Ronsetsu*, pp. 228–229.

38. Tsurumi Yoshiyuki, "Senkyūhyakushichijūnen," p. 56. See Shisō, *Bōhatsu*, p. 112; Mihashi, "Agora," pp. 171–176; Betonamu ni Heiwa, *Shiryō*, 2:106; Harada, *Shōwa*, p. 284; Yoshikawa, "Beheiren to," p. 16; *Shūkan asahi*, May 30, 1969, pp. 20–22.

39. Murakami, *Nihon bōei*, pp. 109–112; Langdon, *Japan's Foreign Policy*, p. 121; Hellmann, *Japan*, p. 24.

40. U.S. Senate, *United States Security*, p. 1167. See Kosaka, "Northeast," pp. 32–34.

41. Haryū, "Hanbaku," p. 126. See *Asahi jānaru*, February 16, 1969, p. 114.

42. *Asahi jānaru*, February 16, 1969, p. 114; Haryū, "Hanbaku," p. 127.

43. Haryū, "Hanbaku," pp. 127, 133; Shisō, *Bōhatsu*, p. 113.

44. Dowsey, ed., *Zengakuren*, pp. 164, 191; Usami, "Zengakuren," p. 234; Tsurumi Kazuko, "Student Movements," p. 205.

45. Duke, "Terror," p. 53.

46. *Far Eastern Economic Review*, December 21, 1967, p. 550.

47. Fukashiro, "New Left," p. 34. See pp. 28–29, 32–33.

48. Usami, "Zengakuren," p. 243. See p. 242; Duke, "Terror," p. 54; Dowsey, ed., *Zengakuren*, p. 214.

49. Yoshimoto, *Jiritsu*. See Wheeler, "Postmodern," pp. 203–204; Tsurumi Kazuko, "Student Movements," pp. 216–218.

50. Wheeler, "Postmodern," pp. 209, 223; Tsurumi Kazuko, "Student Movements," p. 208.

51. Jansen, "United States," p. 31.

52. Wheeler, "Postmodern," p. 207; Stockwin, *Japan*, p. 69.

53. Oda, "Making," p. 125.

54. Shisō, *Bōhatsu*, p. 105.

55. See Fukashiro, "New Left," p. 34.

56. *Ampo*, no. 1 (November 1969), 7; Dowsey, ed., *Zengakuren*, pp. 185–186.

57. *Ampo*, no. 1 (November 1969), 3; *Shōwashi jiten*, p. 656.

58. *Asahi shinbun* (evening edition), December 25, 1969, in Betonamu ni Heiwa, *Shiryō*, 2:185–186.

59. *Ampo*, no. 1 (November 1969), 4. See also p. 12; *Asahi jānaru*, November 2, 1969, pp. 4–6.

60. *Asahi jānaru*, November 2, 1969, p. 5; *Ampo*, no. 1 (November 1969), 12; Dowsey, ed., *Zengakuren*, p. 187; *Shōwashi jiten*, p. 656.

61. *Asahi jānaru*, November 2, 1969, pp. 4–7; Dowsey, ed., *Zengakuren*, pp. 187–188; Takahashi, "Beheiren wa," pp. 108, 111.

62. *Ampo*, no. 1 (November 1969), 4, 12; *Asahi jānaru*, November 2, 1969, p. 4; Dowsey, ed., *Zengakuren*, pp. 187–188.

63. Wheeler, "Postmodern," p. 208; Takahashi, "Beheiren wa," pp. 112–113; Tsurumi Yoshiyuki, "Senkyūhyakushichijūnen," p. 55.

CHAPTER 7: THE PROTESTS PEAK

1. See Kendrick, *Wound*, pp. 293–298, 306.

2. Sneider, *U.S.–Japan*, pp. 34–35.

3. *Japan Times*, August 5, 1969, quoted in Mendel, "Japanese-American Relations," p. 318.

4. Iwadare, "Hansen," p. 232. See Selden, "Okinawa," p. 288; Mendel, "Japan, Okinawa," p. 10. I am grateful to Iwadare Hiroshi for comments on this point. Iwadare interview, November 28, 1984.

5. Arasaki, "Okinawa's Reversion," p. 289; Nihon Heiwa, *Heiwa undō*, p. 285; *Far Eastern Economic Review*, February 13, 1969, p. 270.

6. *Far Eastern Economic Review*, February 13, 1969, p. 270; Harada, *Shōwa*, p. 278; Miyamoto, *Keizai*, pp. 259–261; Saitō et al., eds., *Nichibei*, pp. 455–456.

7. Irie, *Sengo*, p. 154.
8. *Far Eastern Economic Review*, November 20, 1969, p. 396. See *Shōwashi jiten*, p. 658.
9. J. Clark, *Japanese Foreign Policy*, p. 138.
10. Urushiyama, *Shinbun*, pp. 3–4; Asahi, *Pacific Rivals*, pp. 181–182.
11. *Ampo*, no. 2 (1970), 11–12; Togawa, *Satō*, p. 231.
12. Saitō et al., eds., *Nichibei*, pp. 457–458. See Togawa, *Satō*, p. 231.
13. *Asahi jānaru*, November 30, 1969, pp. 5–6; Dowsey, ed., *Zengakuren*, p. 189.
14. *Asahi jānaru*, November 30, 1969, p. 9; *Ampo*, no. 2 (1970), 12; Dowsey, ed., *Zengakuren*, pp. 188–189.
15. Saitō et al., eds., *Nichibei*, pp. 457–458; Dowsey, ed., *Zengakuren*, pp. 189–190; *Ampo*, no. 2 (1970), 3, 11; *Asahi jānaru*, November 30, 1969, p. 5.
16. Dowsey, ed., *Zengakuren*, pp. 188–191; *Asahi jānaru*, November 30, 1969, p. 5; *Ampo*, no. 2 (1970), 3, 12.
17. Haryū interview, November 22, 1984.
18. Morris-Suzuki, *Showa*, p. 309.
19. *Asahi shinbun*, November 18, 1969, in *Nichibei*, ed. Saitō et al., p. 458.
20. *Asahi shinbun*, November 22, 1969, in *Nichibei*, ed. Saitō et al., p. 464.
21. For the communiqué, see Saitō et al., eds., *Nichibei*, p. 461; on American nuclear weapons, see *New York Times*, August 11, 1985.
22. U. A. Johnson, *Right Hand*, pp. 508–509; Asahi, *Pacific Rivals*, pp. 228–229; Shibusawa, *Japan*, p. 70.
23. Saitō et al., eds., *Nichibei*, p. 460.
24. Irie, *Sengo*, p. 156.
25. Saitō et al., eds., *Nichibei*, p. 460.
26. *New York Times*, November 22, 1969. See Dower, "Superdomino," p. 135.
27. *Asahi shinbun*, November 22, 1969, in *Nichibei*, ed. Saitō et al., p. 464; Emmerson, *Arms*, p. 90.
28. Rōyama, "Japan," p. 7.
29. Saitō et al., eds., *Nichibei*, pp. 461–464; Hayashi Risuke, "Where," pp. 260–261; Guillain, "New Pacific Age," pp. 488–490.
30. Rōyama, "Japan," p. 9.

31. Barnet, *Alliance*, pp. 309–310; Destler, "U.S.–Japanese," p. 197.
32. *Asahi shinbun* (evening edition), November 22, 1969, in *Nichibei*, ed. Saitō et al., p. 464.
33. Ibid., p. 465.
34. Ibid.
35. *Nihon kingendaishi jiten*, p. 931; Emmerson, *Arms*, p. 98; NHK, *Zusetsu*, p. 171; Mendel, "Japanese-American Relations," p. 323; Mainichi, *Ichiokunin*, 8:244.
36. Mutō, "December," pp. 504–507; *Ampo*, nos. 3–4 (March 1970), 14.
37. NHK, *Zusetsu*, p. 179.
38. Tsurumi Yoshiyuki, "Senkyūhyakushichijūnen," p. 51.
39. *Ampo*, nos. 3–4 (March 1970), 9–12; *Asahi jānaru*, May 10, 1970, p. 8.
40. Mendel, "Japan's Defense," p. 1068. See Lambert, "Le Japon," p. 63.
41. *Asahi jānaru*, June 28, 1970, p. 4. See July 5, 1970, p. 108; Tsurumi Kazuko, "Student Movements," p. 222.
42. *Asahi jānaru*, June 28, 1970, pp. 4–5.
43. *Mainichi shinbun* (evening edition), June 18, 1970, in Betonamu ni Heiwa, *Shiryō*, 2:360–362.
44. Ōmori, "June," p. 384; *Ampo*, no. 6 (Autumn 1970), 19.
45. See Ōmori, "June," pp. 391–392.
46. Rōyama, "Japan," p. 18.
47. Ōmori, "June," p. 389. See Black, "*Ampo*," p. 9.
48. Minaguchi, *Anpo*, p. 271.
49. Horii returned to Japan on June 19. See *Far Eastern Economic Review*, July 2, 1970, p. 72; Ōmori, "June," p. 388.
50. Iwadare, "Heiwa," p. 47–48; Ōmori, "June," pp. 384, 389.
51. *Asahi jānaru*, June 28, 1970, p. 5. See G. Clark, "Saying," p. 75.
52. *Asahi jānaru*, June 28, 1970, p. 5.
53. *Yomiuri shinbun*, June 24, 1970, in Betonamu ni Heiwa, *Shiryō*, 2:373.
54. Krauss, *Japanese Radicals*, p. 153.
55. *Yomiuri shinbun*, June 24, 1970, in Betonamu ni Heiwa, *Shiryō*, 2:373. See Tsurumi Shunsuke, *Sengo*, p. 180; *Ampo*, no. 6 (Autumn 1970), 18.
56. Betonamu ni Heiwa, *Shiryō*, 2:373; *Ampo*, no. 6 (Autumn 1970) 19; Iwadare, "Heiwa," p. 48; Ōmori, "June," pp. 384–385.
57. *Asahi shinbun*, June 23, 1970, quoted in Rōyama, "Japan," p. 18.

CHAPTER 8: PREPARING FOR THE POST-VIETNAM ERA

1. Oda interview, December 9, 1984.
2. Ishida interview, December 5, 1984.
3. Rōyama, "Japan," p. 13.
4. *Asahi jānaru*, July 12, 1970, p. 17.
5. *Asahi jānaru*, November 1, 1970, p. 8; Iwadare, "Heiwa," pp. 48–49; Katō Bunzō et al., *Nihon rekishi*, 3:265–266.
6. Asahi, *Pacific Rivals*, p. 354.
7. Wheeler, "Postmodern," p. 208; Bowen, "Narita," p. 600.
8. Iwadare, "Hansen," p. 232. See Dowsey, ed., *Zengakuren*, p. 132; Bowen, "Narita," p. 605.
9. Apter and Sawa, *Against*, p. 211. Tokuoka thinks the potential military use of the airport was a minor factor in the protests; Iwadare sees the Narita struggle as partly antiwar. Tokuoka interview, December 3, 1984; Iwadare interview, November 28, 1984.
10. *Far Eastern Economic Review*, May 19, 1978, p. 20.
11. Harada, *Shōwa*, pp. 287, 298; Kirk, "Rebels," pp. 14–15; Mainichi, *Fifty Years*, pp. 402, 406–415.
12. Yoshikawa, "Beheiren to," p. 20. See Takabatake, "Citizens' Movements," pp. 190–195; Suzuki, "Declining," pp. 121–123; Kuroda, "Protest," pp. 947–949; "Citizens Movements," pp. 368–372.
13. Ishida interview, December 5, 1984.
14. *Asahi jānaru*, November 10, 1972, p. 101.
15. Ishida Takishi, *Japanese Political Culture*, p. 152; Mainichi, *Ichiokunin*, 8:163. On Beheiren and the bases, see Betonamu ni Heiwa, *Shiryō*, 2:420, 3:140; Asahi, *Pacific Rivals*, p. 368; *Ampo*, nos. 13–14 (May-July 1972), 30–31. I am grateful to Yoshikawa Yūichi for advice on this point. Yoshikawa interview, January 7, 1985.
16. *Ampo*, nos. 9–10 (1971), 51–55; Mainichi, *Ichiokunin*, 8:138; *Mainichi nenkan 1972*, p. 327; *Shōwashi jiten*, p. 679.
17. Hirose, "Okinawan Disappointment," p. 409; Harada, *Shōwa*, p. 290; *Japan Quarterly* 18:2 (April 1971), 228–229.
18. Mainichi, *Ichiokunin*, 8:197; *Asahi jānaru*, May 14, 1971, p. 99; Harada, *Shōwa*, p. 294; *Far Eastern Economic Review*, May 19, 1971, p. 4.
19. Hirose, "Okinawan Disappointment," pp. 409–412.
20. Mainichi, *Ichiokunin*, 8:197; Mainichi, *Fifty Years*, pp. 388–389;

Selden, "Okinawa," p. 296; Hirose, "Okinawan Disappointment," p. 408; Harada, *Shōwa*, p. 296.

21. Miyake interview, December 28, 1984. See Hellmann, "Confrontation," p. 154.
22. Shibusawa, *Japan*, pp. 51–54, 62–64; Reischauer, *Japan the Story*, pp. 324–325; Kataoka, *Waiting*, pp. 24, 29–30.
23. Rōyama interview, November 26, 1984; Destler, "U.S.–Japanese," p. 197; Mainichi, *Fifty Years*, pp. 364–372.
24. Saxonhouse, "Employment," p. 79; *Far Eastern Economic Review Yearbook 1972*, p. 36; Rōyama interview, November 26, 1984.
25. See Shibusawa, *Japan*, pp. 69–71.
26. Dower, "Superdomino," p. 112.
27. Shibusawa, *Japan*, pp. 63–64; Lu, "Sato," p. 41.
28. Mainichi, *Ichiokunin*, 8:189; Mainichi, *Fifty Years*, p. 391; Harada, *Shōwa*, p. 296.
29. Yoshikawa interview, January 7, 1985; *Asahi jānaru*, January 7, 1972, p. 123; Nichols interview, November 28, 1984.
30. Maruyama, *Betonamu—sono tatakai*, p. 70; Maruyama, *Ronsetsu*, pp. 184–186.
31. *Mainichi nenkan 1973*, p. 376. See Higuchi, "Betonamu," p. 117.
32. NHK, *Zusetsu*, p. 181.
33. Mainichi, *Ichiokunin*, 8:231.
34. Togawa, *Satō*, p. 308; *Far Eastern Economic Review*, April 29, 1972, p. 4.
35. *PHP Intersect* 1:2 (February 1985), 6.
36. Hayashi Risuke, "Where," pp. 259–263; Shibusawa, *Japan*, pp. 66–68, 97.
37. Destler, "U.S.–Japanese," p. 196.
38. *Ampo*, no. 15 (December 1972), 4.
39. Ishida Takeshi, *Japanese Political Culture*, p. 116; *Ampo*, no. 15 (December 1972), 4–6; Heiwa, *Sensō*, pp. 266–267; *Japan Quarterly* 20:1 (January 1973), 3–4.
40. *Asahi jānaru*, August 25, 1972, p. 5.
41. Ibid.; *Ampo*, no. 15 (December 1972), 6–8; Ishida interview, December 5, 1984.
42. *Ampo*, no. 15 (December 1972), 10. See also p. 9; *Japan Quarterly* 20:1 (January 1973), 4–5.
43. *Asahi jānaru*, November 10, 1972, p. 102.
44. Ibid. See Suzuki, "Declining," pp. 125–126; Kirk, "Rebels," pp. 16–17.

45. Maruyama, *Betonamu—sono tatakai*, p. 284.
46. *Asahi shinbun*, January 21, 1973, in Betonamu ni Heiwa, *Shiryō*, 3:293–295; Iwadare, "Hansen," p. 230.
47. *Chūō kōron*, March 1973, p. 38. See Forbis, *Japan*, p. 412.
48. Tonooka, *Genronjin*, p. 229.
49. Ibid., pp. 226, 230.
50. Ibid., pp. 230–231.
51. Ibid., pp. 187–190.
52. Oda Makoto, in Oda and Honda, "Waga," p. 299. See Iwadare, "Hansen," p. 238.
53. See Tonooka, *Genronjin*, p. 179.
54. Rōyama interview, November 26, 1984.
55. Morikawa Kinju, *Betonamu*, pp. 219–221.
56. NHK, *Zusetsu*, pp. 179, 185.
57. Momoi interview, January 9, 1985; Daniels, "Japanese Foreign Policy," p. 86.
58. *Asahi shinbun*, April 22, 1973, in Betonamu ni Heiwa, *Shiryō*, 3:368.
59. Ibid., pp. 363–368.
60. Betonamu ni Heiwa, *Shiryō*, 3:476. See also pp. 368, 464; Sodei, "What Vietnam War Means," p. 316.

CHAPTER 9: ADJUSTING TO PEACETIME

1. Hatada, "Betonamu," p. 66.
2. *Asahi shinbun*, May 1, 1975. See Irie, *Sengo*, p. 144.
3. *Far Eastern Economic Review*, November 14, 1975, quoted in Weinstein and Lewis, "Post-Vietnam," p. 135.
4. Rōyama interview, November 26, 1984; Murakami interview, December 20, 1984. See Tonooka, *Genronjin*, pp. 236–258.
5. Oda interview, December 9, 1984.
6. *Japan Quarterly* 26:3 (July 1979), 417.
7. Yoshikawa interview, January 7, 1985.
8. Mutō, *Nihon kokka*, p. 24.
9. Katō Mikio interview, November 28, 1984; Kamiya interview, November 30, 1984; "Peace Research," pp. 377–381; Kawata, *Tasks*, p. 1; Lummis interview, December 27, 1984.
10. Tsurumi interview, December 24, 1984.
11. Ibid.

12. Ibid. I am also grateful to Douglas Lummis for comments on this point. Lummis interview, December 27, 1984.
13. Tsurumi interview, December 24, 1984.
14. Ibid.
15. Oda interview, December 9, 1984.
16. *Japan Quarterly* 22:3 (July 1975), 276. See 23:1 (January 1976), 10–11; Kosaka, "Northeast," p. 37.
17. Karasawa, "Indoshina," pp. 137–138.
18. *Far Eastern Economic Review Asia Yearbook 1976*, pp. 193–194.
19. Weinstein and Lewis, "Post-Vietnam," p. 137. See Shibusawa, *Japan*, pp. 92–93. I am grateful for comments on these points to Kamiya Fuji, interview, November 30, 1984; Etō Shinkichi, interview, December 20, 1984; and Momoi Makoto, interview, January 9, 1985.
20. *Japan Quarterly* 22:4 (October 1975), 308.
21. Shibusawa, *Japan*, pp. 95–96; *New London Day*, September 19, 1985.
22. Rōyama interview, November 26, 1984.
23. *Japan Quarterly* 23:1 (January 1976), 9.
24. Honda interview, November 28, 1984; Shibusawa, *Japan*, p. 95; Etō interview, December 20, 1984; Kamiya interview, November 30, 1984; Kosaka, "Northeast," pp. 37–38; Momoi interview, January 9, 1985.
25. Onishi, "Japan's Self-Defense," pp. 147, 158. See Shibusawa, *Japan*, p. 95.
26. Momoi interview, January 9, 1985. See Sneider, *U.S.–Japan*, pp. 40–41. I am grateful also to Rōyama Michio, interview, November 26, 1984.
27. *New York Times*, May 14, 1978, quoted in Ha and Guinasso, "Japan's Rearmament," p. 246.
28. *Asahi Evening News*, November 20, 1984; *Japan Times*, December 27, 1984.
29. Tanigawa, *Betonamu*, p. ii.
30. Shibusawa, *Japan*, p. 9.
31. Maruyama, *Ronsetsu*, p. 231.
32. Maruyama, *Betonamu kaihō*, p. 259; Karasawa, "Indoshina," pp. 135–136; *White Papers of Japan 1974–75*, pp. 75–76; Maruyama, "Nihon," p. 25.
33. *White Papers of Japan 1970–71*, p. 89. See Murray, "United States," p. 53; Young, "Involvement," pp. 173–174.

34. Murray, "United States," p. 53; *Ampo*, no. 15 (December 1972), 25.
35. *Ampo*, no. 15 (December 1972), 25; Lambert, "Le Japon," p. 63; Ebashi and Yamada, *Shinsei*, pp. 400–401; Maruyama, *Betonamu kaihō*, p. 255.
36. Hasegawa, *Japanese Foreign Aid*, p. 64.
37. Keizai, *Betonamu*, pp. 12–13; Ebashi and Yamada, *Shinsei*, p. 409. See *Far Eastern Economic Review*, March 26, 1971, p. 67.
38. Keizai, *Betonamu*, p. 50.
39. Honda Kenkichi, "Tōnan," p. 165; Blaker, ed., *Development Assistance*, p. 42. See *Japan Quarterly* 21:2 (April 1974), 200–201.
40. Yano, *Tōnan*, pp. 6, 280–281; *Far Eastern Economic Review*, March 10, 1978, p. 31. See Shibusawa, *Japan*, pp. 102–103.
41. Ebashi and Yamada, *Shinsei*, p. 410; Iwai, "Nihon to Betonamu," p. 256; Shibusawa, *Japan*, p. 115.
42. *Far Eastern Economic Review*, January 13, 1978, p. 16.
43. *Far Eastern Economic Review*, May 12, 1978, pp. 52, 55; Shibusawa, *Japan*, p. 115; *Japan Quarterly* 25:4 (October 1978), 481.
44. Japan External Trade, *Economic Cooperation 1980*, p. 10.
45. *Kodansha Encyclopedia of Japan*, 8:192; Blaker, ed., *Development Assistance*, p. 42; *Asahi Evening News*, July 18, 1984; October 4, 1984.
46. *Asahi Evening News*, July 18, 1984; January 8, 1985.
47. Barnds, "United States," p. 245.
48. *New York Times*, August 17, 1983.
49. Maekawa, *Tsumetai*.
50. Katō Mikio interview, November 28, 1984.
51. Shawcross, "Refugees," pp. 4–5; Wain, "Indochina," pp. 163–164; Gaimushō, *Indoshina*, preface.
52. K. Watanabe, "Japan's Response," p. 37; Sekai Seikei, *Indoshina*, p. 133; Miyazaki, "Nanmin," p. 25; *Japan Times*, November 9, 1984; November 23, 1984; *Asahi Evening News*, December 27, 1984; Gaimushō, *Indoshina*, p. 8.
53. Naikaku Kanbō Indoshina, *Indoshina*, p. 7; Gaimushō, *Indoshina*, pp. 42–43, 54.
54. Gaimushō, *Indoshina*, p. 54; Naikaku Kanbō Indoshina, *Indoshina*, p. 20.
55. *Far Eastern Economic Review*, July 13, 1979, p. 26. See Miyazaki, "Nanmin," pp. 23–25; Sekai Seikei, *Indoshina*, p. 124; Komatsu,

"Waga," p. 50; Naikaku Kanbō Indoshina, *Indoshina*, pp. 20, 54; Maekawa, *Tsumetai*, pp. 176–177.

56. Gaimushō, *Indoshina*, p. 53; Komatsu, "Waga," p. 52; *Far Eastern Economic Review*, January 24, 1980, p. 24; Sekai Seikei, *Indoshina*, p. 126; Andō Isamu, "Zainichi," p. 148.

57. *Chūō kōron*, March 1973, p. 38; *Shōwashi jiten*, p. 706.

58. *Far Eastern Economic Review*, January 12, 1979, pp. 12–13; K. Watanabe, "Japan's Response," pp. 35–36; Gaimushō, *Indoshina*, pp. 49–50; Naikaku Kanbō Indoshina, *Indoshina*, pp. 36, 76; Sekai Seikei, *Indoshina*, pp. 129–130.

59. Gaimushō, *Indoshina*, p. 55.

60. Naikaku Kanbō Indoshina, *Indoshina*, p. 76; Sekai Seikei, *Indoshina*, pp. 129–130.

61. *Japan Times*, November 23, 1984; Sekai Seikei, *Indoshina*, p. 125; Shibusawa, *Japan*, p. 115.

62. Naikaku Kanbō Indoshina, *Indoshina*, pp. 33–37, 83; Maekawa, *Tsumetai*, p. 178–180; Gaimushō, *Indoshina*, pp. 54, 65–66, 80–82; Sekai Seikei, *Indoshina*, pp. 135–138; *Japan Times*, January 3, 1985.

63. "Ramen to the Rescue," *Asahi Evening News*, July 7, 1984.

64. Sekai Seikei, *Indoshina*, pp. 128, 143; Naikaku Kanbō Indoshina, *Indoshina*, pp. 39, 68, 71; Miyazaki, "Nanmin," p. 24; Komatsu, "Waga," pp. 47–49, 53; Gaimushō, *Indoshina*, pp. 61–63; *Japan Times*, November 24, 1984.

65. Naikaku Kanbō Indoshina, *Indoshina*, p. 50.

66. *Asahi Evening News*, December 27, 1984.

67. K. Watanabe, "Japan's Responses," p. 43.

68. U.S. House of Representatives, *1980—The Tragedy*, p. 93.

69. Maekawa, *Tsumetai*, p. 182. See Komatsu, "Waga," p. 33; Tonooka, *Genronjin*, p. 313.

70. Maekawa, *Tsumetai*, p. 182.

71. Sekai Seikei, *Indoshina*, p. 140.

72. *Far Eastern Economic Review*, January 12, 1979, p. 14.

73. Tonooka, *Genronjin*, p. 317; *Newsweek*, August 13, 1979, pp. 27–28. See *Far Eastern Economic Review*, January 12, 1979, p. 14.

74. Yoshikawa interview, January 7, 1985. See Tonooka, *Genronjin*, p. 317.

75. Gaimushō, *Indoshina*, p. 8.

76. *Japan Times*, November 27, 1984.

77. Zainichi, *Ryūmin*, pp. 177–178; *Asahi nenkan 1984*, p. 121. See

Andō Isamu, "Zainichi," pp. 163–165; Komatsu, "Waga," pp. 54–55; Gaimushō, *Indoshina*, pp. 45–46; Yamagami, *Nanmin*, pp. 21, 37.

78. Yamagami, *Nanmin*, p. 22.
79. Miyazaki, "Nanmin," pp. 26–28.

CHAPTER 10: FIRE ACROSS THE SEA

1. Katō Shūichi interview, December 10, 1984. I have benefited from discussing many of the ideas in this chapter with Professor Katō.
2. *Japan Times*, October 22, 1984.
3. *New York Times*, August 13, 1985.
4. Katō Shūichi interview, December 10, 1984.

SOURCES CITED

INTERVIEWS

Etō Shinkichi. Professor of international relations, Aoyama Gakuin University. Tokyo, December 20, 1984.

Haryū Ichirō. Art critic. Tokyo, November 22, 1984.

Honda, Roy M. Business director, *Asahi Evening News*. Tokyo, November 28, 1984.

Ishida Takeshi. Professor of political science, Chiba University. Tokyo, December 5, 1984.

Iwadare Hiroshi. Senior staff writer, *Asahi shinbun*. Tokyo, November 28, 1984.

Kamiya Fuji. Professor of international relations, Keio University. Tokyo, November 30, 1984.

Katō Mikio. Associate managing director, International House of Japan, Inc. Tokyo, November 28, 1984.

Katō Shūichi. Literary critic; professor of comparative literature, Sophia University. Tokyo, December 10, 1984.

Lockheimer, F. Roy. Adviser, Toho Life Insurance Company. Tokyo, December 17, 1984.

Lummis, Douglas. Professor of political science, Tsuda College. Tokyo, December 27, 1984.

Miwa Kimitada. Director, Institute of International Relations, Sophia University. Tokyo, November 22, 1984.

Miyake Wasuke. Director-general, Middle Eastern and African Affairs Bureau, Ministry of Foreign Affairs. Tokyo, December 28, 1984.

Momoi Makoto. Professor, Tokyo Gaikokugo University; former dean, Defense Research Institute. Tokyo, January 9, 1985.

Murakami Yoshio. Deputy foreign editor, *Asahi shinbun*. Tokyo, December 20, 1984.

Nichols, Walter. President, Azabu Artists, Inc.; former cultural attaché, United States Embassy, Japan. Tokyo, November 28, 1984.

Oda Makoto. Novelist; former head, Tokyo Beheiren. Tokyo, December 9, 1984.

Rōyama Michio. Professor of international relations, Sophia University. Tokyo, November 26, 1984.
Tokuoka Takao. Senior writer, *Mainichi shinbun*. Tokyo, December 3, 1984.
Tsurumi Yoshiyuki. Author, Tokyo, December 24, 1984.
Yoshikawa Yūichi. Executive secretary, Tokyo Beheiren, 1965–1974. Tokyo, January 7, 1985.

PRINTED SOURCES

Allison, Graham T. "American Foreign Policy and Japan." In *Discord in the Pacific: Challenges to the Japanese-American Alliance*, ed. Henry Rosovsky, pp. 7–46. Washington, D.C.: Columbia Books, 1972.
Andō Isamu. "Zainichi Indoshina nanmin no jittai to Nihon no sekinin." In *Nanmin mondai nyūmon*, ed. Komatsu Ryūji, pp. 137–174. Tokyo: Ronsōsha, 1981.
Andō Shinzō. *Betonamu tokuju*. Tokyo: San'ichi Shobō, 1967.
Aoshima Shōsuke and Shinta Chūji. *Kichi tōsōshi*. Tokyo: Shakai Shinpō, 1968.
Apter, David E., and Nagayo Sawa. *Against the State: Politics and Social Protest in Japan*. Cambridge, Mass.: Harvard University Press, 1984.
Arasaki Moriteru. "Okinawa's Reversion and the Security of Japan." *Japan Interpreter* 6:3 (Autumn 1970), 281–293.
"The *Asahi* Poll on Vietnam." *Japan Quarterly* 12:4 (October 1965), 463–466.
Asahi Shinbun. *The Pacific Rivals: A Japanese View of Japanese-American Relations*. Tokyo: Weatherhill/Asahi, 1972.
Axelbank, Albert. *Black Star over Japan*. New York: Hill and Wang, 1972.
Barnds, William J. "The United States and Japan in Asian Affairs." In *Japan and the United States: Challenges and Opportunities*, ed. William J. Barnds, pp. 231–279. New York: New York University Press, 1979.
Barnet, Richard J. *The Alliance: America, Europe, Japan, Makers of the Postwar World*. New York: Simon & Schuster, 1983.
Beer, Lawrence W. *Freedom of Expression in Japan*. Tokyo: Kodansha International, 1984.

Béraud, Bernard. *La gauche révolutionnaire au Japon*. Paris: Éditions du Seuil, 1970.

Betonamu Hansen Chokusetsu Kōdō Iinkai. *Shi no shōnin e no chōsen*. Tokyo, 1967.

Betonami ni Heiwa o! Shimin Rengō. *Shiryō "Beheiren" undō*. 3 vols. Tokyo: Kawade Shobō Shinsha, 1974.

Betonamu ni okeru Amerika no Sensō Hanzai Chōsa Nihon Iinkai. *Jenosaido*. Tokyo: Aoki Shoten, 1967.

———. *Rasseru hōtei*. Tokyo: Jinbun Shoin, 1967.

"Betonamu ni okeru Amerika no sensō hanzai to Nihon seifu, zaikai no kyōryoku, katan o sabaku Tōkyō hōtei no ketsuron." In Ajia Afurika Kenkyūjo, *Shiryō Betonamu kaihōshi*, 3:809–813. Tokyo: Rōdō Junpōsha, 1971.

Bix, Herbert P. "Report from Japan 1972—Part II." *Bulletin of Concerned Asian Scholars* 4:4 (December 1972), 17–30.

———. "The Security Treaty System and the Japanese Military-Industrial Complex." *Bulletin of Concerned Asian Scholars* 2:2 (January 1970), 30–53.

Black, Lafcadio. "*Ampo Taisei*: The Treaty System." *Concerned Theatre Japan* 1:2 (Summer 1970), 8–15.

Blaker, Michael, ed. *Development Assistance to Southeast Asia: The U.S. and Japanese Approaches*. New York: Columbia University, East Asian Institute, 1984.

Bock, Audie. *Japanese Film Directors*. Tokyo: Kodansha International, 1978.

Borton, Hugh. *Japan's Modern Century*. 2d ed. New York: Ronald Press, 1970.

Bowen, Roger W. "The Narita Conflict." *Asian Survey* 15:7 (July 1975), 598–615.

Buck, James H., ed. *The Modern Japanese Military System*. Beverly Hills, Ca.: Sage Publications, 1975.

Buttinger, Joseph. *Vietnam: A Political History*. New York: Frederick A. Praeger, Publishers, 1968.

"Citizens Movements." *Japan Quarterly* 20:4 (October 1973), 368–373.

Clark, Gregory. "Saying it with Flowers." *Far Eastern Economic Review*, July 9, 1970, pp. 75–76.

Clark, John. *Japanese Foreign Policy and the War in Vietnam, 1964–1969*. N.p.: Self-published, 1972.

Colbert, Evelyn. "National Security Perspectives: Japan and Asia."

In *The Modern Japanese Military System*, ed. James H. Buck, pp. 199–218. Beverly Hills, Ca.: Sage Publications, 1975.

Daniels, Gordon. "Japanese Foreign Policy and Its Problems." In *Japan in the 1980s*, ed. Rei Shiratori, pp. 84–99. Tokyo: Kodansha International, 1982.

Destler, I. M. "U.S.–Japanese Relations and the American Trade Initiative of 1977." In *Japan and the United States: Challenges and Opportunities*, ed. William J. Barnds, pp. 190–230. New York: New York University Press, 1979.

Dore, Ronald P. *Energy Conservation in Japanese Industry*. London, Policy Studies Institute and Royal Institute of International Affairs, 1982.

Dower, John W. "Asia and the Nixon Doctrine: The New Face of Empire." In *Open Secret: The Kissinger-Nixon Doctrine in Asia*, ed. Virginia Brodine and Mark Selden, pp. 128–218. New York: Harper & Row, Publishers, 1972.

———. *Empire and Aftermath: Yoshida Shigeru and the Japanese Experience, 1878–1954*. Cambridge, Mass.: Harvard University Press, 1979.

———. "The Superdomino in Postwar Asia: Japan in and out of the Pentagon Papers." In *The Pentagon Papers: The Senator Gravel Edition*, 5:101–142. Boston: Beacon Press, 1972.

Dowsey, Stuart J., ed. *Zengakuren: Japan's Revolutionary Students*. Berkeley: Ishi Press, 1970.

Duke, Benjamin C. *Japan's Militant Teachers*. Honolulu: University Press of Hawaii, 1973.

———. "Terror Off-Campus: Japan's Violent Student Radicals." *SR/World*, April 6, 1974, pp. 52–54.

Ebashi Masahiko and Yamada Yasuhiro. *Shinsei Betonamu no keizai*. Tokyo: Nihon Bōeki Shinkōkai, 1978.

Economist Intelligence Unit. *The Economic Effects of the Vietnamese War in East and South East Asia*. London: The Economist, 1968.

Eguchi, Bokurō. *Gendai no Nihon*. Tokyo: Shōgakukan, 1976.

Emmerson, John K. *Arms, Yen, and Power: The Japanese Dilemma*. New York: Dunellen Publishing Company, Inc., 1971.

Etō Shinkichi. *Mukoku no tami to seiji*. Tokyo: Banchō Shobō, 1966.

Fall, Bernard B., ed. *Ho Chi Minh on Revolution*. New York: Signet Books, 1968.

Forbis, William H. *Japan Today: People, Places, Power*. New York: Harper & Row, Publishers, 1975.

Fukashiro Junrō. "The New Left." *Japan Quarterly* 17:1 (January 1970), 27–36.

Fukuda, Kan'ichi. "Japan's Reaction to the Vietnam Crisis." *Journal of Social and Political Ideas in Japan* 4:2 (August 1966), 24–31.

Fukuda Tsuneari. "Amerika o koritsu saseru na." *Bungei shunjū*, July 1965.

————. "Let's Not Make the United States Stand Alone." *Journal of Social and Political Ideas in Japan* 4:1 (April 1966), 79–83.

Gaimushō Jōhō Bunkakyoku. *Indoshina nanmin mondai to Nihon*. Tokyo, 1981.

Gomi Masahiko. "Behan gakuren no tachiba kara." *Shisō no kagaku*, no. 81 (November 1968), 50–53.

Gotō Motoo. "Crisis in Japan-U.S. Relations." *Japan Quarterly* 15:4 (October 1968), 421–429.

Griffin, Stuart. "Politics in Command." *Far Eastern Economic Review*, July 28, 1966, pp. 148–151.

Guillain, Robert. "A New Pacific Age." *Pacific Community* 1:3 (April 1970), 487–497.

Ha, Joseph M., and John Guinasso. "Japan's Rearmament Dilemma." *Pacific Affairs* 53:2 (1980), 245–268.

Halliday, Jon. *A Political History of Japanese Capitalism*. New York: Pantheon Books, 1975.

————, and Gavan McCormack. *Japanese Imperialism Today*. New York: Monthly Review Press, 1973.

Harada Katsumasa. *Shōwa no sesō*. Tokyo: Shōkakukan, 1983.

Harrison, James P. *The Endless War*. New York: The Free Press, 1982.

Haryū Ichirō. "Hanbaku." *Gendai no me*, October 1969, pp. 126–135.

Hasegawa, Sukehiro. *Japanese Foreign Aid*. New York: Praeger Publishers, 1975.

Hashii Senji. "Shichijūnen tōsō to Hansen Seinen Iinkai." In *Han'anpo no ronri to kōdō*, ed. Kanba Toshio and Koyama Hirotake, pp. 213–250. Tokyo: Yūshindō, 1969.

Hatada Shigeo. "Betonamu sensō to Nihon." *Ajia Afurika kenkyū* 15:8 (1975), 64–72.

Hayakawa Osamu. "Raishawā hatsugen to Nihon no hōdō kikan." *Bunka hyōron*, no. 51 (January 1966), 134–139.

Hayashi Chikio. "Chōsa Betonamu o dō miru ka." *Jiyū*, October 1965, pp. 36–43.

Hayashi Risuke. "Where Do We Go From Here?" *Japan Quarterly* 21:3 (July 1974), 258–264.

Heiwa Undō 30nen Kinen Iinkai. *Sensō to heiwa no Nihon kindaishi.* Tokyo: Ōtsuki Shoten, 1979.

Hellmann, Donald C. "The Confrontation with *Realpolitik*." In *Forecast for Japan: Security in the 1970s*, ed. James W. Morley, pp. 135–168. Princeton: Princeton University Press, 1972.

———. *Japan and East Asia: The New International Order.* New York: Praeger Publishers, 1972.

Hidaka Rokurō. "Chokusetsu minshushugi to 'Rokugatsu Kōdō.' " *Sekai*, August 1968. Reprinted in Betonamu ni Heiwa o! Shimin Rengō, *Shiryō "Beheiren" undō*, 1:371–379. Tokyo: Kawade Shobō Shinsha, 1974.

Higuchi Shinji. "Betonamu jinmin o shien suru bunkajin bunka dantai no katsudō." *Bunka hyōron*, no. 137 (December 1972), 116–120.

Hirose Michisada. "Okinawan Disappointment." *Japan Quarterly* 18:4 (October 1971), 408–413.

Honda Katsuichi. *Betonamu sensō.* Tokyo: Suzusawa Shoten, 1973.

Honda Kenkichi. "Tōnan Ajia to Nihon." *Sekai*, no. 368 (1976), 155–169.

Horie Tan. "Sasebo ni okeru gensen ijō hōshanō jiken to kokumin yoron." *Kokusai seiji*, no. 1 (1969), 77–97.

Iida Momo. "Shimin minshushigi undō no ronri to shinri." *Gendai no me*, September 1965. Reprinted in Betonamu ni Heiwa o! Shimin Rengō, *Shiryō "Beheiren" undō*, 1:24–35. Tokyo: Kawade Shobō Shinsha, 1974.

Inaba Michio. "Nikkan, Betonamu, Okinawa, Chūgoku." In *Kōza gendai jānarizumu*, ed. Kido Mataichi, 1:255–276. Tokyo: Jiji Tsūshinsha, 1974.

Inoue Kiyoshi. "Betonamu sensō hantai no imisuru mono." *Bungei*, special issue, September 1965, pp. 33–37.

Irie Michimasa. *Sengo Nihon gaikōshi.* Kyoto: Sagano Shoin, 1978.

Ishida Ikuo. *Anpo, hansen, Okinawa.* Tokyo: San'ichi Shobō, 1969.

———. "Sasebo shimin to Zengakuren." *Tenbō*, no. 111 (March 1968), 58–68.

Ishida Takeshi. "Emerging or Eclipsing Citizenship?" *The Developing Economies* 6:4 (December 1968), 410–424.

———. *Japanese Political Culture.* New Brunswick, N.J.: Transaction Books, 1983.

————. *Japanese Society*. New York: Random House, 1971.

————. *Seiji to bunka*. Tokyo: Tōkyō Daigaku Shuppankai, 1969.

Ishiko Jun. "Senkyūhyakushichijūnen to minshuteki eiga undō." *Bunka hyōron*, no. 94 (July 1969), 43–47.

Itō Shin. "Hansen no ronri to 'kojin no genri.' " *Minshu bungaku*, July 1967, pp. 107–117.

Itō Yoshiaki. "Shinryaku sensō to shizen kagakusha no sekinin." *Bunka hyōron*, no. 124 (December 1971), 24–35.

Iwadare Hiroshi. "Hansen undō o mitsumete." *Sekai*, no. 329 (April 1973), 230-238.

————. "Heiwa undō." In Tōyō Keizai Shinpōsha, *Kakushin seiryoku*, pp. 29–62. Tokyo, 1979.

Iwai Koshirō. "Nihon to Betonamu no bōeki kankei." In Ajia Afurika Kenkyūjo, *Betonamu*, 2:255–273. Tokyo: Suiyōsha, 1978.

Iwasaki, Ikuo. *Japan and Southeast Asia, a Bibliography of Historical, Economic, and Political Relations*. Singapore: Institute of Southeast Asian Studies, 1983.

Jansen, Marius B. "The China War and the Vietnam War." In *Fukuoka UNESCO: From the Second International Seminar on Japanese Studies*, pp. 19–28. Fukuoka: Fukuoka Yunesuko Kyōkai, 1975.

————. "The United States and Japan in the 1970s." In *Japanese-American Relations in the 1970s*, ed. Gerald L. Curtis, pp. 20–47. Washington, D.C.: Columbia Books, 1970.

"Japan and the Manila Conference." *Japan Quarterly* 14:1 (January 1967), 3–6.

"Japan and the Vietnam War." *France-Asie* (Saigon) 20 (1965/66), 239–251.

Japan External Trade Organization. *Economic Cooperation of Japan 1980*. Tokyo, 1980.

Johnson, Chalmers A. "Japanese Relations with China, 1952–1982." Paper presented to "Japan and the Pacific Quadrille" Conference, Tokyo, June 10–11, 1983.

Johnson, U. Alexis, and Jef O. McAllister. *The Right Hand of Power: The Memoirs of an American Diplomat*. Englewood Cliffs, N.J.: Prentice-Hall, Inc., 1984.

Kaiko, Takeshi. *Darkness in Summer*. Translated by Cecilia Segawa Seigle. New York: Alfred A. Knopf, Inc., 1973.

————. "Fukuda Tsunearishi e no hanron." *Bungei*, September 1965, pp. 18–31.

Kajima, Morinosuke. *Modern Japan's Foreign Policy*. Rutland, Vt. and Tokyo: Charles E. Tuttle Company, 1969.

Kajitani Yoshihisa. "Hannin wa hankō o kakusu." *Gekkan sōhyō*, no. 170 (August 1971), 33–38.

Kameyama Asahi. *Betonamu sensō*. Tokyo: Iwanami Shoten, 1972.

Karasawa Kei. "Indoshina kaihō to kakkoku no taiō." In Ajia Afurika Kenkyūjo, *Betonamu*, 2:127–144. Tokyo: Suiyōsha, 1978.

Kataoka, Tetsuya, *Waiting for a "Pearl Harbor": Japan Debates Defense*. Stanford, Ca.: Hoover Institution Press, 1980.

Katō Bunzō et al. *Nihon rekishi, kaiteiban*, 3 vols. Tokyo: Shin Nihon Shinsho, 1978.

Katō Shūichi. "Ushinawareta kuni no risō." *Asahi jānaru*, November 10, 1972, pp. 16–19.

Kawata, Tadashi. *Tasks for Peace Research in Japan*. Tokyo: Sophia University, Institute of International Relations, 1976.

Keizai Hatten Kyōkai. *Betonamu sengo fukkō kaihatsu to Nihon no yakuwari*. Tokyo, 1973.

Kendrick, Alexander. *The Wound Within*. Boston: Little, Brown and Company, 1974.

Kennan, George F. "American Involvement in Vietnam." In *International Politics of Asia*, ed. George P. Jan, pp. 322–327. Belmont, Ca.: Wadsworth Publishing Company, Inc., 1969.

Kesavan, K. V. "The Vietnam War as an Issue in Japan's Relations with the United States." *International Studies* 16:4 (October 1977), 501–519.

Kikuchi Yūgi. *Sugao no Hansen Seinen Iinkai*. Tokyo: Nihon Sono Shobō, 1969.

Kim, Tai Sung. "Japan's Security Policy: A Study of the Relationships among the Decision Makers' Perceptions, the Press, and Public Opinion during 1952–1971." Ph.D. dissertation, Michigan State University, 1974.

Kim, Young C. "Japan and the Vietnam War." In *The Role of External Powers in the Indochina Crisis*, ed. Gene T. Hsiao, pp. 152–164. Edwardsville, Ill.: Southern Illinois University, 1973.

———. *Japanese Journalists and Their World*. Charlottesville, VA.: University Press of Virginia, 1981.

———. "Japan's Security Policy Debate." In *Japan in World Politics*, ed. Young C. Kim, pp. 51–82. Washington, D.C.: Institute for Asian Studies, 1972.

Kirk, Donald. "Rebels in Kyoto." *Worldview* 16:9 (September 1973), 13–17.

Kobayashi Tomi. "Koe naki koe no wakamonotachi." *Shisō no kagaku*, no. 81 (November 1968), 44–49.

Kodansha Encyclopedia of Japan, 9 vols. Tokyo: Kodansha Ltd., 1983.

Komatsu Ryūji. "Waga Kuni ni okeru nanmin seisaku no seiritsu to kadai." In *Nanmin mondai nyūmon*, ed. Komatsu Ryūji, pp. 31–59. Tokyo: Ronsōsha, 1981.

Konaka Yōtarō. *Tezukuri no ronri*. Tokyo: Gōdō Shuppan, 1969.

———. *Watakushi no naka no Betonamu sensō*. Tokyo: Sankei Shinbunsha Shuppankyoku, 1973.

Kosaka, Masataka. "Northeast Asian Security after Vietnam: A View from Japan." In *Northeast Asian Security after Vietnam*, ed. Martin E. Weinstein, pp. 28–51. Urbana, Ill.: University of Illinois Press, 1982.

———. *100 Million Japanese: The Postwar Experience*. Tokyo: Kodansha International, 1972.

Krause, Lawrence B., and Sueo Sekiguchi. "Japan and the World Economy." In *Asia's New Giant*, ed. Hugh Patrick and Henry Rosovsky, pp. 383–458. Washington, D.C.: The Brookings Institution, 1976.

Krauss, Ellis L. *Japanese Radicals Revisited: Student Protest in Postwar Japan*. Berkeley and Los Angeles: University of California Press, 1974.

Kugai Saburō, ed. *Shiryō Betonamu sensō*. 2 vols. Tokyo: Kinokuniya Shoten, 1969.

Kumakura Hiroyasu. *Nihon heiwa undō no rekishi to dentō*. Osaka: Heiwa Shobō, 1968.

Kuroda, Yasumasa. "Protest Movements in Japan." *Asian Survey* 12:11 (November 1972), 947–952.

Kurzman, Dan. *Kishi and Japan: The Search for the Sun*. New York: Ivan Oblensky, Inc., 1960.

Kyōdō Tsūshinsha Shakaibu. *Kono Nihon rettō*. Tokyo: Gendai Shobō, 1968.

Lambert, Jean. "Le Japon et l'après-Vietnam." *Défense nationale* 31 (November 1975), 61–74.

Langdon, Frank C. *Japan's Foreign Policy*. Vancouver: University of British Columbia Press, 1973.

Lee, Jung Bock. "The Professional and Political Attitudes of Japanese

Newsmen." *Asian Perspective* (Seoul) 4:1 (Spring-Summer 1980), 97–124.

Lockheimer, F. Roy. "Further Vietnamese Reflections in a Japanese Mirror." *American Universities Field Staff Reports, East Asia Series* 16:11 (September 1969), 1–17.

———. "Vietnam through a Japanese Mirror." *American Universities Field Staff Reports, East Asia Series* 16:7 (April 1969), 1–13.

Lu, David J. "Sato Eisaku and Close Working Relations with the United States." In *Perspectives on Japan's External Relations*, ed. David J. Lu, pp. 36–42. Lewisburg, Pa.: Bucknell University, Center for Japanese Studies, 1982.

Maekawa Makoto. *Tsumetai Nihonjin*. Tokyo: Eeru Shuppansha, 1980.

Mainichi Daily News. *Fifty Years of Light and Dark: The Hirohito Era.* Tokyo: The Mainichi Newspapers, 1975.

Mainichi Shinbunsha. *Anpo to bōei seisan.* Tokyo, 1969.

———. *Anpo to seiji.* Tokyo, 1969.

———. *Ichiokunin no Shōwashi*, vol. 8: *Nihon kabushiki kaisha no kōzai.* Tokyo, 1976.

Marcot, Neal Abel. "The Japanese Foreign Policymaking Process: A Case Study—Okinawa Reversion." Ph.D. dissertation, Georgetown University, 1981.

Maruyama Shizuo. *Betonamu kaihō.* Tokyo: Asahi Shinbunsha, 1975.

———. *Betonamu—sono tatakai to heiwa.* Tokyo: Asahi Shinbunsha, 1974.

———. "Japanese Opinion and the Vietnam War." *Japan Quarterly* 12:3 (July 1965), 303–310.

———. "Nihon no Indoshina gaikō." *Sekai*, no. 355 (June 1975), 18–30.

———. *Ronsetsu iin.* Tokyo: Chikuma Shobō, 1977.

———. *Tōnan Ajia to Nihon.* Tokyo: Ajia Keizai Kenkyūjo, 1968.

Matsuda Nobuo. *Nihon no shinsei.* Tokyo: Yomiuri Shinbunsha, 1968.

Matsueda, Tsukasa, and George E. Moore. "Japan's Shifting Attitudes toward the Military: *Mitsuya Kenkyu* and Self-Defense Force." *Asian Survey* 7:9 (September 1967), 614–625.

Matsumoto, Sannosuke. "Introduction." *Journal of Social and Political Ideas in Japan* 4:2 (August 1966), 2–19.

Matsumoto Shigeharu. "The Future of U.S.-Japanese Relations." *Japan Quarterly* 13:1 (January 1966), 17–26.

Matsumoto Shun'ichi. "Seifu wa shinsō ni serō to shinakatta." *Shūkan asahi*, July 9, 1971, pp. 21–23.

McGovern, Raymond L. "Moscow and Hanoi." *Problems of Communism* (May-June 1967), 64–71.

McNelly, Theodore. *Politics and Government in Japan*. 2d ed. Boston: Houghton Mifflin Company, 1972.

Mellen, Joan. *Voices from the Japanese Cinema*. New York: Liveright, 1975.

———. *The Waves at Genji's Door: Japan through Its Cinema*. New York: Pantheon Books, 1976.

Mendel, Douglas H., Jr. "Japan, Okinawa, and Vietnam." Paper presented to the annual meeting of the Association for Asian Studies, Chicago, March 20–22, 1967.

———. "Japanese-American Relations in 1970." *Pacific Community* 1:2 (January 1970), 318–332.

———. "Japanese Opinion on Key Foreign Policy Issues." *Asian Survey* 9:8 (August 1969), 625–639.

———. "Japan's Defense in the 1970s: The Public View." *Asian Survey* 10:12 (December 1970), 1046–1069.

———. "Security without Arms." *Far Eastern Economic Review*, January 16, 1969, pp. 102–103.

Mihashi Kazuo. "Agora o genshutsu saseta fuōku gerira no majutsu." *Poppusu*, August 1969. Reprinted in *Beheiren to wa nanika*, ed. Oda Makoto, pp. 169–178. Tokyo: Tokuma Shoten, 1969.

Minaguchi Kōzō. *Anpo tōsōshi*. Tokyo: Shakai Shinpō, 1968.

Mishima Yukio. "Nihon to wa nani ka." *Bungei shunjū*, December 1985, pp. 192–209.

"Mr. Satō's Visits to Southeast Asia." *Japan Quarterly* 15:1 (January 1968), 3–6.

Mita, Munesuke. "Political Attitudes: Social Discontent and Party Support." *Developing Economies* 6:4 (December 1968), 544–565.

Miyamoto Ken'ichi. *Keizai taikoku*. Tokyo: Shōgakukan, 1983.

Miyaoka Masao. *Sunagawa tōsō no kiroku*. Tokyo: San'ichi Shobō, 1970.

Miyazaki Shigeki. "Nanmin to Nihonjin." In *Nanmin mondai nyūmon*, ed. Komatsu Ryūji, pp. 1–30. Tokyo: Ronsōsha, 1981.

———. "The Political Rights of Aliens in Japan and Compulsory Deportation." Translated by Douglas Paine. *Law in Japan* 12 (1979), 82–98.

Mori Kyōzō. "Judgments of Paris." *Japan Quarterly* 15:3 (July 1968), 298–300.

―――. "Two Ends of a Telescope: Japanese and American Views of Okinawa." *Japan Quarterly* 15:1 (January 1968), 14–21.

Morikawa Kinju. *Betonamu ni okeru Amerika sensō hanzai no kiroku.* Tokyo: San'ichi Shobō, 1977.

Morinaga Kazuhiko. "Shinbun hōdō no jirenma." *Jiyū*, October 1965, pp. 10–19.

Moriyama Tadashi. "Minshuteki bijutsu dantai no genjō to mondaiten." *Bunka hyōron*, no. 94 (July 1969), 51–55.

Morris-Suzuki, Tessa. *Showa.* London: Athlone Press, 1984.

Murakami Kaoru. *Nihon bōei no kōsō.* Tokyo: Saimaru Shuppankai, 1970.

Murray, Martin. "The United States' Continuing Economic Interests in Vietnam." *Socialist Revolution*, nos. 13–14 (January–April 1973), 1–65.

Mutō Ichiyō. " 'Beheiren' undō no shisō." In *shimin undō to wa nanika*, ed. Oda Makoto, pp. 82–99. Tokyo: Tokuma Shoten, 1968.

―――. "The December 1969 Elections." In *Postwar Japan, 1945 to the Present*, ed. Jon Livingston, Joe Moore, and Felicia Oldfather, pp. 504–512. New York: Pantheon Books, 1973.

―――. *Nihon kokka no kamen o hagasu.* Tokyo: Shakai Hyōronsha, 1984.

Nagai Yōnosuke. *Takyoku sekai no kōzō.* Tokyo: Chūō Kōronsha, 1973.

Naikaku Kanbō Indoshina Nanmin Taisaku Renraku Chōsei Kaigi Jimukyoku. *Indoshina nanmin no genjō to kokunai engo.* Tokyo, 1980.

Naikaku Kanbō Naikaku Chōsashitsu. *Betonamu sensō no keizaiteki eikyō.* Tokyo, 1968.

Narita Tomomi. *1970nen no kadai.* Tokyo: Rōdō Daigaku, 1968.

NHK Hōsō Yoron Chōsa Kenkyūjo. *Zusetsu sengo yoronshi.* Tokyo, 1975.

Nihon gaikōshi jiten. Tokyo: Ōkurashō Insatsukyoku, 1979.

Nihon Heiwa Iinkai. *Heiwa undō 20nen undōshi.* Tokyo: Ōtsuki Shoten, 1969.

―――. *Nihon no kokusho.* Tokyo: Rōdō Junpōsha, 1967.

Nihon Keizai Chōsa Kyōgikai. *Betonamu jōsei no henka to sono keizaiteki eikyō.* Tokyo, 1968.

Nihon Keizai Shinbun Shakaibu. *Kore ga Beigun kichi da*. Tokyo, 1970.

Nihon kingendaishi jiten. Tokyo: Tōyō Keizai Shinpōsha, 1978.

Nihon Kyōsantō. *Betonamu mondai to Nihon Kyōsantō*. Tokyo, 1965.

"Nihon no Betonamu hōdō." *Sōgō jānarizumu kenkyū* 4:2 (February 1967), 33–48.

" 'Nihonsei' napāmu tama no nazo." *Sandē mainichi*, July 25, 1971, pp. 150–151.

Nikkan Rōdō Tsūshinsha. *Kensetsu naki hakai no yume*. Tokyo, 1970.

Oberdorfer, Don. *Tet!* Garden City, N.Y.: Doubleday, 1971.

Oda Makoto. *"Betonamu" no kage*. Tokyo: Chūō Kōronsha, 1974.

————. "Demo kōshin to piramiddo." *Tenbō*, June 1969. Reprinted in Betonamu ni Heiwa o! Shimin Rengō, *Shiryō "Beheiren" undō*, 2:49–57. Tokyo: Kawade Shobō Shinsha, 1974.

————. *Gimu to shite no tabi*. Tokyo: Iwanami Shoten, 1967.

————. *Heiwa o tsukuru ronri*. Tokyo: Kōdansha, 1967.

————. " 'Ikitsuzukeru' to iu koto—senkyūhyakushichijūichinen igo." *Tenbō*, January 1971. Reprinted in Betonamu ni Heiwa o! Shimin Rengō, *Shiryō "Beheiren" undō*, 2:441–453. Tokyo: Kawade Shobō Shinsha, 1974.

————. "Making Democracy Our Own." In *Listening to Japan*, ed. Jackson H. Bailey, pp. 122–137. New York: Praeger Publishers, 1973.

————. *Mao Zedong*. Tokyo: Iwanami Shoten, 1984.

————. *Nan de mo mite yarō*. Tokyo: Kawade Shobō, 1961.

————. "Nani ka ga hajimatte iru." *Sekai*, no. 285 (August 1969), 100–110.

————, ed. *Shimin undō to wa nani ka*. Tokyo: Tokuma Shoten, 1968.

———— and Honda Katsuichi. "Waga Betonamu taiken no sō kessan (taidan)." *Asahi jānaru*, February 9, 1973. Reprinted in Betonamu ni Heiwa o! Shimin Rengō, *Shiryō "Beheiren" undō*, 3:299–321. Tokyo: Kawade Shobō Shinsha, 1974.

————, Suzuki Michihiko, and Tsurumi Shunsuke, eds. *Kokka to guntai e no hangyaku*. Tokyo: Taihei Shuppansha, 1972.

———— and Tsurumi Shunsuke, eds. *Hansen to henkaku*. Tokyo: Gakugei Shobō, 1968.

Okakura Koshirō. *Betonamu sensō to watakushitachi*. Tokyo: Rōdō Junpōsha, 1966.

Oketani Shigeo. "Chishikijin no Betonamu kanjō." *Jiyū*, October 1965, pp. 29–35.

Olson, Lawrence. *Japan in Postwar Asia*. New York: Praeger Publishers, 1970.

Ōmori Minoru. *Ishi ni kaku*. Tokyo: Ushio Shuppansha, 1971.

———. *Kita Betonamu hōkoku*. Tokyo: Mainichi Shinbunsha, 1965.

Ōmori Shigeo. "June 1970." *Japan Quarterly* 17:4 (October 1970), 383–392.

Ōmura Yasuo. *Shōwashi o kangaeru*. Tokyo: Gakushū no Tomosha, 1983.

Onishi, Seiichiro. "Japan's Self-Defense Requirements and Capabilities." In *The Common Security Interests of Japan, the United States, and NATO*, pp. 143–163. Cambridge, Mass.: Ballinger Publishing Company, 1981.

Ōuchi Hyōe et al. "A Petition to the Japanese Government Concerning Vietnam." *Journal of Social and Political Ideas in Japan* 4:1 (April 1966), 73–75.

Packard, George R. III. "Living with the Real Japan." In *Japan and the United States in Asia*, ed. Robert E. Osgood, George R. Packard III, and John H. Badgley, pp. 29–47. Baltimore: The Johns Hopkins University Press, 1968.

———. *Protest in Tokyo*. Princeton: Princeton University Press, 1966.

Parker, Tom. *In One Day*. Boston: Houghton Mifflin Company, 1984.

"Peace Research." *Japan Quarterly* 20:4 (October 1973), 377–381.

The Pentagon Papers: The Senator Gravel Edition, 5 vols. Boston: Beacon Press, 1971–1972.

Reischauer, Edwin O. *Japan the Story of a Nation*. 3d ed. New York: Alfred A. Knopf, Inc., 1981.

———. "The Role of the Intellectual in the U.S. and Japan." *Japan Quarterly* 13:3 (July 1966), 325–329.

———. "Watakushi no hatsugen wa gokai sarete iru." *Sekai shūhō*, September 7, 1965, pp. 28–37.

Rōyama Michio. "The Domestic Factors Affecting Japanese Foreign Policy." *Annual Review, Japan Institute of International Affairs* 4 (1965–1968), 1–7.

———. "Japan: Economic Power in Search of a Political Role?" *Peace Research in Japan*, 1970, pp. 1–20.

Saeki Kiichi. "Betonamu sensō wa dō naru." *Getsuyōkai repōto*, no. 238 (April 26, 1965), 1–55.

Saeki Shōichi. *Kyōki no jidai*. Tokyo: Sankei Shuppan, 1979.

Saitō Makoto, Nagai Yōnosuke, and Yamamoto Mitsuru, eds. *Nichibei kankei*. Tokyo: Nihon Hyōronsha, 1970.

Sasebo Jūkunichi Shimin no Kai. *Shimin undō no shuppatsu*. Tokyo: Shakai Shinpō, 1969.

Satō, Eisaku. "Pacific Asia." *Pacific Community* 1:1 (October 1969), 1–3.

Satō Katsuaki. "Ongaku, buyō bunya no anpo tōsō." *Bunka hyōron*, no. 94 (July 1969), 47–51.

Sato, Tadao. *Currents in Japanese Cinema*. Translated by Gregory Barrett. Tokyo: Kodansha International, 1982.

Saxonhouse, Gary R. "Employment, Imports, the Yen, and the Dollar." In *Discord in the Pacific*, ed. Henry Rosovsky, pp. 79–116. Washington, D.C.: Columbia Books, 1972.

Scalapino, Robert A. *The Japanese Communist Movement, 1920–1966*. Berkeley and Los Angeles: University of California Press, 1967.

Sekai Seikei Chōsakai. *"Indoshina nanmin" mondai no suii to genjō*. Tokyo, 1980.

Seki, Hiroharu. "International Environment and the Postwar Japanese Diplomacy." *Developing Economies* 6:4 (December 1968), 425–445.

Seki Hiroharu. *Kiki no ninshiki*. Tokyo: Fukumura Shuppansha, 1969.

Seki, Yoshihiko. "Introduction." *Journal of Social and Political Ideas in Japan* 4:1 (April 1966), 2–10.

Selden, Mark. "Okinawa and American Security Imperialism." In *Remaking Asia*, ed. Mark Selden, pp. 279–302. New York: Pantheon Books, 1974.

Shawcross, William. "Refugees and Rhetoric." *Foreign Policy*, no. 36 (Fall 1979), 3–11.

Shepler, Cora E., and Leonard G. Campbell. "United States Defense Expenditures Abroad." *Survey of Current Business* 49:12 (December 1969), 40–47.

Shibata Shingo. "Gendai no handō shisō." *Bungei hyōron*, no. 66 (April 1967), 28–52.

Shibusawa, Masahide. *Japan and the Asian Pacific Region*. London: Croom Helm, 1984.

Shinobu Seizaburō, ed. *Nihon gaikōshi 2*. Tokyo: Mainichi Shinbunsha, 1974.

Shisō no Kagaku Kenkyūkai. *Tenkō*. 3 vols. Tokyo: Heibonsha, 1959–1962.

Shisō Undō Kenkyūjo. *Bōhatsu suru shinsayoku*. Tokyo: Zenbōsha, 1969.

Shōwashi jiten. Tokyo: Kōdansha, 1984.

Sneider, Richard L. *U.S.–Japan Security Relations: A Historical Perspective*. New York: Columbia University, East Asian Institute, 1982.

Sodei Rinjirō. "What the Vietnam War Means to Us." *Japan Quarterly* 22:4 (October 1975), 314–317.

"Sono toki no Satō naikaku no genkō o sōtenken suru." *Shūkan asahi*, July 9, 1971, pp. 16–21.

Stockwin, J.A.A. *Japan: Divided Politics in a Growth Economy*. New York: W. W. Norton & Company, Inc., 1975.

Storry, Richard. "Repercussions in Japan." *Studies on the Soviet Union* 6:2 (1966), 74–82.

Suzuki Sunao. "The Declining Role of Ideology in Citizens' Movements." *Japan Quarterly* 23:2 (April 1976), 121–126.

Takabatake, Michitoshi. "Citizens' Movements." In *Authority and the Individual in Japan*, ed. J. Victor Koschmann, pp. 189–199. Tokyo: University of Tokyo Press, 1978.

Takagi, Sakae; Akira Enoki; and Masahiko Seki. "Secrets of the Longevity of the Sato Administration." *Contemporary Japan* 29:2 (March 1970), 308–312.

Takahashi Yoshio. " 'Beheiren' o meguru shisō." *Bunka hyōron*, no. 69 (July 1967), 22–44.

———. "Beheiren wa doko e iku." *Bunka hyōron*, no. 100 (January 1970), 108–126.

———. "Betonamu shien no tame no bunkajin geijutsuka no tōsō." *Bunka hyōron*, no. 59 (September 1966), 108–116.

Takami Keishi, ed. *Hansen Seinen Iinkai*. Tokyo: San'ichi Shobō, 1968.

Tanigawa Yoshihiko, ed. *Betonamu sensō no kigen*. Tokyo: Keisō Shobō, 1984.

Togawa Isamu. *Satō Eisaku to kōdo seichō*. Tokyo: Kōdansha, 1982.

Tonooka Akio. *Genronjin no seitai*. Tokyo: Takagi Shobō, 1981.

Tsurumi, Kazuko. "Student Movements in 1960 and 1969." in *Postwar Trends in Japan*, ed. Shunichi Takayanagi and Kimitada Miwa, pp. 195–227. Tokyo: University of Tokyo Press, 1975.

Tsurumi Shunsuke. "Beheiren to wa nani ka?" In *Shimin undō to wa nani ka*, ed. Oda Makoto, pp. 1–7. Tokyo: Tokuma Shoten, 1968.

————. *Sengo Nihon no taishū bunkashi.* Tokyo: Iwanami Shoten, 1984.

————, Kaikō Takeshi, and Oda Makoto, eds. *Heiwa o yobu koe.* Tokyo: Banchō Shobō, 1967.

Tsurumi Yoshiyuki. "Beheiren." *Japan Quarterly* 16:4 (October 1969), 444–448.

————. "Senkyūhyakushichijūnen to Beheiren." In *Beheiren,* ed. Oda Makoto, pp. 47–66. Tokyo: San'ichi Shobō, 1969.

U.S. Congress, House of Representatives Subcommittee on Asian and Pacific Affairs of the Committee on Foreign Affairs. *1980— The Tragedy in Indochina Continues: War, Refugees, and Famine.* February 11, May 1, May 6, and July 29, 1980. Washington, D.C.: U.S. Government Printing Office, 1980.

U.S. Congress, Senate Committee on Foreign Relations. *United States Security Agreements and Commitments Abroad, Japan and Okinawa: Hearings before the Subcommittee on United States Security Agreements and Commitments Abroad,* 91st Congress, 2d Session, Part 5, January 26, 27, 28, and 29, 1970. Washington, D.C.: U.S. Government Printing Office, 1970.

Urushiyama Shigeyoshi. *Shinbun ronchō e no hanron.* Tokyo: Nisshin Hōdō, 1975.

Usami Shō. "Zengakuren." *Japan Quarterly* 15:2 (April 1968), 233–244.

"Vietnam Special Procurement and the Economy." *Japan Quarterly* 14:1 (January 1967), 13–16.

Wain, Barry. "The Indochina Refugee Crisis." *Foreign Affairs* 58:1 (Fall 1979), 160–180.

Watanabe, Akio. *The Okinawa Problem.* Carlton, Australia: Melbourne University Press, 1970.

Watanabe, Koji. "Japan's Response to Indochina Refugees' Problem." *Asia Pacific Community,* no. 5 (Summer 1979), 35–44.

Weinstein, Franklin B., and John W. Lewis. "The Post-Vietnam Strategic Context in Asia." In *U.S.–Japanese Relations and the Security of East Asia,* ed. Franklin B. Weinstein, pp. 127–166. Boulder, Colo.: Westview Press, 1978.

Wheeler, Donald F. "Japan's Postmodern Student Movement." In *Changes in the Japanese University,* ed. William K. Cummings, Ikuo Amano, and Kazuyuki Kitamura, pp. 202–216. New York: Praeger Publishers, 1979.

Whitmore, Terry, as told to Richard Weber. *Memphis—Nam—Swe-*

den: The Autobiography of a Black American Exile. Garden City, N.Y.: Doubleday, 1971.

Williams, William Appleman, Thomas McCormick, Lloyd Gardner, and Walter LaFeber, eds. *America in Vietnam: A Documentary History.* Garden City, N.Y.: Doubleday Anchor Books, 1985.

Yamagami Susumu. *Nanmin jōyaku to shutsunyūkoku kanri gyōsei.* Tokyo: Nihon Kajo Shuppan, 1982.

Yanaga, Chitoshi. *Big Business in Japanese Politics.* New Haven: Yale University Press, 1968.

Yano Tōru. *Tōnan Ajia seisaku—utagai kara shinrai e.* Tokyo: Saimaru Shuppankai, 1978.

Yara, Chobyo. "Report from Okinawa." *Pacific Community* 2:2 (January 1971), 283–296.

Yasutomo, Dennis. *Japan and the Asian Development Bank.* New York: Praeger Publishers, 1983.

Yoshikawa Yūichi. "Beheiren to wa nani ka." In *Beheiren*, ed. Oda Makoto, pp. 7–22. Tokyo: San'ichi Shobō, 1969.

———. "Beheiren wa awa to hae datta ka." *Pengin*, February 1984, pp. 20–22.

Yoshimoto Ryūmei. *Jiritsu no shisōteki kyoten.* Tokyo: Tokuma Shoten, 1966.

Yoshioka Shinobu. "Tenki ni tatsu Beheiren." *Asahi jānaru*, September 1, 1968. Reprinted in *Beheiren to wa nani ka*, ed. Oda Makoto, pp. 67–74. Tokyo: Tokuma Shoten, 1969.

Young, Kenneth T. "The Involvement in Southeast Asia." In *Forecast for Japan: Security in the 1970s*, ed. James W. Morley, pp. 169–203. Princeton: Princeton University Press, 1972.

Zagoria, Donald S. *Vietnam Triangle.* New York: Pegasus, 1967.

Zainichi Indoshina Ryūmin ni Rentaisuru Shimin no Kai. *Ryūmin.* Tokyo: Ronsōsha, 1980.

Zinn, Howard. *Vietnam: The Logic of Withdrawal.* Boston: Beacon Press, 1967.

Zusetsu Nihon bunkashi taikei 13 gendai. 2d ed. Tokyo: Shōgakukan, 1968.

Minaguchi Kōzō, 209
Minobe Ryōkichi, 124, 131, 156
Mishima Yukio, 67-68
Mita Munesuke, 126
Mitsubishi, 99, 219
Miyake Wasuke, 48, 68, 222
Miyamoto Masao, 162
Miyanohara Sadamitsu, 121
Miyazawa Kiichi, 65, 237, 241
modern theater, *see* Shingeki
Momoi Makoto, 34, 91, 244
Mondale, Walter F., 243
Mononobe Nagaoki, 56
Mori Kyōzō, 125
Morita Akio, 100, 139
Morse, Wayne, 108
Muchaku Seikyō, 65, 256
Murakami Hiroshi, 233
Murakami Yoshio, 91, 97
Muro Kenji, 215
Mutō Ichiyō, 56, 198, 204, 239
My Lai massacre, 192, 196

Nakamura Shin'ichi, 75
Nakano Shigeharu, 56
Nakasone Yasohiro, 50, 65, 92, 111, 202, 249-50
napalm, 98-99
Naramoto Tatsuya, 56
Narita airport, 159, 162, 174, 215-17
Narita Tomomi, 161
National Liberation Front (NLF), 17, 28, 31, 36, 50-51, 65, 121, 128, 244; film, 75; Japanese antiwar movement and, 56, 216
New Left, 179-81, 186, 189-90, 204-206, 208, 210, 214, 225, 229-30, 261; defined, 169
New York Times, 65
newspapers, 27-28, 33, 35-42, 64, 125, 145, 151-53, 158-61, 213, 228, 233, 243. *See also Asahi shinbun; Mainichi shinbun; Yomiuri shinbun*
Ngo Dinh Diem, 16-17

Nguyen Cao Ky, 26, 135
Nguyen Khanh, 26
Nguyen Van Choi, 75
Nguyen Van Thieu, 135, 226, 234, 246, 248
NHK, 139
Nichols, Walter, 74, 116
Nihon Hōshi Sentā; *see* Japan Volunteer Center
Nihon Kōhō Sentā (Japan Information Center), 125
Nihon Terebi (NTV), 39, 80, 116
Nihon University, 186
Nihonzan Myōhōji, 117
Ninagawa Torazō, 131
Nishi Yoshiyuki, 68
Nixon, Richard M., 55, 172-73, 192-93, 213, 224-26, 243; Guam doctrine, 183; meets with Satō, 199-204, 221-22; 1971 shocks, 4, 44, 221-26
NLF, *see* National Liberation Front
Noda Uichi, 26
Noma Hiroshi, 56
nonnuclear principles, 151-52, 242
North Korea, 151
North Vietnam, *see* Democratic Republic of Vietnam
Nozaka Akiyoshi, 56
NTV, *see* Nihon Terebi
nuclear weapons, 146-47, 151-52, 199-200, 212

Oda Makoto, 27, 30, 32, 119, 133, 141-44, 158, 173, 180, 199, 213, 218, 231, 233, 241, 262; antiwar principles, 57-63, 120-21; antiwar tactics, 63-67, 180, 186-87; artists and, 72-76; criticized, 67-72, 111; founds Beheiren, 56-57; leads June Action, 165-69, 206-12; post-Vietnam War activities, 238-41; students and, 188. *See also* antiwar movement; Beheiren
Ōe Kenzaburō, 56, 73, 206

LIBRARY OF CONGRESS CATALOGING-IN-PUBLICATION DATA

Havens, Thomas R. H.
Fire across the sea.

Bibliography: p.
Includes index.
1. Vietnamese Conflict, 1961-1975—Japan.
2. Japan—History—1952-   . 3. Vietnamese
Conflict, 1961-1975—Protest movements—Japan. I. Title.
DS558.6.J3H38 1987   959.704'33'52   86-22630
ISBN 0-691-05491-6 (alk. paper)
ISBN 0-691-00811-6 (pbk. : alk. paper)